BILL BRAND

TREVOR GRIFFITHS

Bill Brand

The Screenplays

SPOKESMAN

First published in 2010 by Spokesman
Russell House, Bulwell Lane
Nottingham
NG6 0BT
Phone 0115 970 8318. Fax 0115 942 0433
e-mail elfeuro@compuserve.com
www.spokesmanbooks.com

ISBN-13: 978 085124 763 2
A CIP catalogue is available from the British Library

Printed by the Russell Press Ltd (www.russellpress.com).

CONTENTS

Bill Brand was a Thames Television production for ITV.
The series was broadcast in the summer of 1976.

This book is dedicated to the memory of
Stella Richman and Stuart Burge

Introduction

'I knew from very early on that I wanted to work in television. Television seemed then and still seems a massively powerful means of intervening in society's life.'
Trevor Griffiths, 1982

By January 1974 Britain was in political turmoil. Edward Heath's Conservative Government had been forced to impose power cuts and a three-day week in an attempt to conserve energy stocks during the miners' overtime ban, which was supported by the rail and electricity unions. Trevor Griffiths' television play *All Good Men* was transmitted during this period, cut from 75 to 63 minutes to fit in with the 10.30 pm television curfew. *All Good Men* dealt with the history of labourism, the struggle between the Left and Centre-Right, and the perennial conflict between principle and pragmatism within the Party.

It was in many ways the precursor of the eleven-part series *Bill Brand,* which was conceived in 1974, written and produced over the following two years, and transmitted in the summer of 1976.

*   *   *

The following extract from the book Powerplays *is reproduced here by kind permission of the authors, Michael Poole and John Wyver. Their book about Trevor Griffiths' television work was published by the British Film Institute in 1984.*

On 1ˢᵗ February 1974 the result was announced of the crucial miners' ballot about stepping up the overtime ban which they were then enforcing. 81% authorised the NUM Executive to call an all-out strike, promptly scheduled to begin a week later. Within those seven days, Edward Heath was forced to set an election for 28ᵗʰ February.

Political debate was defined, on television as elsewhere, by the question of a 'strong' Government versus the demands of the unions. 'The choice before the nation today, as never before,' the Tory manifesto asserted, 'is a choice between moderation and extremism.'

Constructed from an opposing viewpoint, with a different vocabulary, this was also to be a central dynamic of *Bill Brand.* As Brand says, 'I have these two voices … they say: might, right; power, principle; pragmatism, precept; slow, quick; one day, now …'

Such was the choice before at least part of the nation. That February, however, 'the nation' found it hard to make up its mind. For the first time since 1929 no party gained an overall majority. A weekend of talks between the Conservatives and the Liberals failed to bring forth a coalition and Harold Wilson formed the first minority government since 1931.

On election night, Griffiths met for the first time the independent television drama producer Stella Richman, in the bar of Mayfair's 'White Elephant' restaurant, which she owned. *[She had very recently watched Griffiths'* The Party

at the National Theatre and had decided he was someone she wanted to work with.]
They watched television coverage of the election results together, and she later told the *Daily Express*: 'Suddenly the idea came and I asked him if he would like to do a series about the beginnings of the life of a Labour MP. We sat up until three in the morning trying to get the bones of something. Within a week he had the notes on paper. The man has the mind of a filing cabinet. It is the equivalent of a novel.'

The subsequent detailed research and writing of the eleven hour-long episodes were to occupy Griffiths for much of the next two years, and the scripting continued well into the production process.

'Stella was going to do *Bill Brand* as a kind of independent production', recalls Stuart Burge, who became the series' producer. 'But in those days that never worked out, with the complete dominance of the big companies. So I was brought in when some of the scripts were there and we all went to Thames with it. And Stella sold the whole idea to Verity Lambert.'

After a successful career herself as a drama producer, Verity Lambert had recently been appointed Thames TV's Controller of Drama by Jeremy Isaacs. Isaacs, as Director of Programmes, and Lambert began with a long-term strategy. In Isaacs' words, 'She and I said let us do drama in the next couple of years that will make everybody sit up and take notice.' Ratings and advertising revenue in the early '70s were both buoyant, and a company like Thames could afford to take some risks, even though the executives were certain that demanding contemporary drama would not pull high peak-time ratings. When Verity Lambert started at Thames she made two important decisions: no costume drama in the first eighteen months, and a commitment to drama with a London base. She wanted 'a kind of style and a kind of feeling about our drama which meant it couldn't have come from any other company, it had to come from a London company.'

Griffiths saw the project as a clear complement to his writing on revolution: 'It seemed an important thing to do, if you're talking about politics in Britain now, to examine and to explore social democracy as well as revolutionism. What I've tried to do is present as full a picture as I can of a Member's life in all its complexity and its density. So I spend quite a lot of time in the constituency, quite a lot of time in Parliament, in Committee, in the desk room, the bar, wherever. We're investigating the stuff, the actual tissue and texture, of the social democratic processes within a major party. About which people know next to nothing. They really don't.'

While the series was in production, in the late autumn of 1975, Granada transmitted *The Nearly Man*, a series written by Arthur Hopcraft which also dealt with the life of a Labour MP. *The Nearly Man* had different concerns and a different politics, since Hopcraft's MP was on the right wing of the party. And in a later review, the then Labour MP Christopher Price wrote: 'Hopcraft took a snapshot; Griffiths has tried to portray a political odyssey.'

None the less, the similarity was close enough to threaten *Bill Brand's* chances of a primetime network slot. The ITV Controllers' Committee wanted it to go out at 10.30pm in the summer. The production team were adamant that it had to be shown at 9pm. Usually the Controllers would have overridden this wish, despite Jeremy Isaacs' passionate backing for the series. Then, as Griffiths recalls it, 'We put the word out and something like seventy people turned up for this meeting with

Isaacs on the rehearsal room floor and he got a lot thrown at him … He went back and fought for 9 o'clock, which we got, in the summer.'

So eventually episode one of *Bill Brand* went out on Monday night 7th June 1976 in a slot previously occupied by an American thriller series, *Manhunt*. Preceding it in the schedule was *World in Action*; and directly after it came *News at Ten*, which it was to parallel fortuitously on several occasions in the coming weeks.

* * *

Despite the misgivings of the ITV Controllers, the series achieved an audience of ten million viewers (including many MPs, who gathered to watch it in the House of Commons each week), and generated great interest and debate. It received extensive press coverage from across the political spectrum.

'The series not only depicts an MP who is honest, intelligent and real; it also tells us more about Parliament, constituency politics and the Labour Party than the combined writings of most of the Westminster drama critics who masquerade as political commentators.'   *New Statesman*, 30.7.76

'There are two little games to play while watching: one is to spot the veiled and not-so-veiled caricatures of real politicians such as Michael Foot and Roy Jenkins; and the other is to award Griffiths marks for the accuracy of his foresight when he wrote the scripts months ago. There has, occasionally, been an uncanny sense of déjà vu in watching *News At Ten* immediately after *Bill Brand*.'
Financial Times, 21.7.76

'Last night's episode was concerned with the battle for the leadership of the Labour Party, with left and right at war as much with themselves as with each other. The details of the script must have been incomprehensible to large numbers of viewers, as it ploughed through the internecine warfare. Yet … the line of Trevor Griffiths' argument carried through. It is a series that in this way defies criticism: I find it fascinating, despite its defects. Others – MPs included – may disagree. But that does not stop it being the most interesting TV drama of the season.'   *The Guardian*, 3.8.76

'I find myself following the series grudgingly but attentively, as a sharper insight into such matters than that afforded by many a current affairs programme. And in the light of recent exploits by the Parliamentary Left, I suppose that even Bill Brand's bleak and unremitting humour is lifelike.   *Sunday Telegraph*, 27.6.76

'I can only hope that this insight into the workings of the House of Commons is fictional – if not the future looks bleak.'   *Evening News*, 24.6.76

'The most remarkable serial ever seen on the box.'   *Sunday Times*, 15.8.76

Author's note

Any reader who is fortunate enough still to have videotapes of the eleven episodes of *Bill Brand* may find that the televised version of some of them differs slightly from the plays published in this book.

In some cases this is because of post-production editing and in others because the actual shooting scripts are no longer available to work from.

This book has been prepared from such texts as are still extant, more than thirty years after they were written – some of them first draft typescripts, some rehearsal scripts. The texts were then compared with the videotapes of the series and amended as necessary and as appropriate.

Occasionally, dialogue or scenes that were cut from the finished programmes in order to fit them into the 53 minute straitjacket which was an ITV hour have been reinstated, for the reader's interest.

Apart from that, each episode is as close as possible to the programmes as broadcast. Whatever minor variations there may be, everything you will read here is true to the narrative line and character development of the series and to my intentions at the time.

Finally, I would like to thank the many people who made invaluable contributions to this series during the time I was researching and writing it, in particular Professor Lewis Minkin, political advisor for the series and an authority on the history of the Labour Party; Mike Noble MP, for his help with parliamentary procedures; and my longtime friend and comrade the writer Jeremy Pikser.

Trevor Griffiths
2009

Episode 1

In

was broadcast on Monday 7th June 1976

The cast was as follows:

Bill Brand   Jack Shepherd

Michael Brand   Philip Cox

Miriam Brand   Lynn Farleigh

Jane Brand   Karen Silver

Alf Jowett   Allan Surtees

Albert Stead   John Barrett

Elsie Wright   Lynne Carol

Lily Atherton   Nellie Hanham

Frank Hilton   Clifford Kershaw

Pru   Peter Ellis

Martin   Alan Luxton

Alex Ferguson   Cherie Lunghi

Eddie Brand   Dave Hill

Mrs Brand   Anne Dyson

Mr Brand   Harry Markham

Woman Interviewer   Jan Harvey

Mrs Watson   Myrtle Devenish

Gladys   Jeanne Doree

Bernard Shaw   Colin Jeavons

Angie Shaw   Carol Hayman

Returning Officer   Alan Bowlas

Conservative candidate   James Drake

Liberal candidate   Rosemary Frankau

Designers: David Ferris, Harry Clark

Executive Producer: Stella Richman

Producer: Stuart Burge

Director: Michael Lindsay-Hogg

PART ONE

A court of ten or twelve houses on a modern private estate. Morning. April. A light drizzling fume in the air. A Ford Escort 1300 Estate parked in front of the still, quiet houses.

Inside the car, Bill Brand, mid-thirties, stares through the window at No.10, whose curtains are drawn. A 'For Sale' sign on the seven-foot white slatted fence that secludes the house from the court. He smokes a Winterman's Senorita without liking it. Surveys the houses one by one; notes the 'individual' differences between two-, three-, and four-bedroom versions; the identical up-and-over garages and dead patios shielding house from world; the miserable silver yew trying to survive in the tarmac of the court. From the car radio, the flabby sounds of Terry Wogan exhorting the white-collar world to do its duty.

Brand checks his watch: 8.10. He fiddles through the medium wave band until he strikes the news on Radio Manchester. He stares at the curtained windows of No.10 through the stumbling news roundup, read by a young woman in a clean Manchester accent.

NEWSCASTER: ... Miners' leaders in the North West are meeting in Manchester later today to decide their attitude to the Coal Board's latest 8½% pay offer. We'll have on-the-spot reports for you in bulletins throughout the day. *(Scrape of papers on mic.)* And today, of course, is polling day in the crucial Leighley by-election, caused by the death of the sitting Labour member, where the Labour government will obviously be looking for a positive indication of its standing in the country. Radio Manchester will be covering events in Leighley throughout the day, and will hope to bring you interviews and reports direct from the Town Hall as the by-election reaches its climax round about midnight tonight. *(A boy, about 7, parts an upstairs curtain, stares down at the car)* Labour candidate William Brand ... *(Brand switches the radio off, opens car door, gets out, waves to the boy in the window. The boy smiles)*

Brand lets himself into the house.

Int. White-walled kitchen. *The table is set for three, cups turned down on saucers. He fills the kettle, plugs it in, searches for bread, lights the gas grill, begins cutting bread for toast. Michael, the boy at the window, arrives, still in pyjamas.*

BRAND: Hi, Mike.

MICHAEL: *(tipping cornflakes into his dish)* Hello.

BRAND: Toast?

MICHAEL: No thanks.

Brand slides two pieces under the grill, spoons tea into pot.

BRAND: Your mum up?

MICHAEL: *(studying Kellogg packet offer)* What? *(he looks up eventually)* Yes, she's in the bathroom.

Brand crosses to the table, puts a small embossing tape on it.

BRAND: Got you the tape.

MICHAEL: *(picking it up)* Oh great. Ta.

BRAND: Give us a kiss then.

Michael puts his arms round Brand's neck, offers his lips. Brand kisses him, full, a love kiss.

Miriam Brand in. Early thirties, wearing, pale after sleep, dressed, effortfully neat already. She crosses to the stove, taking in the kiss on the way. Pulls out the dark brown toast.

MIRIAM: This yours?

Brand takes the pan from her, turns the toast. Miriam switches kettle off, brews tea precisely.

MIRIAM: *(to Michael)* You should be dressed.

MICHAEL: *(holding tape up: pleased smile)* Look.

MIRIAM: *(not impressed)* Mmm. *(checks watch)* Christ. *(calling)* Jane! *(pause)* Jane!! *(indistinct call from upstairs)* Do you want toast or cereal? *(another indistinct call from upstairs. To Michael)* Hurry up.

She turns the three cups up, pours tea into them. Takes a fourth from a cupboard. Pours that. Brand butters his toast, places one round on Jane's plate. Jane in, dark, round, almost ten. She sulks her morning sulk, nothing serious as long as it's left unpressured.

BRAND: Hi chicken.

JANE: Hello. *(to mother)* Where's my brown skirt?

MIRIAM: I've no idea. Eat your breakfast, we're late.

JANE: *(picking Michael's tape up)* What's that?

MICHAEL: *(menacing, protective)* Leave it, it's mine ... it's for my mini-printer.

JANE: *(to Miriam)* It's not fair, he's always getting things bought him ...

MIRIAM: Look, don't start, for God's sake. It's half past eight.

JANE: Well it isn't. *(pause)* It was in my wardrobe last night ...

The breakfast proceeds, four separate cubicles of process; not happy. Brand drains his cup; leaving.

BRAND: Three minutes ... *(he leaves)*

MIRIAM: *(to Jane, who sulks quietly on)* What's wrong with that one? It looks lovely.

Int. Bathroom. Mirror area only. Brand shaves with electric razor. Fastens red wool tie on clean white shirt; settles collar under the good suit he's changed into. Michael pees at the lavatory, dressed for school; zips up.

BRAND: Got your glasses? *(Michael pats his little schoolbag)* O.K. In the car. *(Michael out. Calling after him)* Get your sister …

Ext. Car. They drive through suburban Manchester, the kids in the back. Jane reads a book. Miriam applies a smidgin of make-up, cool, withdrawn.

The kids straggle their separate ways from the car to the school. Michael turns to wave.

They drive on, the traffic building, in silence. He stops in the grounds of a Victorian hospital. They sit for a moment in silence.

BRAND: O.K?

MIRIAM: Fine.

She begins to get out.

BRAND: Listen, Mim. *(she holds door open, looks back at him)* I know I've no right to ask, but it would help if you were to … put in an appearance, later on …

She looks at him levelly for a few moments.

MIRIAM: I didn't marry you to … put in appearances.

She closes the door, turns, walks off. He rubs his nose and eyes, staring after her. Finally:

BRAND: Glad to know I can count on your support, Mrs Brand.

He shoves into second, drives off.

***Central Committee Rooms, Leighley.** Brand parks his car, passes a poster of himself on his way in.*

Agent's office. Alf Jowett, late forties, Labour Secretary-Agent, stands in front of an action map of the constituency, glaring at the blue and yellow pins that seem to sprout from every street and alley. Albert Stead, from North West Regional Executive, old, bullet-headed, in brown striped suit, red tie, rosette, drinks a cup of tea in silence, studying a pile of undistributed election literature. The cramped office sags under the weight of printed material; files, correspondence, collection boxes, dance tickets, bingo cards, Labour publications, union papers, rules, standing orders. Jowett lights his eighth cigarette from the stub of the seventh. He's thin, small, wiry, aggressive; meanly single-minded.

JOWETT: *(jabbing blue pin in fiercely)* Where the bloody hell is he? Look at the time. *(the old clock on the wall says 9.20)* Lecturers, Albert, I ask you. Don't know they're bloody born. *(he sees Brand approaching through the open door)* He's here. Oh Christ, he's got a blue suit on.

BRAND: *(arriving)* Good morning.

JOWETT: *(heavy look at his watch)* Are you sure? It's today, you know.

Brand smiles coolly, refusing to rise, used to and yet not wholly unnettled by the frontal irony of the man. Crosses to large brown metal teapot, feels it, pours tea into plastic beaker.

BRAND: You said half nine, Alf. I'm early.

JOWETT: I said half nine at the latest. You don't listen.

BRAND: *(blowing on tea, grinning)* That's what makes me such a good candidate.

Jowett blinks, annoyed by his ferocious cool.

JOWETT: *(eventually)* Bill Brand, Albert Stead, North West Region.

BRAND: *(hand out, smiling)* Hello, Albert.

STEAD: *(standing, taking hand; a nice man)* Greetings, brother. Nice to meet you.

JOWETT: *(ironic)* Albert's going to look after the nerve centre *(waving at his office)* when we hit the road.

BRAND: Good.

JOWETT: Right. *(moving to desk, spreading map)* We'll make a start. We're gonna keep this bugger, right? *(close up map of Leighley)* All we've got to do is let this sodding lot know.

STEAD: Well, we've got two of the opinion polls behind us …

JOWETT: In spite of which, we will win, brother. *(looking at Brand)* In spite of everything. This seat is not a Tory seat.

Ext. *Jowett drives his fawn minivan, Brand beside him. The drizzle has thickened. They pass a junior school polling station, the gate littered with party tellers and others. A small boy holds up a placard with 'Vote Labour' printed in red.*

JOWETT: Don't worry about rain. It'll clear up. Nobody votes in the morning. Not our lot, anyway. *(he drives in silence for a moment, the cigarette dangling)* You might have to go on the speaker, later on. We'll see. *(Brand lights a Wintermans)* Cigars. *(He shakes his head wearily)*

BRAND: *(ironic)* Do they bother you?

JOWETT: It's not me, sonny. I don't give a toss. *(They drive on in silence. Finally)* What time can we expect the wife?

BRAND: I'm not sure. She's a bit tied up at the hospital …

JOWETT: You what? I hope you're joking. Listen, this isn't a bloody game we're playing ...

BRAND: *(fast, toughening)* I *know* that. All right?

JOWETT: Like hell it is! *(He stops the car with a jerk)* I don't care if you have to push her round in a wheelchair, our workers expect a wife, and by Christ they're gonna get one. Right?

Brand looks out at the blackened terrace ahead. One house bears a Labour Committee Rooms placard in the window. He opens the door, turns back in to Jowett.

BRAND: *(mild, deliberate)* Comrade. Go straight home tonight. Don't hang about. Because win or lose, I might just want to kick your teeth in.

He gets out, pulls his coat collar up against the rain, strides off to the rooms. Jowett pecks after him, a racing pigeon of a man, busty on the wind.

JOWETT: *(calling after him)* Bigger men than you have tried it, comrade. Believe you me ... And where's your bloody rosette?

Int. Local Committee Room. *The front room of a two-up two-down terrace. The clock on the mantelpiece has 10.10. Two oldish women work busily at ham sandwiches, Reading Slips and tea.*

MRS ATHERTON: *(on Reading Slips)* S'elp me God, I'll never understand these, I won't. Where does the pink go, Elsie?

ELSIE: *(on sandwiches)* Don't ask me, Lily. *(smiling)* I'm on sandwiches.

Jowett opens the door without knocking.

JOWETT: Morning, ladies. Hard at it, are we. That's the stuff. I've just brought er ... *(he turns into the passage)* Come in, come in ... I've just brought your next Member of Parliament round to see you ... Mr Brand.

ELSIE: Oh that's nice.

JOWETT: He wanted to thank you personally for all the work you've done for him during the campaign...

MRS ATHERTON: *(pleasantly)* Nay, it were for t'party, Mr Jowett. I've done it all me life and don't want thankin'.

BRAND: *(stepping forward)* I would like to say a word, though. If that's all right.

ELSIE: Of course it's all right. Sit you down lad, have a cup of tea and a sandwich, it'll be a long day will this one ...

JOWETT: *(too late)* We can't ... stop, Mrs Wright ... *(a cup and saucer reach Brand's left hand, a plate his right)*

BRAND: Thank you. Can I just say ... how much I appreciate what you're doing ... for the party. And I really do hope that ... when I'm elected *(smiling gently)* ... I'll not let you down.

MRS ATHERTON: Very nice. Nice, Elsie.

ELSIE: Very nice.

JOWETT: Good. Right, now any problems?

MRS ATHERTON: Well, I know you've shown me before Mr Jowett, but I can't seem to get the hang of these slips ...

She draws Jowett over to the table, where he begins to instruct her on the vote-return system. Brand places his plate on a sideboard, sips his tea, smiles at Elsie.

ELSIE: Not from Leighley, are you Mr Brand?

BRAND: Manchester. *(smiling)* Down the road. *(pause)* I work here though. At the tech.

ELSIE: Oh really. Our Mildred's girl works there. Cleaner. *(Brand nods, no comment possible)* Will your wife be coming?

BRAND: *(slowly)* Yes, I think so. She's a medical social worker ... in a hospital, you know? ... It's erm ... quite a job getting away.

ELSIE: *(unimpressed)* Mmm.

Jowett has heard the electric hare and twitches in his trap.

JOWETT: All right, Mrs Atherton. You'll get the hang of it. *(turning to the room)* Well, there we are ladies. I'll probably be back when it's busier. Thank you again. *(to Brand)* All right?

BRAND: Goodbye.

They begin to leave, Jowett herding Brand before him. A small boy arrives carrying half a dozen white slips in his hand.

JOWETT: There we go, Mrs Atherton. We're on the way!

We follow them out into the wet road. They walk in silence to the van. Clamber heavily in. Jowett lights a cigarette, starts the engine. The wipers clear the screen. Silence for a moment.

JOWETT: *(eventually)* Take it easy on the tea, lad. You've another eighteen before you're finished.

Brand looks at him. Smiles, almost fondly.

BRAND: You'd still take me round if I were *dead*, wouldn't you!

JOWETT: *(into gear)* With pleasure,

They grind off into the murk.

Ext. The rain has stopped, the sky brightened a fraction, but the damp hangs dully in the air. A dormobile with twin speakers affixed crawls around a busyish shopping area. The van's sides are heavily plastered with Labour stickers and pics of Brand. Brand's voice veers and wobbles onto the pavements through the far from perfect system he operates.

BRAND'S VOICE: ... remember, a vote for Labour is a vote for the future. By voting Labour today, you have a chance to show the country that you support the present Labour government in its efforts to build a society in which equality, social justice and co-operation carry more weight than private profit, exploitation and manipulation. Vote Brand, vote Labour, vote for a better future. *(pause)* This is Bill Brand, your Labour candidate, making a final appeal to you to vote today to keep Leighley Labour ...

The van dwindles with the address at the bottom of the street,

Int. Central Committee Rooms. *The large bare hall is milling with party workers, young socialists, constituency party executive members, trade unionists, tea brewers, ham sandwich makers. A throng of Young Socialists surround Jowett's doorway, appropriate Reading Slips and other messages in their hands.*

Bill Brand and the driver of the dormobile in from the street. When he's spotted, a cheer goes up from those closest, good luck cries and handshakes accompany his slow progress to the agent's office.

Office. Jowett, on phone and dealing with two teenage girls at the same time, sees Brand in the doorway over the moil of heads. He waves him in without shifting attention from his two existing interactions.

JOWETT: *(to phone. Minatory, interrupting)* ... Albert, you promised a van for midday and it's half one and there's no van here. *(He shows the two girls in mime how to deal with Reading Slips throughout, a facial performance of some richness and subtlety)* ... I know that, Albert ... *(short pause)* Look, it's a simple enough decision: either you bring it here or you don't, I'm not interested in what you're going to do with it if you don't lend it to us. *(pause. Still teaching the girls)* So let your wife get a taxi. Good. We're counting on you, Albert. *(He puts the phone down. To two girls)* O.K?

He turns to Brand.

JOWETT: How'd it go?

BRAND: Fine. Fair bit of interest round the Centre.

JOWETT: We're going to be five cars light in North Ward. *(Several of the Young Socialists begin singing 'Why are we waiting'. Jowett smiles sourly at them, turns back to Brand)* See if you can get any of your lecturer friends to chip in this evening ... it's important.

BRAND: All right. What next?

JOWETT: You'd better get some lunch. Take your time, there's nowt left for you to do and you'll only be in the way ...

BRAND: *(moving to go)* Whatever you say, Herr Kommandant ...

JOWETT: Hang on. Where is it? (*he sees the rosette on the desk, picks it up, pins it on Brand's lapel. Quietly, touching nose with fore-finger*) There's even time for a quick visit to the barber's, if the fancy took you ...

BRAND: (*leaving, smiling*) I'll see what I can do about cars ...

JOWETT: (*calling*) There's a crowd in the Nelson, if you need company ... Hey, I don't suppose there's any word on Mrs Brand is there?

BRAND: No word.

JOWETT: (*to moil, as Brand leaves*) Right, who's next ...?

Int. Central Committee Rooms. Hall. Brand exchanges smiles with the rough young people outside the door.

TEENAGE BOY: Gonna win, Bill, are we?

BRAND: *No* danger.

A cheer, faintly ironic in tinge, from the others.

PART TWO

Ext. Brand parks his car, locks it, close to the Admiral Nelson Arms. As he approches it, he unpins his rosette and sticks it in his pocket.

Int. The Nelson. An overdone almost empty bar by the Town Hall, still early for the rush. Stead drinks a pint of Guinness at the bar with Councillor Frank Hilton, Chairman of the C.L.P., Labour Councillor, Chairman of the Finance Committee, a huge, fleshy corporation bus driver in his late fifties, uniformed, on his lunch hour.

HILTON: We'll hold it, I think ... He's a good lad. He'll make a good member if he buckles down. He's liked. (*Draws on his pint*) The right think he's a bit wild. But the right's never held the reins in these parts. And it's balanced by the young thinking he's a bit tame.

STEAD: I'd be happier if some of the promises of help we've had would start materialising ...

HILTON: (*dry*) Promises, Albert. Fragile things. You've gotta kick a few arses ... (*he's spotted Brand arriving*) Bill! (*Brand sees him, already in mid-stride towards one of the rooms. Hilton touches one of the barmaids through the dark wood frame as she passes*) Pint of bitter, Mary. (*he puts the money on the bar. Looks at Stead*) You?

STEAD: Nay, it's my turn.

HILTON: No, no. I'm due back at two. (*to Mary, as he counts out more money with the accuracy of habit*) ... And another pint of guinness, love. (*Brand arrives*) How are you, Bill? Bearing up? Better than working, I bet. Pint on the way.

BRAND: Thanks, Frank. Do you want the truth? *(seeing Stead)* Hello, Mr Stead. *(to Hilton)* I'm glassy-eyed with boredom. *(his pint arrives, he takes it, drinks)* Cheers.

STEAD: Nay, you'll have more than enough to do before this day's out, brother …

BRAND: No, I don't mean that. *(he looks at Hilton, who's lighting a Woodbine)* We've, us … England … we've perfected the process of ruthlessly reducing what we do to its most fundamentally trivial elements. You'd think an election could be something more … significant … than the price of sugar and the availability of Albert Hudson's van in North Ward. *(the tone is steady but mild, an irony there to soften it)*

HILTON: *(to Stead)* He talks well on this subject. I had it for twenty meetings from him with the WEA.

BRAND: Right. I'll shut up. Pint.

HILTON: *(draining glass, fitting peaked cap on)* I've got to go. See you this evening. You'll be all right. Once you settle down. *(Brand grins at the crack. Hilton slaps him on the shoulder, elbows his way to the street.)*

BRAND: That's a good chairman.

STEAD: *(drinking up)* He's a good sort is Frank. *(pause)* Well, I must be off meself. There's unfortunately no shortage of work for the likes of me.

BRAND: Won't you have another, Mr Stead?

STEAD: I won't, if you don't mind. Two's my limit at lunchtime. You won't have got round to your prostate yet, but you will … *(He takes his steelrim glasses off, boxes them. Then, almost shyly)* There was a time I thought of trying … *(he waves his glasses case at the rosette he wears)* After the war, you know. *(long pause)* I never did. *(another)* I hope you make it, lad.

BRAND: Thanks.

Stead leaves, pocketing his glasses case. Brand watches him a moment, takes a long pull on his pint. A group of people arrive in doorway noisily, the first of the moil, three youngish men and two women. Pru (long blonde hair) leads the group to the bar, his arm on Alex's shoulder. Martin (long unkempt black beard) follows them, a pocket chess set open in his hand, which he studies. Alex is about 24; sturdy; dark-haired.

PRU: *(seeing Brand first)* It's the candidate himself. How's the seduction of social democracy grabbing you, Bill?

MARTIN: *(studying Brand. Mock sotto voce)* I swear he's put weight on …

BRAND: *(ignoring bearded man)* Piss off, Pru. *(he looks at Alex, winks, for her alone. She smiles, looks away. To bearded man)* How's Liberal Studies then, Martin? Missing me?

MARTIN: Liberal Studies is what it's always been: the opium of the working classes. *(drinking)* You'd better watch yourself, you know. If you're not careful you'll get in.

PRU: *(ordering drinks)* And then it's Hail and Farewell. Hail Parliament, Farewell Politics. What's yours, Privy Counsellor? Large gin maybe ...? *(some laughter, some interjections from others)*

BRAND: *(low, leaning across to Alex)* I'm parked in Wellington Street. Any chance of a word?

The variations on Pru's theme and the accompanying laughter dying.

MARTIN: I suppose it's all of a piece really. He's always been a bit of an infiltrationist, haven't you, Bill. *(Alex nods undemonstratively at Brand)* Chairman of the College Council, member of the Labour Party ... I bet you were a prefect, weren't you, Bill?

Brand raises his glass, smiles, cool, self-possessed, at the bar table, and then at the bearded man.

BRAND: What you and the Fourth International will *never* forgive me for, Martin, is not having all the answers. I do know how unreliable that makes me. Cheers, comrades.

He leaves, amiably enough.

PRU: He's very good at the parting thrust, is Bill.

Ext. Brand in car. Alex looms in window, opens door, slides in beside him.

BRAND: Hi.

ALEX: Hi.

BRAND: What time are you back?

ALEX: 2.15.

He hands her his box of Wintermans, she takes one, he lights hers, then his.

ALEX: What did you want?

BRAND: Nothing special. I'm going out of my skull.

ALEX: *(tough)* You made the bed, comrade ...

BRAND: Yeah, right, fine, forget it.

They sit for a moment, tense. Finally

ALEX: *(softer)* Soon be over.

BRAND: Yeah. *(pause)* Do you have to go back, Al? I'm free till four or so ...

ALEX: Yeah, I do. I've got two supplementary benefit tribunals tomorrow and a mountain of forms to process ... *(pause)* I suppose you'll ... have other things tonight ...

BRAND: I don't know. I'll call you.

ALEX: I should be in from nine or so. *(looks at watch)* O.K? *(she begins opening the door, he puts his arm out, draws her towards him suddenly, kisses her with some passion on the lips)*

BRAND: *(gently)* Come if I can. *(he stares at her face)* Is that eye-shadow?

ALEX: *(softly)* Nights without sleep. See you soon.

Ext. Brand drives down Stockport Road towards Ardwick and the centre of Manchester. He smokes a Winterman's, listens to the radio. Music, which fades abruptly. Through the following newscast Brand's face remains expressionless.

ANNOUNCER: Radio Manchester on 206 metres medium wave. We interrupt this repeat of our Leighley Decides programme to bring you further news of the bomb blast that took place in London this morning. A statement just issued by the police states that the toll of dead has now reached five, following the death of a young woman, believed to be a secretary, discovered in the basement of the Bridge Street premises and rushed to Westminster Hospital an hour or so ago. The possibility of still further bombs in the street, which houses MP's offices as well as offices of private businesses, continues to hamper search and rescue operations by police and firemen. A statement in the House is due in about an hour's time, and we'll be bringing you a full report and more news in our five o'clock news round-up. Now, with apologies, back to ...

Brand clicks it off.

Int. He climbs a dark, narrow, wooden stairway. Sounds of a band-knife at work upstairs. Emerges into a longish, gaunt room, filled with bolted or racked shirt and pyjama material and rubbish, a few wooden chairs, scarred wooden floor, a long table full of old milk bottles, mugs, old newspapers, an old black phone. At the top of the room, at an old cutting table, Eddie Brand, late thirties, short, wiry, concentrates on his cut.

Brand watches him for a moment; the skill, the unsentimental care, the absorption, the honesty. Eddie removes his foot from the switch, studies his pattern.

BRAND: Thought you were getting your own place.

EDDIE: *(turning)* Hiya, kid, what you doing here?

BRAND: Just thought I'd call. Filling in time.

EDDIE: Did me mam get you?

BRAND: No. Been out all day.

EDDIE: She was trying. She rang here. They brought me dad home from work this morning ...

BRAND: What's wrong?

EDDIE: I dunno. He's had another attack of some sort.

BRAND: *(checking watch)* He should never have gone back. I'll get up there.

EDDIE: He dunt sound so bad. You can never tell with me ma. Maybe I'll see you later. When I've finished here.

BRAND: *(moving back towards stairs)* I'll probably have to push, Ed. *(he shows him the rosette, a little ruefully)*

EDDIE: Christ, it's today innit. I'd forgotten all about it.

BRAND: We're short of transport. How're you fixed for a couple of hours this evening?

EDDIE: Hopeless, tonight. We play top of the league at snooker, Conservative Club.

BRAND: *(making face on top stair)* OK. See you. I'll ring if you're needed at me ma's.

EDDIE: I took some shirts up. Tell her to show 'em to you. Smashing.

BRAND: Right. Go easy.

EDDIE: Oh aye. Hey. *(Brand turns to look up)* Big day.

BRAND: Yeah.

They smile gently at each other, closest when they're parting. Brand disappears into the gloom of the stairwell. Eddie lights a Craven A, returns to the table, studies the half-finished cut, lines up the material, kicks on the band-knife. Over this, Mrs Brand's voice.

MRS BRAND: *(over)* Eeh, thank God you've come, son. I've been out to that box a dozen times to call you. Come in, come in …

***Int. Front room.** East Manchester. Hundred-year-old redbrick terrace of two-up, two-downs with back yards and outdoor lavatories.*

BRAND: *(entering room)* I saw our kid in town. How is he? *(he turns, kisses her on the cheek)* You look tired.

MRS BRAND: *(sixty, perhaps in the year she will accept the fact)* There's nowt wrong with me. They brought your father home again. Ten o'clock.

BRAND: Yeah, Eddie said. What's the doctor say?

MRS BRAND: The usual. You know him. *(pause)* Sit you down, I'll make some tea.

BRAND: I'll slip up and have a look at him, if it's all right.

MRS BRAND: I'll see if he's awake …

She leaves. He hears her clump up the straight stairs that split the front of the house from the back. Looks round the room, at the 23" tv, on racing from Lingfield, no sound, the tiny tile fireplace, old three piece suite too large for this room, and other remnants of a marginally more sumptuous past. Crosses to the mantelpiece, picks up a green vase, revealing two pound notes and a handful of change, her housekeeping. Feels in his back pocket, places a fiver under the vase. His mother returns.

MRS BRAND: He's awake. The doctor gave him something. I'll make a pot. *(she moves into the kitchen, Brand takes the stairs)* Ask him if he wants a mug. I don't think he will.

Brand enters the small bedroom over the living room, sparsely furnished, thin curtains drawn. His father lies half-propped in the brown double bed, drowsy still from the shot. They stare at each other a moment across the room.

MR BRAND: *(finally, weak)* It's a bugger intit. First week back …

BRAND: *(crossing to chair by bed)* How do you feel?

MR BRAND: Not so good, son. Not so good.

BRAND: He should never have signed you off.

MR BRAND: It's not his fault. I thought I were fit. Bloody hell.

He lies there, exhausted. Brand looks covertly around the strange cramped room he's hardly ever seen before.

MR BRAND: I'll be all right. Bit of rest. Jenkins didn't seem bothered.

BRAND: I'll pop down to the surgery if I get the chance, have a word with him.

Silence. Mr Brand wheezes a little, eyes closed, sweat glistening under thin silver hair on his forehead.

BRAND: Anything you want, dad?

Mr Brand opens his eyes, stares at his half-stranger son.

MR BRAND: Aye. I want to get back to work. *(he smiles faintly)* I want that pension I've been slaving for these fifty years.

BRAND: You'll have your pension. Just … don't rush it. *(he stands uncertainly, wanting and unable to say more)* Get your bowls out. Enjoy the summer.

He's preparing to leave, still uneasy.

MR BRAND: Will you win, Bill? It's today, isn't it.

BRAND: Yeah. I don't know. I've a chance, they seem to think.

MR BRAND: *(eyes closed)* You were never like us, even as a little lad. Allus had your head stuck in a book somewhere. I never told you … I worried about you sometimes, how you'd end up, with all that learning. *(pause. He raises his hand very slowly, his eyes open, stares at his tough, gnarled, segged palms and fingers)* There's pain in itching when you cannot scratch. *(he puts the hand down. Looks at Bill)* Do someat … good, won't you?

BRAND: Yeah. *(pause. At door, softly)* I'll fetch the kids over Saturday, if you're feeling up to it. *(he starts down the stairs, comes back up again, head in doorway)* Ma's got some tea on.

MR BRAND: *(tired again, eyes closed)* No thanks.

Int. Living room. Brand's mother is pouring the tea. She looks up as he enters.

MRS BRAND: How does he seem, Billy?

BRAND: He's sharp enough. I'll speak to the doctor …

MRS BRAND: I'd be glad if you would. Here's your tea. Have a sandwich, they're salmon.

BRAND: *(taking cup)* Look, I can't stop, ma. I've got to get back to Leighley.

MRS BRAND: S'elp me God it's today. I'd forgotten all about it. Eeh, I wouldn't have bothered you if I'd known.

BRAND: I'm free most of the afternoon. But it'll pick up from now on.

MRS BRAND: You don't look excited, but then you never did, always hid what you were feeling. *(handing plate of sandwiches)* Have one, I made 'em for you.

BRAND: Thanks.

He sits down on the settee, stares at the mute horses in the ring. A show of betting superimposed.

MRS BRAND: How's Miriam and the children?

BRAND: They're fine. She's back to work now.

MRS BRAND: Till the next one. *(staring at the screen)* I've had a bet on this one I think. *(she studies a slip of paper drawn from her pinny pocket)* No I haven't, it's the 4.15. *(pause. Sipping her tea)* I shall have to do something if your dad's going to be ill again. *I* can't take any more time off work, they just won't keep it open.

BRAND: Maybe they'll take you half-time.

MRS BRAND: I'll have to do something.

BRAND: *(uneasy again)* Ed said he'd try and call after work.

MRS BRAND: He calls to see if I've got any money for him, selling his 'foreigners'. I've a room packed with his stuff up there. If a policeman were to come here I don't like to think, I don't …

BRAND: *(smiling, used to the complaint)* What would a policeman be doing here? You've never had a policeman in your house in your life.

MRS BRAND: I'm saying if. *(pause. She thinks)* I have anyway. Cemetery Road. During the war. I set the chimney on fire during the black-out and a policeman came and helped me put it out. Your dad was on nights. You wouldn't remember, you were in a cot in the Morrison shelter.

BRAND: Well, if there's another war, I'll help you get shut of 'em. *(he drains his cup)*

MRS BRAND: Another cup?

BRAND: No, I'd better get off.

MRS BRAND: Have you made all your plans then?

BRAND: What for?

MRS BRAND: You know. If you go down to London. I suppose Miriam'll want to be with you. And the children.

BRAND: *(standing)* No, not really. *(pause)* We're selling the house, anyway ... as it happens.

MRS BRAND: You never said.

BRAND: *(slowly, covering)* Miriam's not very keen on it, the area more than anything.

MRS BRAND: Northenden? It's lovely. I'd swop her any day.

BRAND: Anyway ... I suppose we'll just ... let things happen.

MRS BRAND: They will, son. They always do.

BRAND: *(near door)* Listen, I've got to go. Thanks for the tea. I'll talk to Jenkins.

MRS BRAND: Thanks, Bill. Take care.

He kisses her cheek, leaves. She watches at the door for a moment, then returns to the room, crosses to the vase, lifts it, stares at the notes.

Ext. *Phone box on main road, Leighley. He dials a number from his pocket book, stares at the Tory candidate's big bold poster on the hoarding outside: Vote Conservative, the party that will unite the country ... He slips in his 2p.*

BRAND: Could I speak to Miriam Brand, please ... Thank you. *(he waits, reads a fragment from the Tory candidate's address, stares at the man's clean, honest, managed face ... 'I promise to serve all sections of the community equally, to the best of my ability ...')* Hello, is Mrs Brand there please? *(listens)* I see. No, no message. *(he sniffs, stares at the phone a moment, puts it down on the rest)*

PART THREE

Int. Evening. Central Committee Rooms, hall, now pretty well packed with helpers, watchers and supporters. Streams of people move from the main doors to the four tables, manned by Jowett and assistants, outside his office. A thin thread of purposive sense runs through seeming chaos. The tension is now evident: a campaign, a seat, face, pride – all stand in the balance of the next few hours. The clock says 7.05.

Slow track through the main hall, isolating Jowett, Stead, Hilton and several new clusters of professional middle-class party members – university lecturers, schoolteachers, a doctor, progressive ICI middle-managers et al – most of them dressed more for the town hall count than for here. We stop at Jowett's door, which is unfamiliarly closed.

Int. Jowett's office. Brand is being interviewed by the Radio Manchester woman reporter whose voice we heard on the car radio this morning.

WOMAN: *(young, fresh)* You have the reputation of being some way to the left of centre in the Labour Party, Mr Brand. How would you describe your politics?

BRAND: *(smiling)* Couldn't you ask me something easier? How I'd describe my face or something? I'm a socialist. Of the sort that Bernard Levin and his trail-blazing claque would call reactionary. I actually believe in public ownership of the means of production, distribution and exchange. I actually believe in workers' control over work, community control over the environment. I actually believe that the real wealth of any society is its *people*. All of them, not just the well-off, the educated and the crafty. Which I suppose makes me a democrat too.

WOMAN: Have you found much evidence that the electors of Leighly see your ... fundamental approach to politics of relevance to their everyday worries and concerns? I'm thinking of inflation, food prices, the cost-of-living, rents, mortgages, jobs ...

BRAND: Some. But elections – and particularly by-elections critical of the government of the day – are more to do with the mobilisation of support than the education of the electorate. There's a difference.

WOMAN: Is that an admission, then, that you've found yourself having to ... tone down your left-wing views, to make them more palatable ... ?

Brand looks at her for a moment, smiles dryly, holds the pause.

BRAND: Those weren't the terms on which I accepted the party's nomination and they're not the terms on which I'll take my seat in the House of Commons as MP for the Leighley constituency.

WOMAN: You think you'll win, then ...?

BRAND: The votes are there. As of an hour ago we were short of maybe a dozen cars to drive people to the polling stations. Did you ever hear of the Conservatives being short of cars at an election? *(he grins again, perfectly friendly, yet serious)* I still think we'll win.

WOMAN: I've asked the Conservative and Liberal candidates, and I must ask you ... Assuming you *are* returned, what if anything do you expect to be able to do for the people of Leighley, given that Parliament is now dominated by the government of the day and the opposition front bench and given that the individual back-bencher is treated more and more as lobby fodder by the party whips? Can you honestly put your hand on your heart and say: I can do this or this for the people of Leighley, whatever it is?

Brand takes a deep breath, impressed by her astuteness. Leans forward.

BRAND: Listen. I thought very carefully before I decided to seek selection. I was doing a good job, teaching liberal studies at the local tech. *(pause)* I wouldn't be here now if I didn't think I could do something *better* as an MP. *(pause)* I should find it ... very hard ... to think of myself as fodder.

A surge of noise as the door opens causes the interviewer to switch off her tape recorder. Brand sees Miriam in the doorway. Stands.

MIRIAM: *(looking at woman's back)* I'm sorry, Mr Jowett said I'd find you in here.

BRAND: Come in, come in. I think we've just about finished? *(the woman nods, standing, beginning to pack the gear)* This is my wife, Miriam ...

WOMAN: Oh marvellous. Do you think I might er ... *(she waves the mic in Miriam's direction. Brand looks at Miriam, who looks back at him uncertainly)* Five minutes, no more, I promise. Something for my Manchester Woman programme, goes out tomorrow ...

MIRIAM: *(finally)* All right. It's up to you ...

WOMAN: Thanks. Here'll do, if we shut that door.

MIRIAM: Mr Jowett seemed ... keen to have a word with you ...

BRAND: Yeah? *(to interviewer)* Excuse us a moment, will you ...

He leads Miriam out into the throbbing hall.

BRAND: *(close to her)* Thanks.

MIRIAM: Mother's got the children. They'll stay the night.

BRAND: You look good. New suit?

MIRIAM: No. *(he purses his lips, looks away)* Go and do your work while I tell the world what a wonderful person you are.

BRAND: Yeah.

He shoves a way towards Jowett's register tables. Miriam watches a moment, turns back into Jowett's office.

Jowett conducts an aggressive phonecall with some outlying committee room in North Ward. He promises more help, more transport, but implies they ought to have been able to sort it out themselves. Stead controls operations at the four tables: huge stacks of appropriate Reading Slips in piles of fifty on each of the tables. People clamour to get their slips accepted and registered. Messengers – mainly young boys and girls – from polling stations and local committee rooms stream in and out.

Brand reaches Jowett, who's doing some calculations on a pad.

BRAND: Alf.

JOWETT: Oh, you're there. Finish the interview?

BRAND: Ahunh.

JOWETT: *(calling)* Frank, Albert, got a minute?

Stead and Hilton join them. Hilton, in sports coat and slacks, sweats heavily.

JOWETT: I've just been doing some reckoning ... I think we're a nose in front, but it's too bloody close. *(he opens a book on the table)* Now, we're an hour behind in North Ward. I reckon that's eighty, maybe a hundred votes up the spout by ten. *(checks watch)* I've a promise of four cars at nine from the AEUW, but I'd like to get cracking up there right away. I can't go, obviously. Frank, what about you?

HILTON: All right by me. Can you cover the table?

JOWETT: Yeah yeah, don't worry about that. Albert, see if there's anybody reliable on your table who could handle a couple of streets in my van.

STEAD: Will do.

BRAND: What about me?

JOWETT: No, they'll want you up at t' Town Hall directly. Have the tv people been in touch...?

BRAND: Look, sod them, Alf, give me the streets, I'll do it. That's what it's about, isn't it?

STEAD: Doesn't look so good, candidate on the knocker on the day, Bill ...

BRAND: So I'll wear a false nose.

HILTON: Executive'd have someat to say ...

BRAND: They'll have someat to say if we lose, Frank. *(he looks at each of them in turn)* Look, I'm not arguing. I'm going. Right?

They look at each other, shrugging, struggling for the consensus.

JOWETT: Right, I'll sort out the division.

Stead and Hilton retire to their stations.

JOWETT: *(grinning)* You're going to be one long problem you, aren't you.

BRAND: *(seriously)* How does it really stand, Alf?

JOWETT: *(holding book and slips up)* According to the collective wisdom of the Reading Slip, we're in the lead. Just. *(pause)* I don't think I'd want to lay more than ... 50p on it, nevertheless. *(Brand nods, lips tight suddenly)* Did you see your wife?

BRAND: Yes.

JOWETT: *(returning to table)* Give me five minutes. Wear your rosette, will you.

Brand turns towards Jowett's office. People pat him on the back and shoulders, wish him luck. He pushes his way into the office.

Int. Jowett's office.

BRAND: Has she gone?

MIRIAM: *(drinking tea from a mug)* Ahunh.

BRAND: *(crossing to phone, checking number in directory)* I'm going on the knocker. Do you want to come?

MIRIAM: Trouble?

BRAND: Maybe. Can't tell. Jowett says not but he'd say that if there'd been a Tory landslide. Till ten o'clock anyway. *(he begins to dial)* Do you want to come?

MIRIAM: All right.

BRAND: Won't be a minute. *(waits. New voice, cool, efficient)* Dr Jenkins? My name's Brand. You saw my father this morning, Wilfred Brand ... yes, that's right. *(listens a moment)* Ahunh. Mmm. And damage? *(listens)* Ahunh. Yes, two things. I don't know if you noticed, but my mother's looking pretty weary, perhaps you could give her something, a tonic? Fine. And ... er ... you might consider having a word with the Social Services department about home help ... Ahunh. Well, she works, and she can't afford not to. *(listens)* Well, I'd be grateful if you'd do what you can. Many thanks. Goodbye.

He puts the phone down. Miriam frowns a question at him.

MIRIAM: Dad?

***Int. Tower block**, corridor. Brand, fixing rosette, knocks at no.8. Waits. Stares down at the corridor floor, at a largeish clump of dogshit about eighteen inches from his shoe. He knocks again. The door is opened by an old lady, over 70, small, balding, arthritic.*

MRS WATSON: What do you want?

BRAND: Labour Party, Mrs Watson. I've come to take you down to the poll.

MRS WATSON: Can't go now. It's me favourite programme. They said they'd come this morning, they said.

BRAND: Won't take a minute, Mrs Watson.

MRS WATSON: Will you bring me back then?

BRAND: Certainly.

She waits, thinking, undecided.

MRS WATSON: I'll get me coat. *(peers at the rosette, half blind)* You did say Labour, dint you?

BRAND: That's right.

She turns back into her flat. He hears the tv go off. Looks around him at the bleak, patched, peeling walls, the shabby lift, the cold brick floor. The woman returns, in a long brown coat.

MRS WATSON: Have I to bring anything?

BRAND: You'll need your voting card ...

MRS WATSON: Is that it? *(she hands him a card)* I'm not so good without my glasses.

BRAND: Yes, that's it.

MRS WATSON: *(checking)* Keys. Right then. *(she closes door. Brand presses for the lift)* There'll be another election 'fore that's mended. Two months or more that's been out of order, it's the kids, they play in it, they've nowhere else ... *(she walks towards the dogshit. Brand steers her past it)*

BRAND: Here, I'll give you a hand.

MRS WATSON: *(at top of stairs)* Oh. What about Gladys? You must take Gladys. She'd never forgive me if I went without her …

BRAND: Gladys?

MRS WATSON: *(turning)* Number nine. Here. *(she walks towards the door. Brand checks his list, frowning)* She might be in bed. *(she knocks)*

BRAND: Mrs Watson, I don't seem to have … Gladys down. Do you happen to know if she's Labour…?

MRS WATSON: I've no idea. Wouldn't dream of asking her. It's a secret ballot, you know.

The door opens. Gladys is a year or two younger, thin, wiry, alert.

GLADYS: Martha.

MRS WATSON: Hello Gladys. This young man's come to take us to the vote, so get your coat and we'll have a nice ride in his car.

GLADYS: Well, I'm expecting the clubman any minute, Martha, I don't really want to miss him …

MRS WATSON: He'll bring us back. He's promised. It'll be a bit of an outing.

GLADYS: I'll get me coat.

Mrs Watson turns to Brand with a nice smile.

MRS WATSON: I told you she'd come.

Car. The two old women chatter away in the back. Brand drives past a Volksmobile with Tory posters neatly affixed, its quadruple speakers pumping out a final message. Miriam checks the address file.

MIRIAM: So that's er, eight and what? Ten?

BRAND: Nine.

MIRIAM: Nine's not on the list.

BRAND: Nevertheless.

MIRIAM: How come?

BRAND: It seems … they always go together.

MIRIAM: Well, I suppose a vote's a vote. *(he doesn't answer. She peers at him in the gloom)* She is … Labour, I take it?

BRAND: *(grinning in spite of it all)* Well, I suppose it's no more than a three to one chance …

Miriam lifts her eyes in mock horror, grins back.

MIRIAM: Are you *sure* you want to win this seat?

Ext. Town Hall. Night. A blackened white building floodlit at front and side from the narrow lawns. A BBC outside broadcast van parked next to a Granada van. Quite dark now, the clock showing 9.50, as Brand's Escort draws up. Brand and Miriam walk up the steps and enter.

Int. Entrance to Town Hall. Brand and Miriam enter. Cheers go up from the Labour support in the hall. Tories and Liberals jeer a little. In their path, a cluster of middle class professionals, ruddy with gin and anticipation, whom they cannot avoid. Among them, Bernard Shaw and his wife Angie.

SHAW: *(detaching, with wife, from larger crowd)* They're looking for you, Bill. Think you've lost your deposit.

Brand smiles dryly. He doesn't like him.

BRAND: Bernard and Angie Shaw, my wife Miriam.

SHAW: Delighted to meet you. *(Miriam smiles, though minimally)*

ANGIE: *(cool)* We've met, I think.

MIRIAM: *(cool)* Yes, I think we have.

An announcement lurches cracklingly across the P.A. system.

ANNOUNCEMENT: Would Mr William Brand, Mr William Brand, please go to Room 2 behind the stage, where the Returning Officer is waiting to receive him. Mr William Brand to Room 2 please. Thank you.

A whine as it's switched off.

BRAND: See you later then. Come on. *(he takes Miriam by the arm, pushes her towards the hall)*

ANGIE: I thought you were going to invite them back ...

SHAW: *(smiling)* He's got to win first, my love. *(pause)* She seems nice.

ANGIE: *(with some contempt mounting)* Nice?

SHAW: Nicer than him anyway. Smug bastard.

Int. Town Hall. The candidates' room. Long and narrow, an oak panelled door at one end. The Tory and his wife, the Liberal and her husband, and the two agents are already there, drinking shorts and talking tersely, stop and start, as a group. A uniformed waitress stands by a white linen-covered drinks table, waiting to serve. The Returning Officer and one of his assistants study the procedures manual for disputed ballot papers. Brand and Miriam arrive. The other candidates stare into their drinks, the only sign they give of having seen him. The Returning Officer sees him.

RETURNING OFFICER: Ah, Mr Brand ...

BRAND: I'm sorry I'm late ... your worship ... hope I've not kept you waiting ... you know my wife, I think.

RETURNING OFFICER: How do you do, Mrs Brand. Very glad you could come along. *(clearing throat)* Well ... ladies and gentlemen, if I could have your attention for a moment ... *(he checks his watch)* The polls will close in ... sixty seconds time. I'm hoping to have all ballot boxes inside this building within the next forty minutes, when the count will begin. Assuming a clear result, there's no reason why the announcement shouldn't be ready by midnight or a few minutes later ... That calculation is based, I should add, on a no higher than 75% turn-out, so don't hold me to it. At about a quarter to twelve I shall ask you to assist me in allocating those voting slips which, for one reason or another, are what we call 'in dispute'. I hope we'll be able to show the same amicability and forbearance in that as we've shown in the remainder of this hard but fairly fought contest. My assistant Mr Petty will show each of you in turn between now and then the rules and guidance manual relating to disputed slips, so that you can see the sorts of examples that do crop up from year to year ... *(clears throat again)* I'd be grateful if you would keep your speeches of thanks one: non-controversial and two: as brief as possible, so that my staff can get off to their beds with the least possible delay. I think that's all. Thank you very much, ladies and gentlemen.

TORY: Thank you, Mr Mayor.

Mutters of thanks from the others.

BRAND: *(to Miriam)* Drink?

MIRIAM: I'll have a sherry.

Brand crosses to the table, asks the waitress for a sherry and a brown ale. The Returning Officer arrives, chain clanking.

RETURNING OFFICER: *(low, slightly broader voice)* Where the bloody hell were you, then? Nearly give me heart failure.

BRAND: Shorthanded, Percy. I've been on the knocker.

RETURNING OFFICER: Bloody hell. It's Dunkirk every day in this bloody party. Eeeh. *(he clicks his false teeth at the thought of it, moves off out of the room)*

Brand returns with the drinks, stands with Miriam, apart from the others, but staring at them. The Tory turns his way finally.

TORY: Good evening.

BRAND: Good evening.

Silence. The odd throat clearing.

LIBERAL LADY: Good evening.

BRAND: Good evening.

Silence. Brand drains his glass, three gulps. Stares at the group. They begin their terse exchanges again, stop, start, with much pivoting on toes and heels.

Montage sequence of count. TV commentator, speaking to lip mic. His monitor. Increasing tension as the count develops. We watch the piles mount: the work of the scrutineers: the recounting of dubious piles: the candidates trying to agree allocation of disputed slips: loudspeaker requests for silence from supporters while the count is in progress: the candidates prowling up and down the long lines of tables.

Int. Candidates' room. Brand stands by window, looking out into night, through the room's reflection. Miriam sits, close but remote.

The Tory candidate is checking some figures with his agent. The Liberal candidate talks to a member of the Returning Officer's staff. Door opens at far end of room. Jowett in. Sees Brand at the other end, approaches, an open notebook in his hand. Stops a couple of feet from Brand, the same alert whippet he was at 9.30 this morning. Jowett hands Brand the notebook. Brand studies it. Looks back at Jowett. Jowett winks.

We see the Returning Officer beginning his address and announcement on a tv screen. Pull out to show Mrs Brand nodding, half-sleeping, on the settee. She wakes up suddenly as she hears the first name:

RETURNING OFFICER: *(on tv)* Geoffrey James Arnold Anderson ... *(commentator's voice: 'Conservative')* ... 18,172. *Close shot of Anderson.*

Another tv screen, the Returning Officer continuing. Pull out to reveal Eddie cutting a red into the middle pocket, the club tv in the background.

RETURNING OFFICER: *(on tv)* Katherine Wyatt Bairstow ... *(commentator's voice: 'Liberal')* ... 11,486.

Another tv screen. Pull out to show Alex in bed, watching, impassive.

RETURNING OFFICER: *(on tv)* William Brand... *(commentator's voice: 'Labour')* ... 19,332.

(close shot of Brand. 'Lab Hold' flashes onto the screen as the Returning Officer continues)

RETURNING OFFICER: ... and that the aforesaid William Brand is duly elected member for this constituency ...

Huge cheering from the Labour supporters. Over,

COMMENTATOR'S VOICE: So Labour hang on to Leighley, but with a considerably reduced majority, and an anti-government swing of what seems to be around ... five per cent ... *(quietens as Brand steps forward)*

Alex closes her eyes, opens them as Brand approaches the microphone to give his speech of thanks. Closes them again.

Int. Central Committee Rooms. *1.20 am by the clock. The celebrations have already thinned out to a couple of dozen Young Socialists and a few members of the Executive. Brand and Miriam stand in a group of Young Socialists, drinking and arguing. Down the room, another group at the piano, singing the*

Internationale badly. Jowett sits in his office, door ajar, staring at the mounds of paper on the rolltop desk, a bottle of Newcastle Brown in his hand. Albert Stead, trilby on head, says goodnight to Jowett from the door. They shake hands. Stead comes down the room to Brand's group.

STEAD: I'll say goodnight then, brother.

BRAND: *(hand out)* Goodnight, Albert. Thanks for everything.

STEAD: I'll look out for you at Region. *(pause)* Miners said no, did you hear?

BRAND: Yeah.

STEAD: S'gonna be interesting. Good night, Mrs Brand. Well done the pair of you.

He tips his hat smilingly, leaves. Cries of 'What about a song then, Bill?' from the bottom of the room. The group he's with take up the entreaty.

BRAND: *(calling)* Hang on, hang on, I'll sing in a minute, all right? *(to Miriam)* I want a word with Jowett. We'll go soon.

MIRIAM: Whenever you say.

Miriam is drawn by the Young Socialist people towards the piano, to cheers from those already there. A glass falls to the floor with a crash. Another cheer. Brand reaches Jowett's office, stares at Jowett for a moment, knocks on the open door.

Int. Jowett's office. Jowett throws down his pencil, leans back in his chair.

JOWETT: Come in.

BRAND: Thanks. *(he half sits, half leans on a table by the wall, drinks his pale ale a moment)*

JOWETT: Just ... *(he waves at the impossibility surrounding him, smiling crookedly)*

BRAND: *(quiet)* I wanted to say thanks.

JOWETT: We did all right.

They look at each other for a moment. Jowett reaches down for his little battered briefcase, flicks the flap to, pockets three pencils and a biro. Stands, stretches a little, scratches the back of his head with some vigour.

JOWETT: I suppose I'd better get back. *(ribald shrieks, another glass crashing, from the bottom of the hall)* Before the revolution gets under way in earnest ... *(turns to look at Brand)* I'm ... glad you came back. *(Brand frowns. Jowett waves at the hall)* You could have gone off to the *party* with the Heaton Moor brigade ... the Leighley elite.

BRAND: *(smiling softly)* There was only one party tonight, Alf.

JOWETT: *(sniffing)* I'll figure you out. It'll take a while, but I'll figure you out. *(he leaves)* I'll shut up shop ...

BRAND: I just need to make a call, OK?

JOWETT: *(gone)* Help yourself ...

Brand closes door, crosses to desk, dials a number, waits for answer, unwraps and lights a Winterman's.

BRAND: Hi. Yeah. Amazing. *(listens a moment)* I'm at Adelphi Street ... No, just a bit of a do ... *(checks watch)* I don't think so, love ... What? *(listens, biting the inside of his mouth with growing tension)* Well, we'll talk about it tomorrow- *(listens again, angering a fraction)* Whenever you say, baby- *(listening again)* I'm sorry, it was a perfectly harmless expression- *(listens again)* All right. All right. Fine.

He puts the phone down, crushes his Winterman's in the overflowing ashtray, turns. Miriam stands watching him from the door. Long silence.

Car. Night.

MIRIAM: *(who's been crying)* You bastard. You bastard.

BRAND: I'm sorry. I didn't ... Look, you've known about this for two-

MIRIAM: You were with *me*. You *asked* me. You're a selfish, egotistical uncaring swine of a man.

BRAND: That's me. Fine. Leave it.

MIRIAM: Is that all you can say?

BRAND: *(terse, tense)* What is there to say? I've said it all. There's nothing new in the world. There is you and the children and there is Alex. I don't like it, I wish I could handle it with a little more grace and so on, but I *get no help* ... *(seeking control again)* You're not interested in ... rational solutions ...

MIRIAM: 'Rational solutions'! Oh my God! Life isn't a series of resolutions for Annual Conference. I won't have these children's future ... *composited.* Understand?

BRAND: You're being hysterical, Mim ...

MIRIAM: I'm not, I'm being emotional. There's a difference, though *you* couldn't be expected to see it, because you long ago decided that *feelings* were just a bit ... embarrassing, childish ... not rational, mm? *(pause. Right)* You make me *puke.*

They drive in silence, arrived on the estate. The car draws up outside the house. Brand dips the lights.

MIRIAM: *(tightly)* Look, don't come in. I don't want you to.

BRAND: Oh Christ, don't start that agai-

MIRIAM: I mean it. *(pause)* I mean it, Bill. *(pause. then quickly)* I think we should get a divorce.

Brand puts his head back, breathes deeply, rubs his face.

BRAND: We've been ... over this ... a hundred times, Mim. A hundred times. Tomorrow you'll say something else ...

MIRIAM: *(decisive)* No. No I won't.

Silence.

BRAND: *(finally)* Jesus Christ. You've got a magnificent sense of timing, Mrs Brand ...

MIRIAM: *(tiny voice)* I just want to survive.

She gets out of the car swiftly, moves off towards the house.

BRAND: Mim ...

She walks on. He sits a moment, then flicks on the lights, sees her, through the open carport, fumbling for her key, simple, pretty, alone.

Int. Alex's flat. A spoon stirring a mug of tea. Reveal Brand, in blue bathrobe, preparing a second mug, with tea bag, at the kitchen area of Alex's room. Alex, sleepy but awake now, watches him from the bed. She sleeps in an old faded denim shirt. Brand carries the mugs over, hands her hers, sits down on the bed.

BRAND: Cheers.

ALEX: Cheers.

They sip in silence for a moment.

BRAND: Sorry about the stuff on the phone.

ALEX: My fault. I was childish. And a bit frightened.

BRAND: It'll be all right, love.

ALEX: Will it? With you in London and me here?

BRAND: We'll think of something ...

ALEX: What? Correspondence by cassette?

BRAND: *(delicate)* You could work in London ...

ALEX: Until yesterday, you could've worked here. *(he turns away)* God, I wouldn't mind if it were something you'd always wanted, a passion. Two years ago, when I first met you, you called the House of Commons a club for fleas, a place where the fleas on the body politic could swap leaps and pirouettes before returning to their pelts for the serious business of sucking our democratic life blood ... mmm? So what happened?

BRAND: *(turning to face her)* I changed my mind.

ALEX: Ah.

BRAND: I woke up one morning ... and examined my store of ... exquisitely turned metaphors ... and realised I hadn't *done* anything in fifteen years, beyond add to that store. *(pause)* I've got to do something, Al. *(pause)* Something has to be done. *(he shrugs, stands, paces a bit)* I've few illusions. But the illusion I'm most glad to be rid of is the one that says we're all *impotent* in face of the juggernaut, the system.

ALEX: And you think you can really *do* something down there?

BRAND: *(slowly)* Yes. I think I can.

ALEX: *(finally, putting down her cup, lying down in bed)* I wish you luck.

He watches her for a moment.

BRAND: Would you ... marry me? If it were ... possible, I mean.

Long silence.

ALEX: I'd live with you. Not marry.

Car. Day. Brand comes on to the M6 just south of Manchester. Signs to Birmingham and London. We see his suitcase and other effects in the back of his estate car. He wanders across stations on the radio. A church service establishes it's Sunday. He arrives at 'Pick of the Week' on Radio 4. Drives, giving it minimal attention, until

WOMAN PRESENTER: And now for something from local radio, an item that took our fancy in Radio Manchester's 'Manchester Women' series broadcast last Friday. Mrs Miriam Brand, whose husband Bill is now the newly returned Labour MP for Leighley in Lancashire, was asked to describe what qualities she thought her husband possessed that would make him a good politician. Her answer: *(Brand turns it up a little)*

MIRIAM'S VOICE: He's honest. He's open. He's got roots in the community. He's never suffered from what you might call an excess of personal ambition. There's something else, though, very difficult to put into words without sounding pompous, pi, you know what I mean. He ... he's ... trying to be a good man ...

We watch the car pick up speed, heading south.

- *end* -

Episode 2

You wanna be a hero, get yourself a white horse

was broadcast on Monday 14th June 1976

The cast was as follows:

Bill Brand   Jack Shepherd

Waverley   Richard Leech

Sandiford   William Hoyland

Mapson   Richard Butler

Paxton   Frank Mills

McNab   James Giles

Winnie Scoular   Rosemary Martin

Michael Brand   Philip Cox

Jane Brand   Karen Silver

Miriam Brand   Lynn Farleigh

Mosley   Michael Atha

Alf Jowett   Allan Surtees

Alex Ferguson   Cherie Lunghi

Reg Starr   Douglas Campbell

Maddocks   Peter Copley

Ticket Collector   Stanley Dawson

Designers: David Ferris, Harry Clark

Executive Producer: Stella Richman

Producer: Stuart Burge

Director: Roland Joffe

PART ONE

Ext. Palace of Westminster. Small queue for Visitors Gallery. MPs arriving in cars, on foot. Police.

Int. House of Commons. Brand introduced by Sandiford, an assistant Whip, to the House from below the bar. Brand affirms (i.e. no oath). The bewigged Speaker accepts the affirmation. All this in close-up, the sound alone suggesting a fairly full chamber.

Int. Desk Room, House of Commons. Five desks crammed in irregularly, in a badly shaped room. A tallish man of about 60, well-dressed, silver-haired, sits at a desk in a corner, reading the Financial Times attentively, half-rim glasses on end of nose.

Brand in, balancing files, letters and other effects on his black attaché case. He looks around the room, seeking ways of discovering which desk is his. Waverley, the other man, stares over glasses and paper at the new arrival. Brand takes the look. Waverley nods him to a desk on the far wall. Brand smiles, dumps his gear on it, begins to sort it all out.

WAVERLEY: *(across room)* Brand, is it? Did I catch it right?

BRAND: Brand.

WAVERLEY: You took old Willie Horton's seat at Leighley.

BRAND: *(small smile)* Kept.

Slight pause. Waverley folds his paper, checks his fob watch. Stands.

WAVERLEY: Tea or something I think. *(to Brand)* Waverley, Worcester North.

BRAND: How do you do.

WAVERLEY: *(smiling)* Not in the market for a pairing, are you? *(Brand grins)* No, I suppose not. I need a couple of days away to get my business in some sort of order. *(pause)* I'm Waverleys. *(Brand doesn't understand)* The boat firm. *(Brand nods, polite, still no wiser)* Chaos. You don't understand *business*, Brand. Wrong people at the helm. And *this* place ... I've had three days off in the last year. I can remember when the House was like a club.

Sandiford in. Stands in doorway.

WAVERLEY: *(looking at Sandiford with distaste)* It's more like a damned ... assembly line now. Drop in at the Bar, we'll have a chat.

He leaves. Sandiford takes his place. Brand studies order papers, whips' instructions; piles Hansards and other books and pamphlets in front of him.

SANDIFORD: *(smooth, about Brand's age, southern, clever)* You found it then. Good. Not too painful, eh. *(a gesture in direction of absent chamber)*

BRAND: *(reading)* No no.

SANDIFORD: The Tories prefer the oath. They prefer God to be in there somewhere. They think we're pretty godless creatures, all in all.

BRAND: *Aren't* we?

Sandiford smiles blandly.

SANDIFORD: The word on you is you find it difficult to agree with a Tory on anything ...

BRAND: *(grinning dryly)* Anything ... fundamental.

Mapson in, MP for Ribble, grizzled, past 50. He walks to his desk by the window.

SANDIFORD: Evening, Tom.

MAPSON: Richard.

Mapson sits down, begins rooting in his desk.

SANDIFORD: *(thinking of introducing Brand, deciding against)* Let me know if there's anything you need by way of help. You'll be getting the call from our office pretty soon, I should think, the state things are in just now. Not sure who *your* whip is. Not me, I know. Could be Dennis Paxton. Still, we're all ... reasonable men. *(He smiles at his irony, Mapson turns to look at him, gnarled, impassive, on this last line)* Be good.

He leaves. Brand runs through an order paper. He pairs it eventually with its whips memorandum: two-line. Puts it down. Picks up small sheaf of mail, begins to open first envelope.

Mapson has turned in his chair to study Brand.

MAPSON: How do. Tom Mapson, Ribble.

He stands, hand outstretched. Brand stands, takes it.

BRAND: Hello. Bill Brand, Leighley.

MAPSON: Aye. Welcome. Sit down, sit down.

Brand sits, Mapson daws up a spare chair, to sit at the edge of the desk. He wears a fraying, shiny navy blue suit, cracked shoes, a red tie on whiteish shirt. Hair cropped short, where it survives on the cragged skull.

MAPSON: Watch them buggers. *(points to door)* Whips. They'll put you through hoops if you give 'em an opening.

BRAND: I think that one was trying to kill me with blandness.

MAPSON: Sandiford? Oh, he'll get on, don't you worry. PPS next, then junior minister ... you won a good seat there, Bill. A good campaign. Full of principle.

BRAND: *(ironic)* I've got a good agent.

MAPSON: The modesty of real arrogance, too. Bodes well, does that. This place is stacked high with lobby fodder. *(Brand opens another letter, studies it)* Had a word with Bert Stead at North West Region last weekend ... *(Brand nods, acknowledging)* He rates you.

BRAND: He's a good feller.

MAPSON: Will you be applying to join the Journal group?

BRAND: *(guarded)* I'm thinking about it.

MAPSON: I spoke with Reg Starr this morning. I think he's keen to have you aboard.

BRAND: I'll get my bearings first, I think.

MAPSON: Aye.

BRAND: *(studying letter)* Excuse me a minute, will you. *(hand on phone)* How do I use this thing?

MAPSON: Nine gives you a line out.

BRAND: *(clicks 9, then taps out Leighley code + 2746. Waits. To Mapson)* Some dates gone haywire ... Hello. Alf? Bill. Yeah, fine. Look, I've got your letter about the Victory Dance. I think the girl was drunk, it was *Saturday*, wasn't it? She's put Thursday. *(listens)* But, I can't get away Thursdays ... *(listens again)* Yeah, I know that ... *(listens again)* I *know* it's important, Alf ... Yes, I'll do what I can ... No, I see that ... All right, I'll call you back. Probably tomorrow. Cheers... And you. *(puts phone down)*

MAPSON: Cock-up?

BRAND: Yeah. They've had to fix the victory celebration for a week Thursday. I imagine that might prove ... a trifle difficult?

MAPSON: No harder than flying. Still. Where do you stay?

BRAND: Hotel at the moment, sixteen quid Monday to Thursday, special rate.

MAPSON: What're your plans?

BRAND: I suppose I'll try and find somewhere.

MAPSON: We rent a house in Clapham, three of us. We're looking for a fourth. Of similar persuasion, of course.

BRAND: All Journal Group, you mean.

MAPSON: All Journal Group.

BRAND: I'd like a look.

MAPSON: *(card from wallet)* Just off the South Circular Road. Lynnett Drive. What about tonight?

BRAND: Fine. I'll have to pick up the car ...

His phone rings. He answers it.

BRAND: Speaking. How do you do. Yes, I think so. *(checking watch)* Could you make that twenty minutes? ... Well, I'll get there as soon as I can ... *(he puts receiver down)* Paxton?

MAPSON: The CSM. He's got a pace-stick where his mind used to be. Watch him … they're all on edge just now … *(he retires to his own desk)*

BRAND: *(standing, frowning at Jowett's letter)* See you tonight then, Tom.

MAPSON: Yeah.

BRAND: Where's … Er … where's the Bar?

MAPSON: Nowhere near the Whips Office, lad.

BRAND: Pity.

He leaves.

Int. House of Commons Bar. *Waverley sits at a table on his own, the Financial Times open at the arts page. He sniffs with incredulity from time to time. Chatter, some laughter, from room. Brand looms above him. Waverley looks up.*

WAVERLEY: Do you ever read this thing?

BRAND: Occasionally.

WAVERLEY: Full of communists. The arts page is crawling with 'em.

BRAND: Pink paper too.

WAVERLEY: Get a drink, sit yourself down.

BRAND: I'm en route. How's next Thursday sound?

WAVERLEY: What?

BRAND: For a pairing. You and me.

WAVERLEY: *(disbelieving)* Sounds bloody marvellous. Have you cleared it?

BRAND: No. I'm seeing the Whips now.

WAVERLEY: *(subsiding)* I see. Best of British to you. Though God knows what good that particular commodity will do you in this year of grace …

BRAND: I'll let you know.

Turns, leaves. Waverley reads the tv review with crescent disbelief.

Int. Whips' Office. *Brand knocks, enters. A number of desks around the room. Paxton sits at his desk, ticking or querying names – about twenty of them – on a clipboarded duplicated sheet. He's in his mid-40s, a South Londoner, with a round, hard, crinkled face and stiffly parted dark hair.*

PAXTON: Come in. I'm Paxton. You'll be answerable to me in divisions.

He offers no seat, no ground even. Brand draws up a chair, sits facing him across the desk. Stares briefly at the door that connects the Assistant Whips' office to the Chief Whip's.

PAXTON: Chief Whip's on his regular Monday meeting with the other parties. *(pause)* Not that he expressed any particular wish to meet you. *(Brand says nothing)* I take it you know the present state of the House. *(Brand nods)* 301 votes, that's how we see it. If we get them all out, we have a majority of four over all other parties – Tories, Liberals, Scots Nats, Welsh Nats, Irish, and other assorted odds and sods. If we don't ... *(he leaves it. Picks up a folder from the desk)* The ... Foreign Secretary's offer to speak in your constituency during the campaign was ... not taken up. *(looks at Brand over folder)* What was that about?

BRAND: There's a lot of feeling in the CLP about the new pattern of arms deals. *(pause)* The consensus was ... he'd've been a liability.

PAXTON: Don't Metro-Prince Small Arms have a division in Leighley?

BRAND: Ahunh. Six hundred men.

PAXTON: Does the local party want to see them unemployed then?

BRAND: *(quiet, deliberate)* I think you know the answer to that.

Slight pause.

PAXTON: I know the answer to a great many things. That's my job. No government can function efficiently without information and ... management, ie discipline. We expect your co-operation. These are perilous times. One tilt, one shift, one foot out of place ... and we're all in the mire, Government, Party, country. We're on the right road. Your victory at the polls is a clear enough indication of that. The Government has a right to your loyalty. Total; unquestioning, if necessary. *(pause)* What were you before this?

BRAND: Lecturer in a tech ... I taught-

PAXTON: Don't tell me: Liberal Studies? *(Brand grins, nods)* Figures. I was going to say, if you'd worked in industry you'd know what I'm driving at ... Forget it. Do you have any questions?

BRAND: Just one. What are the chances of leaving early Thursday week?

Pause. Paxton thinks he's being joshed.

PAXTON: Supposed to be funny?

BRAND: Not that I'm aware.

PAXTON: Why?

BRAND: My CLP's organised a Victory Celebration. I'd like to be there. *(pause)* Naturally, if there's a chance of a division ...

PAXTON: *(contemptuous)* There's a chance every day, sonny. Every single day ...

BRAND: There is a pairing available ... *(Paxton wide-eyed)* A Tory in the same desk-room. *(innocent)* If that will help ...

PAXTON: *(a reluctant smile developing: not pleasant)* You slippy man, you. Mmm? I'll be in touch. We'll see how you go, shall we?

Brand is dismissed. He stands.

BRAND: His name's Waverley. Worcester North.

PAXTON: *(unyielding)* Right. I don't suppose I need to spell out the *powers* of this office, do I?

BRAND: No no. I used to teach the history of the Constitution. Charting the growth of our freedoms.

He leaves, nodding to Sandiford who's just entering. Sandiford crosses to his desk, picks up phone, asks for a number, replaces receiver.

SANDIFORD: *(eyeing door)* Yours?

PAXTON: I don't know where they dig them up, I don't. Flash Harry …

SANDIFORD: Ambition. *(Paxton frowns his incomprehension)* Take him … *(finger and thumb in delicate conjunction)* … by the heel.

Int. Clapham flat. *Bedroom. Brand stands inside doorway, turns on the light. An irregular, fair-sized room with a mattress on the floor, blankets and pillows folded at its head. Assorted styleless furniture, but neither grubby nor particularly bad. A free-standing two-bar electric fire from a point on the near wall. A window overlooking an entry. He switches off the light, goes back into the living room.*

Living room. Mapson stands near the door. This room is marginally better-furnished, with small green-topped desk, table, divan and chairs. A corner of the room, half-screened, contains the kitchen area: sink, cooker, utensils, small fridge.

MAPSON: What do you think?

BRAND: How much?

MAPSON: Ten quid a week.

BRAND: I'll take it.

MAPSON: Good. I'll tell old Brierley. When would you like to move in?

BRAND: Now. *(Mapson's surprise)* My gear's in the car. That be OK?

MAPSON: *(smiling)* I don't see why not. You'll need sheets.

BRAND: I'll manage.

MAPSON: I'll see if Winnie's got any. She's got the ground floor.

Jim McNab in, small, wiry, early forties, rimless glasses, emigré Scot.

MAPSON: Jim and I share the first floor. Jim McNab, Bill Brand. Jim's got Nottingham Park.

BRAND: *(shakes hands)* Hi.

MCNAB: Good to meet you. Great win, that.

BRAND: Thanks.

MAPSON: Bill's joining us.

MCNAB: *(acute)* Journal Group, you mean?

MAPSON: That too, when he's ready.

MCNAB: Look forward to that. *(to Mapson)* What's the latest on the Economy Bill?

MAPSON: Starr's meeting Maddern again tomorrow. I think they'll shift.

MCNAB: *(unconvinced)* Do you? *(leaving)* I've a quid says they won't. *(to Brand)* Drop in any time. First door on the landing ... *(he's gone)*

Pause

BRAND: I'll get my stuff, I think.

MAPSON: I'll see Winnie about those sheets. Oh ... the phone's got extensions throughout the house ... and there's a buzzer thing ... *(he locates it on the desk)* ... for internals ... one for Winnie, two Jim, three me ... you'll be four. *(indicates)* And plenty of lead for phoning the wife ... *(he indicates the bedroom, flashing an unexpected grin at Brand)* ... all right?

PART TWO

Int. Clapham living room. Day. Winnie Scoular stands inside the doorway, holding a pair of sheets and pillow cases. She's a tough, good-looking woman in her late thirties, hair greying already. She wears a good woollen suit and boots. She surveys the room, now littered with two suitcases, opened, books, box files, folders, newspapers, pamphlets, typewriter, radio, portable tv and other personal paraphernalia.

Brand in from stairs, carrying last armful, crumpled coat and trousers on a hanger and a carrier bag of groceries.

BRAND: Hello.

SCOULAR: Hello. I brought you these. Winnie Scoular.

BRAND: Thanks. S'very kind of you. Bill Brand.

She puts them on the table. He dumps his gear. They shake hands.

BRAND: I'm just gonna make some cocoa ...

SCOULAR: That'll be nice.

BRAND: Have a seat.

He fishes a packet of cocoa, some sugar and a carton of milk from the carrier, begins to prepare the drinks, fishing for a pan below the sink, cups from the cupboard above. Scoular sits in an armchair facing the kitchen area.

BRAND: South coast somewhere, aren't you?

SCOULAR: Churton.

BRAND: Went there once to watch City. Manchester. Before you slipped into the second. Bit of a dump.

SCOULAR: Careful. I've been to Leighley.

BRAND: *(grinning round screen)* Ah. Now you're talking. Sugar?

SCOULAR: One. *(he retires behind the screen)* Are you sponsored?

BRAND: No.

SCOULAR: You're going to find it hard then. Unless your wife has money. Or your bank manager.

Brand appears with the cocoa, hands her hers.

BRAND: *(sitting opposite her)* I'm drawing my superann. Fourteen hundred for fourteen years hard. Should see me through to the end of the month.

SCOULAR: You might pick something up from the papers, if you're that way inclined.

BRAND: The Journal, for example?

SCOULAR: *(laughing)* Hardly. The Journal barely has enough to pay the rent on the offices, let alone fees.

BRAND: I suppose I'll make out.

She drinks a little, watches him. He lights a Winterman's Senorita.

SCOULAR: You're very adept at saying nothing. Is that a style, or just an absence of content?

Brand puts down his cup, looks at her: grins suddenly.

BRAND: That wouldn't be a proposal, would it?

SCOULAR: *(smiling; very softly)* There you go again.

BRAND: What do you want me to say?

SCOULAR: *(again, very soft, direct)* I'm a *comrade*, comrade.

Slight pause.

BRAND: *(carefully)* Forgive me. *(pause)* I've met a good many ... comrades today. Paxton, do you know Paxton? It was an encounter not calculated to loosen the tongue.

SCOULAR: Ex-docker. Did you know? *(Brand didn't)* Entered parliament from the left.

BRAND: What the man called ... 'parliamentary cretinism'...?

SCOULAR: *(ironic)* Ah. He's read his Marx.

BRAND: *(Bogart. Even)* That's ... erm ... some aggression you've got going there, Mrs Scoular.

Silence. They look at each other. Brand smiles. She doesn't. The phone dings as a receiver is lifted somewhere in the house. A series of muted bell trills chart the number being dialled. They both look at the phone.

SCOULAR: *(checking watch)* That'll be Tom ringing home. His wife has cancer. He wanted to resign the seat to look after her ... she told him not to be so silly.

Pause

BRAND: *(hand out for cup)* More?

SCOULAR: No thanks.

He gets up, crosses to the pan of milk on low light, pours some into cup, froths cocoa on it, stirs.

SCOULAR: *(picking a delicate way)* I thought it might have been ambition ... kept you guarded.

BRAND: *(stirring cocoa carefully)* There are things I want to do. Or see done. Sure.

SCOULAR: And ... does that involve ... office?

BRAND: *(returning, scratching head, developing the conceit, stretching back in his chair)* Well ... let's think now. I don't suppose I'd mind being a member of a socialist government seriously committed to the elimination of all eliminable inequalities – of wealth, possession, education, opportunity – not just here but abroad too. *(pause)* I might just ... overcome my ingrained modesty enough to answer that call, if it were ever to come ...

SCOULAR: *(joining the irony)* I see. But in the event of its not happening immediately, you'll presumably be seeking a way of making your presence felt, will you not?

BRAND: *(with care; above the line)* Yes. I suppose so.

SCOULAR: And it's unlikely to take you too long to realise that, on your own, you're a sitting target for the party managers ...

Brand sits up, drains his cocoa, sets the cup down.

BRAND: You mean: do I intend joining the Journal Group?

SCOULAR: Yes.

BRAND: Do I receive a certificate of ideological purity on entry?

SCOULAR: I'm afraid you have to bring that with you ...

BRAND: *(fast, not at all light)* How many men have you got in office, Winnie? Three, is it? One in Cabinet, two junior ministers ... what's that about?

SCOULAR: I don't defend it. I think it's a mistake ...

BRAND: A mistake! There's nearly a million unemployed out there, Winnie. That's not an act of God, it's an act of government. People's lives are being sliced into ribbons in this pathetic attempt to shore up the crumbling edifice of British capitalism, which is, of course, the historic function of this great Party of ours. And comrades – Journal people – preside over it all, locked away behind their 'collective Cabinet responsibilities', out of reach. On the other side. *(pause. quiet, tough)* Ambitious? I don't *whore* for anyone.

Tom Mapson knocks on the half-open door, enters. He carries a large Newcastle Brown and a beaker.

MAPSON: Everything all right? You've met Winnie, that's good. *(to Scoular)* Is he all right?

SCOULAR: *(standing, placing cup on table)* He's fine. And what he doesn't know, he'll have to learn. Thanks for the cocoa. Ground floor if you need anything. *(to Mapson)* How's home? *(Mapson nods, smiles. She touches his arm gently)* Good night.

She leaves. Mapson swells around doorway.

MAPSON: Good lass. Eats fire.

BRAND: Do you want cocoa?

MAPSON: No, I've got this. Fancy? *(Brand shakes head, stands, surveys the room)* I wanted to talk to you actually. Have you got a minute?

BRAND: Sure. Have a seat.

MAPSON: Here. *(he hands him a White Paper, about 12 or 16 pages in length. Brand takes it, studies the cover: 'White Paper on the State of the Economy: the measures to be taken and a Bill relating to it')* You've probably seen the White Paper already, but read 'em, both of 'em. See what our ... comrades in government are up to. The Bill has its second reading early next week. Probably Tuesday.

BRAND: Will the Tories oppose?

MAPSON: On recent showing, probably not. In any case, it's a Bill their front bench might easily have drafted themselves. *(pause)* But *we* will.

Brand blinks, frowns, stares at Mapson in silence a moment.

BRAND: The Journal?

Mapson nods.

MAPSON: If we have to.

Ext. Moist Saturday morning, around 10.30. Brand, Michael and Jane jump up and down on a fallen tree trunk half in, half out of the river, trapped below the weir. Miriam, wrapped and booted, stands up the bank watching them. Shrieks from the children, enjoying their father's attention.

Long shot of the group. A wooded spot, maybe four miles from Leighley, the thin river hurrying across pebbles on its way to the west. Deserted save for the four and the estate car parked at the end of a track.

MICHAEL: Let's cross the weir, dad.

BRAND: Are you mad? We'd be dashed to pieces.

MICHAEL: Go on.

JANE: Hold me.

Brand takes her hand, as she walks the tree out into the river. Brand's feet meet the water.

BRAND: I'm getting wet, I'm getting wet.

JANE: *(pert)* Farther, father.

BRAND: No farther, daughter!

They laugh. He swings her, hugs her back to the shale of the bank. Michael begins searching for collectable pebbles. Jane studies a small pool for life forms. We see them from Miriam's point of view.

Brand climbs the short, steep bank to the path between the trees. He wears a sweater, jeans, heavy shoes, a jungle hat. Joins Miriam. They stand in silence for a moment, watching the children play.

BRAND: They seem ok. *(she says nothing)* Mim, I do have some rights, you know ... It'd be nice if you'd just let me speak with them when I ring from down there ...

MIRIAM: I'm not prepared to get them out of bed, I've told you. You don't have to get them off in the morning; I do.

BRAND: Jane doesn't sleep before eleven, you know that ...

MIRIAM: *(peremptory)* Are you still seeing her?

BRAND: *(weary)* I drove up this morning.

MIRIAM: I've seen a solicitor.

BRAND: Yeah?

MIRIAM: I'm going through with it.

BRAND: Fine.

MIRIAM: *(calling)* Not too far, Michael. Michael! *(a half-compliant rejoinder from the bank)* I'd sooner you slept somewhere else, if that's all right.

BRAND: Jesus.

MIRIAM: I have a life to lead too.

BRAND: A feller, you mean?

MIRIAM: And see your father while you're up. He's no better.

BRAND: I asked you a question.

MIRIAM: *(calling)* Jane! Michael! Come, we're going, Nana will be waiting. *(to Brand, facing him)* It's none of your business now.

BRAND: *(staring at her)* Isn't it?

MIRIAM: Are you going to keep the car down there or what?

BRAND: No. You can have it. *(he fishes the key from his pocket, looks at it, hands it to her)* Can you drop me at the Adelphi? I've got a surgery.

MICHAEL: *(arriving)* Dad, dad, a fossil, look, incredible ... *(he shields the find in two hands. Brand crouches to look. Michael uncovers it slowly. It's a rusted beer bottle top.)*

BRAND: *(deeply mock-serious)* Amazing! Antiqua botula, genus guinness. I'll ring the Natural History Museum the minute I get back to London ... *(Michael grins, toothy, pleased)*

JANE: Silly. Aren't they, mummy.

Long shot of them ploughing off for the car.

Int. Agent's office. *Brand, seated behind Jowett's desk. He stares at something in front of him, perplexed.*

BRAND: Yes, I don't doubt it for a moment, Mr Mosley ... You don't need to ...

Reverse angle. Mr Mosley, 77, is showing Brand a bullet wound in his wrinkled arse. Brand can't believe it's happening.

MOSLEY: Do you see it? There. There. Do you see it? Just there.

BRAND: Ah yes. Yes. I can see it. That's ... that's fine, Mr Mosley.

MOSLEY: *(drawing up trousers)* Like hellerslike it's fine, it's a bloody national disgrace. Sixty years I've fought for proper compensation for that bullet, and I'm not giving up now. You've got my file ...

BRAND: *(patting it. It's enormous)* Yes. I have it. And I'll do what I can.

MOSLEY: You see you do, young man. Because the last seven have done nothing. Nothing!

Jowett in, as though on cue, pointing to his watch.

JOWETT: You'll miss the meeting, Mr Brand.

BRAND: *(frowning)* Yes ...

MOSLEY: *(a menace)* I'll be back next week, to see how you've got on. That's a promise.

He leaves, bristling at Jowett as he goes. Brand sits back, phased.

BRAND: I don't believe it!

JOWETT: I meant to warn you about him. He's been coming here since 1927 ... He's left his file, has he? I shouldn't lose sleep over it. Seven men testified at the court martial that he put the bullet there himself ... don't ask me how.

Brand sits back gathering the reams of notes he's made on the surgery.

BRAND: I'd better get these in some sort of order ... Is that the lot? *(Jowett nods)* I counted forty three. Half of 'em housing. I'll er ... dictate a few notes for Irene Monday, if that's all right.

JOWETT: Sure. But the sooner you get some secretarial help of your own sorted out the better. Irene's overworked as it is.

BRAND: Yeah.

Jowett moves towards the door.

JOWETT: OK. We're seeing Parfitt tomorrow at the Trades Club. I said about noon.

BRAND: I'd like a word about that before you go, Alf.

Jowett stops, turns, looks at Brand carefully.

JOWETT: Fine. I'll er ... I'll have a word with Ernie about the coke ... five minutes.

Brand nods, Jowett leaves. Brand sniffs, rubs face in hands, picks up phone, dials. Is surprised by a man's voice.

BRAND: Erm ... Is er ... Could I speak to Alex, please.

Brand frowns at the receiver. Waits. Alex at phone eventually.

ALEX'S VOICE: Hello.

BRAND: Hi.

ALEX'S VOICE: *(coolish)* Hi. How are you?

BRAND: Fine.

Pause. Each waits for the other.

ALEX'S VOICE: I was in the bathroom.

BRAND: Ahunh.

Pause.

ALEX'S VOICE: Did you ring with anything particular in mind?

BRAND: *(slowly)* I thought I might come round.

ALEX'S VOICE: Ah, you're around then ...

BRAND: *(steely)* Alex, I'm sorry I didn't manage a call, it's been a hard week ...

Silence from the other end.

ALEX'S VOICE: *(finally)* What time?

BRAND: *(checking watch)* Half seven, eight.

ALEX'S VOICE: Fine. Make it eight.

BRAND: *(deep breath, for control)* Right.

He puts phone down, sees Jowett in doorway.

JOWETT: OK? *(Brand nods, Jowett takes a seat opposite his own desk. Brand kicks back from it, spreading a little)* Parfitt.

BRAND: Yeah. Before I forget, I should be ok for the Victory Ball Thursday. *(Jowett nods impassively, lighting a cigarette)* On the Parfitt thing, depending on what he asks of me, of course, I shall contact the three other textile MPs affected – that's Saddle, Sowerdale and Rochdale Royton – as soon as I get back, to work out tactics. If Parfitt's right, a three-day week's only the beginning. We're less affected than others, but it's the best part of a thousand jobs we're talking about. *(pause)* I'd like you to keep your ears peeled for any overtures from the Employers' Federation. I'd like to speak with them next Friday, say, if you can manage it … *(Jowett makes a note in his diary)*

JOWETT: Parfitt's Regional Secretary, Bill. He'd know best who to approach.

BRAND: Yeah. But it'll do no harm to cover the ground independently. *(pause)* I don't trust Bro Parfitt. He's sold out more men's jobs than I got votes in the election, in his time.

JOWETT: *(non-commital)* Anything else?

BRAND: Yeah. *(he sifts a file, hands the Economy Bill across the desk)* Second reading's due. Probably Tuesday.

JOWETT: Ahunh.

BRAND: You'll be … familiar with its broad contours, I suppose …

JOWETT: *(biding time)* Ahunh.

BRAND: *(dogged, forced to explain)* In essence it aims to take around a thousand million out of the social and welfare services over the next three years. That's schools, hospitals, old folk, the handicapped, the mentally ill, and so on and so on. *(pause)* There's a vague suggestion that defence spending will also be 'pruned'. Which means in *fact* an increase in defence expenditure of not more than one per cent per annum for the corresponding period. *(pause)* Now I know these are difficult times, I know we must look for savings wherever we can make them. But this is *not* a socialist bill, Alf. Millions of people already underprivileged will find themselves further disadvantaged. And the withdrawals of subsidy from direct works departments will result in a further down-turn in housing starts and still greater unemployment in the building sector. *(pause)* Do I need to go on?

JOWETT: *(quiet, tough)* No. Unless you're telling me you're going to vote with the Tories.

BRAND: *(very quiet but decisive)* The Tories are voting with the government.

Long pause. Jowett sniffs. Nods a couple of times, without a hint of concession.

JOWETT: It won't be popular.

BRAND: The whips are gonna take me to the cleaners ...

JOWETT: I'm not talking about the bloody whips, I'm talking about the E.C. here. They didn't select you to vote against the Party.

Silence. Brand taps a pencil.

BRAND: Nevertheless. It may come to it.

JOWETT: *(standing)* All right. I'll have a word with Frank Hilton. It'll need ... handling.

BRAND: Thanks.

Jowett turns to leave, hard, anfractuous, unyielding.

BRAND: Oh ... I might be in need of a sofa tonight ...

Jowett pauses in doorway.

JOWETT: *(slowy)* I keep waiting for the *good* news, Bill. You don't seem to have any. *(pause. Brand smiles, gnomic)* It's your life but *my* problem ... We can't take a scandal. I'm warning you.

BRAND: No scandal. I promise.

JOWETT: *(nodding)* I'm in all night. You've got the number.

He leaves. Brand throws the pencil down, begins to organise the dictaphone and his many notes. Switches on after a moment.

BRAND: *(dictating)* Letter to Housing Manager, Leighley. Headed: Mrs G Pilling: Notice of Eviction ...

Int. Alex's flat. *Brand rings bell. Alex opens door.*

ALEX: Forgot your keys?

BRAND: No.

She frowns, turns back into her ground-floor flat. Brand closes door behind him, following her. She wears a neat print shirt, flared below-knee skirt, boots, tank-top.

Flat. Books, pamphlets, documents, files, papers, litter carpet and other surfaces. Alex has a cushion on the paper ocean: a notepad and biro indicate she's working. Stevie Wonder on record player. She turns it low.

ALEX: *(crouching over record-player)* Coffee? There's a pot on ...

Brand has taken her by the hand, pulled her upright, turned her to him.

BRAND: I don't want coffee. All right?

ALEX: Fine.

He looks at her face, cool, controlled. They're close, not quite touching.

BRAND: Do you have something to tell me?

ALEX: I don't think so.

BRAND: I rang Tuesday, I rang Thursday, you were out both times.

ALEX: I've been filling in at the Advice Centre, I told you ...

BRAND: I've been up to my ears, Al ...

Alex detaches, kneels on her cushion, buttocks on heels, the work in front of her.

ALEX: A letter would've found me, Bill. 'Am alive. See you Saturday.' Nothing grand.

BRAND: *(sitting in armchair)* I'm sorry.

ALEX: *(not harshly)* What does that mean? Christ, I was worried, Bill. Doesn't it occur to you I get worried when you're away, in the car, and I've *no* way of making contact?

BRAND: I was ok ...

ALEX: *You* knew that. *I* didn't.

BRAND: *(finally)* Yeah.

Pause. He's drained. She studies his face.

ALEX: Hey. I'm sorry.

BRAND: No. You're right.

ALEX: There's a beer in the fridge ...

BRAND: Sounds good.

She smiles, stands, touches his hair with her fingers as she crosses to the kitchen area and the fridge.

ALEX: When do you go back?

BRAND: Monday morning. *(he's measuring the resonance of the question: knows she won't ask on)* Who was the guy answered the phone?

She turns, the bottle and a glass in her hand.

ALEX: *(slow, deliberate)* It was ... the guy who answered the phone, Bill.

BRAND: Sorry.

ALEX: He was working here ...

BRAND: Fine.

ALEX: What's this *about*?

BRAND: Nothing.

She uncaps the bottle, hands him bottle and glass, kneels by his chair.

ALEX: I dreamt about you twice this week. Once we were in that hotel in Hull. Remember? With the bath-towel ...?

BRAND: *(touching her lips with his fingers)* The purple soap.

ALEX: The other was on Westminster Bridge. You had this contraption strapped to your back, wings, and a motor, and you were trying to fly over the river ...

BRAND: *(mock-sour)* Yeah? You can stop there, I know how it ends ...

ALEX: If you say so. *(smiling inwardly, but showing him)* I doubt it ...

He grins, sets glass down, draws her to him.

BRAND: Not even your endlessly feverish ... sexual imagination ... could build a scenario of promise out of *that*, Al my love ... *(they're kissing, licking each other's lips, nostrils)* ... Could it? Mmm? Mmm?

ALEX: *(fragments)* I thought ... you said you ... knew ... how it ... ended.

BRAND: Will I stay?

ALEX: Mmm.

She pulls him down onto the floor. They begin to make love.

PART THREE

Int. House of Commons. Bar. Wednesday lunch time. Brand carries a glass of pale ale and a few fragments of bar food to a table by the wall. He passes Winnie Scoular and Jim McNab, who sit with two other members.

MCNAB: Bill. Enjoy yesterday's meeting, did you?

BRAND: Sure thing. I was always told meetings of the Parliamentary Labour Party were exemplary essays in stage-management.

SCOULAR: Well, it depends who's managing the stage, I suppose. *(to large bearded man at the table)* Have you met Bill Brand, Reg? *(he shakes his head)* Reg Starr, Bill Brand. Reg is chairman of the Group ...

BRAND: *(freeing hand, to shake Starr's)* Yes, I know. Pleased to meet you.

STARR: *(Londoner, about 60)* I'd like a chat sometime, when you've a minute.

BRAND: Fine.

He smiles, ploughs on to his table, sits, sorts his tray. Sandiford appears, as from nowhere, silky, smiling.

SANDIFORD: Hello, Bill. Nice weekend?

BRAND: Terrific.

SANDIFORD: Mind if I join you?

BRAND: Help yourself.

Sandiford sits, sideways on, stares for a moment at the Starr table.

SANDIFORD: Lively meeting.

BRAND: Mmm.

SANDIFORD: You've got to admire old Starr. Twenty six years in the House and as
... uncompromised now as when he entered. One of nature's oppositionists.
Motto: if it moves, oppose it. *(he laughs a little. Brand quarters his apple)*
He's helped, I suppose, by his singular lack of office or actual parliamentary
influence. Wasn't it Nye Bevan who said *(Welsh, stammer, brilliantly clever)*
'Purity ... is the worst ... sort of impotence'?

BRAND: Was it? When did he say that?

SANDIFORD: *(easily)* Perhaps it was someone else ...

BRAND: *(simple)* Yeah. Perhaps it was Mussolini.

Sandiford laughs, untouched by Brand's oblique assault.

SANDIFORD: One or the other, anyway ...

*Brand munches a cut of cheese. Sandiford looks briefly out of window at river.
His manner changes imperceptibly, takes on a more sinewy timbre.*

SANDIFORD: It would be a mistake to believe everything you heard in the meeting
this morning. From the PM or Reg Starr and the Journal Group. Monday
meetings are expressly designed to allow members to let rip, criticise ...
threaten even. Nothing has been settled. Maddern and Starr will almost
certainly meet tonight and probably again tomorrow. Assurances will be
sought, entrails will be read ... r.e.a.d., that is ... and nobody will be in the
least surprised if the weather tomorrow afternoon isn't just about perfect for
the debate on the second reading.

BRAND: Let's hope you're right. I was thinking of bringing mac and wellies, to tell
you the truth.

SANDIFORD: Won't be needed. Sure of it.

*Brand takes out his Senoritas, offers Sandiford one. Sandiford smiles his refusal.
Bill strips one, to light it.*

SANDIFORD: I was speaking with Swinson. Sowerdale ...

BRAND: Sordale. Sowerdale's just the way it's spelt ...

SANDIFORD: Looks as though you're going to be in for a busy time getting
ministers to look at these processed yarn quotas ...

Brand screws up his eyes involuntarily, acknowledging Sandiford's acuity.

SANDIFORD: That's quite a job, you know. Tabling questions, trying to speak in
relevant debates, getting private access to ministers and departmental officials
... Quite impossible, I should have thought, without the ... co-operation of
Paxton and the Whips Office.

His meaning hangs between them like signals on a flag-ship.

BRAND: *(slowly)* Amazing.

SANDIFORD: What?

BRAND: You said that without moving your lips ...

Sandiford smiles dazzlingly, pleasant, handsome, urbane.

SANDIFORD: *(standing)* Jokers are never wild in this game, Bill. Try and remember that.

He leaves. Brand stubs his cigar in the ashtray, rather tensely.

Mapson takes Sandiford's place. Puts a telegram in front of Brand.

MAPSON: Here y'are, son. Found this in your tray.

Brand examines it, opens it. Reads. Mapson studies his face for clues. Brand folds it up eventually, pockets it.

MAPSON: All right?

BRAND: Ahunh.

MAPSON: *(big sigh)* Well. Looks like war, Bill.

BRAND: *(weak suddenly)* Yeah. *(standing suddenly)* I just wish somebody'd point me in the direction of the enemy.

Int. Clapham flat. *Bedroom. Brand in bed, phone to ear, mid-call. He wears white bathrobe.*

BRAND: ... Yeah, yeah, OK. Look ma, get some sleep, I'll speak to the doctor first thing tomorrow ... No ... ma, listen, I can't get up till Thursday. Thursday. It's not possible to come up earlier, if it were I would, you know that ... All right, I've got the ward number, I'll speak to somebody at the hospital as soon as I can ... Hey, listen, don't worry eh, he's weathered worse ... Yeah I know ... Yeah ... OK. Get some sleep. Goodnight.

He closes his eyes briefly, replaces the receiver. Stares at the wallet of pics of his children open on the floor by the bed.

The buzzer rings four times. He picks up the receiver.

BRAND: Yeah? Hello, Winnie. Yeah, sure. Fine.

He replaces phone, gets out of bed, moves into the living room, switches on lights. The room is more ordered now, liveable, yet filled with the litter of obsessional application to jobs-in-hand. He strides about it, tense, coiled, teasing upper lip with his teeth. He checks clock: 12.30 am.

Winnie Scoular knocks, enters. She's just in. Looks worn.

BRAND: Do you want a drink? *(indicates Scotch)*

SCOULAR: Fine. As it comes.

She slumps into a chair, closes her eyes, head back. Brand carries the drink to her, taps her hand with it. She opens her eyes.

SCOULAR: Thanks. *(she takes a long gulp)* No shift. We vote against the government in tomorrow's debate.

BRAND: How many's that?

SCOULAR: Fifty eight, fifty nine. *(pause)* It remains to be seen whether we … attract others …

Brand plays with three paper clips on the table, abstracted, remote.

SCOULAR: Something the matter?

He turns, looks over at her, deliberates.

BRAND: My old man's had another coronary. *(pause)* He's er … in intensive care.

SCOULAR: I'm sorry. *(pause)* Is he … in danger?

BRAND: Yes. I think so.

SCOULAR: You could see the Whips first thing. You'd probably get compassionate leave …

BRAND: No. *(long pause)* It's not the way.

She looks hard at him. He takes her stare.

SCOULAR: What does he do, your father?

BRAND: Chemical process worker. Shovels sulphur into moving hoppers the size of this room. Once a week he climbs into these … house-high vats where the sulphuric acid's made and cleans them. There's barely an inch of his body hasn't been burnt at some time or other. *(pause)* When I was a kid I used to take him his dinner of a Saturday when he worked weekends – 'tater hash in a basin with gauze over t'top, keep it warm. We'd sit on t'works wall while he ate it, he'd joke with mates, and I'd feel good just being there next to him. *(pause)* A very honest man. Tool-made for exploitation. A fair day's work … 'Proud' of his lad who was 'given the chance' to go to the university. *(pause)* He never talked politicis. 'Never you mind, I vote the way I vote and that's that …' He probably votes Conservative. Out of respect. *(he looks at Scoular)* Not your world.

SCOULAR: Only by adoption. My father's a doctor. Still practising. My mother died when I was still young. She was a journalist, Daily Worker. They were both Party. She died in the blitz. Direct hit on the house. My brother and I had been taken to the country. *(pause)* My father had been called out to deliver a baby in Wapping …

Long silence.

SCOULAR: *(softly)* You could go. Nobody would blame you.

BRAND: *(quiet)* He would.

SCOULAR: I thought you were just a charmer when I first met you. I don't think that now. *(she drains the glass)* Thanks for this. Good night.

She passes close to him on her way out, doesn't look at him. He keeps his eyes on the clips on the table, pushes them about in regular but aimless patterns.

Int. House of Commons. *Desk Room. Night. Clock on wall says 10.35. The room's lit but empty. Brand bursts in, furious, clenched, throws his pigskin briefcase at his desk, but hits the wall with a slap.*

He sits down angrily at his desk, slaps his knuckles against his teeth, elbows on desk, as though violently suppressing the urge to shout out loud.

Mapson in. He looks at Brand's back for a moment, then crosses to his desk and begins casing files and papers.

Brand can't trust himself to look or speak. Mapson is embarrassed but resolute. He is ready to go. Pauses by Brand's desk.

MAPSON: Shall we talk here or back at the flat?

BRAND: *(clenched teeth)* Piss off, Tom.

MAPSON: *(patient)* They changed the wording ...

BRAND: *(hard)* But not the *meaning* ...!

MAPSON: *We* thought so ... Enough, anyway, for us to say Aye. *(pause)* Some of us wanted to abstain, but the feeling was we shouldn't appear to be supporting the Liberals.

BRAND: *(bursting savagely)* Great! That's great, Tom! They change a 'welcome' to an 'accept' and a 'recommend' to a 'note' and all your principled opposition to a reactionary Bill evaporates like piss in the desert! For Christ's sake, comrade, what game on?

MAPSON: *(fierce, low)* I'll tell you what game on, comrade. It's a game called power. And to get on to the board you need organisation and you need discipline. We reached a decision, in the face of the facts as we saw them, and we acted on it. Fifty eight of us. Like one man. That's a strength. It has to be reckoned with. *(pause)* I'm sorry you weren't ... informed. If you'd joined us you would've been. You wanna be a *hero*, get yourself a white horse ...

He leaves, white, just contained. Brand begins to pack his things.

Paxton in, mottled.

PAXTON: Right. You're wanted. You.

Brand turns, very slowly. Looks at Paxton.

BRAND: Me?

PAXTON: You. Now.

BRAND: *Who* wants me?

PAXTON: Look, don't be clever with me, sonny, it doesn't wash ...

Brand stands very fast, his chair smashing to the floor behind him.

BRAND: *(loud, ferocious)* You call me sonny once more Paxton and I'll thump you
   from here to your constituency and back again! Now that's a promise!

He glares across the room. Paxton has moved several paces towards the door.

PAXTON: Are you coming?

*Brand looks round the room carefully, control seeping back into his jangled
frame. He rights the toppled chair carefully, zips his pigskin case.*

Int. Chief Whip's office. *Brand stands in front of the Chief Whip's desk. Paxton
stands a pace to his left. Sandiford and another whip sit around the room, staring
at Brand. Maddocks's desk is empty. Silence.*

*Maddocks in finally. He's a small man, thin, almost elegant, mid-fifties, his own
version of a ministerial man, grey hair polished onto the round skull, half-rim
spectacles, a hearing aid in his left ear.*

*He walks slowly to his desk. Sits. Opens the Evening Standard he carries, begins
to read it without looking at Brand. Brand stares at him for a moment.*

BRAND: *(finally; polite)* Would anybody mind if I had a seat?

Maddocks looks up, half-quizzical, deceptively gentle.

MADDOCKS: *(his version of received standard English)* I don't know about
   anybody else ... *I* mind you even breathing ...

*Brand almost finds it funny, in contrast to the funereal silence from the rest of the
room. He draws up a chair, sits, at a slight angle to Maddocks, with Sandiford in
his line of vision. Sandiford stares coolly, non-committally, at Brand.*

MADDOCKS: *(folding paper)* Well. you're quite the little shit, aren't you, Brand ...
   Don't answer that, it wasn't a question. I sent you a memorandum. *(he holds
   one up)* It had three thick black lines on it. Which meant, your vote is of vital
   importance to the government. The Labour government whose record these last
   three years enabled you to win your by-election. Now, I don't want to know
   why you entered the No lobby, I'm not interested in your miserable
   'conscience' and pathetic and misguided 'principles'. I'm interested in the *fact*
   that you have deliberately and cynically taken it upon yourself to flout the
   constitutional authority of the Party by asserting your right to vote how you
   think instead of in accordance with Party directive. *(pause)* I shall have to
   consult my colleagues before advising how you should be disciplined.

Personally I would be prepared, as of now, to send you off into the wilderness. To rot. *(pause)* But I can tell you this. While I have anything to do with it, you will find life here very far from easy. You will receive no favours of any kind. You will not be nominated for office, however menial. And I shall be writing today to the Chairman of your Constituency Party ... *(longish pause, letting it sink in. Picks up a pairing application form)* Brand-Waverley: request for pairing. *(smiles thinly as he tears the form neatly in two)* Request received. As you see. Get out.

Brand stands slowly. Sees a picture of 50,000 sheep on the wall behind Maddocks's desk.

BRAND: I hope that's not your last word ...

MADDOCKS: It is. And make that yours. I expect you in the lobby if called on Thursday.

Brand purses his lips, nods his head.

BRAND: Fine.

He leaves. Maddocks looks hard at Paxton.

MADDOCKS: *(smiling thinly)* You'll have to do better than this, Dennis.

PAXTON: *(gruff)* So I see. I think he's a nutter, actually.

MADDOCKS: That's a description fits half the House and more. It won't do.

SANDIFORD: A brilliant coup, Cedric, if I may say so. *(he points in the direction of the Chamber)* We lost a minnow maybe, but you trawled a shoal in there. How did you manage it?

MADDOCKS: Give and take, dear boy. Give and take. The essence of democracy. Something that little ... thing is going to have to learn before very long ...

Close shot of train, engine throbbing, warming. Digital station clock shows Thursday, 4.05 pm.

Brand in public phone booth, head thrust into sound cowl. Long shot, without dialogue. He speaks. Waits. Takes some news impassively. Nods. Replaces receiver.

Long shot of Brand, carrying canvas grip, showing ticket at barrier, rushing for the train. He enters open door, drags it to behind him. Whistle. Flag. The train draws out. It's Euston.

Int. Train. Second class carriage. Brand sits, stone silent, deep in own process. The conductor works his way down the coach, clipping tickets. Brand comes to, hands him his travel warrant. The conductor examines it.

CONDUCTOR: There *is* room in first class, sir, if you're er ...

BRAND: I'm fine here, thanks.

The conductor scratches his nose with his clipper, punches the warrant, hands it back. Brand smiles wanly.

Ext. Manchester Piccadilly. *Brand strides down the platform to the barrier. Jowett waits for him, his dirty mac flapping a little in the trapped winds of the station bowl.*

Brand joins him. They shake hands formally.

JOWETT: *(sombre)* You did it then. *(Brand nods, very grim)* Shaw's put down a motion to censure before the Executive.

BRAND: Yeah?

JOWETT: *(quietly)* I just heard about your dad. Your wife rang the office ... She didn't know if you'd heard. Were you close?

BRAND: Would you call two hundred miles close?

They walk off toward the cars.

- end -

Episode 3

Yarn

was broadcast on Monday 21st June 1976

The cast was as follows:

Bill Brand   Jack Shepherd
Mrs Brand   Anne Dyson
Miriam Brand   Lynn Farleigh
Eddie Brand   Dave Hill
Aunt Ethel   Edith Carter
Alf Jowett   Allan Surtees
Frank Hilton   Clifford Kershaw
Hughie Marsden   James Garbutt
Bernard Shaw   Colin Jeavons
Leighley E.C. members   Enid Irvin
Tommy Wright
William Hamilton
Bowers   Tom Harrison
Swinson   Walter Hall
Wellburn   Richard Ireson
Sandiford   William Hoyland
Reg Starr   Douglas Campbell
Wilkinson   Gary Roberts
Patel   Albert Moses
David Last   Alan Badel
Walton   Alick Hayes
Pearson   Ralph Nossek
Browning   Nigel Hawthorne
Winnie Scoular   Rosemary Martin
Tom Mapson   Richard Butler
Waverley   Richard Leech
Malcolm Frear   Geoffrey Palmer
Parfitt   Fred Feast
Bryant's gateman   Peter Martin
Jane Brand   Karen Silver
Michael Brand   Philip Cox
Designers: David Ferris, Harry Clark
Executive Producer: Stella Richman
Producer: Stuart Burge
Director: Michael Lindsay-Hogg

PART ONE

Int. Small scullery of Mrs Brand's house. Sounds of the funeral tea, well on, some laughter, a slightly raucous edgy note developing with the family talk.

Mrs Brand, pale, thinner, stares, frowning, at tea leaves she's just emptied into the cracked sink; for a moment, deep in herself. Her kept prettiness has drained off; she's old.

Miriam Brand in behind her, the noise lifting as she opens the door. She wears a neat, dark suit.

MIRIAM: I have to go, mum.

MRS BRAND: *(purposive at once)* So soon? You'll have another cup, the kettle's on ...

MIRIAM: My mother has the children, I'd better not. *(smiling)* You know how anxious they make her.

MRS BRAND: You get off then, love.

MIRIAM: Bill's staying.

MRS BRAND: No need. It's over now.

MIRIAM: *(kissing her cheek)* I'll call during the week, after work.

MRS BRAND: You've got thin. Is everything all right?

Miriam inspects her face carefully, silent.

MIRIAM: *(squeezing her hand)* I've been dieting. *(pause)* We shall miss him.

Mrs Brand smiles, nods, the kettle begins to whistle.

MRS BRAND: I'll make the tea ...

Miriam leaves.

Mrs Brand's front room. About a dozen relatives, including two or three early teenage kids, cram into it somehow: among them Eddie and his wife on the settee, and Bill, jacketless, perched on the arm of an armchair. Sweet sherry, bottles of stout, ham and chicken sandwiches. 'World of Sport' has just started on the tv, with a darts tournament. Two of Bill's uncles bet stolidly, very quiet and undemonstrative, on each thrower's score. Notes swap hands regularly, barely perceptibly. An older cousin of Bill's father, pushing eighty, is being led on by Eddie and others. Miriam watches a moment.

EDDIE: Give over, Aunt Ethel. You're having us on.

ETHEL: *(frail, shrill)* It's true. Vesta Tilley saw me and asked me to join her show. My father wouldn't hear of it. Ask your mother, she'll tell you.

EDDIE: But what were you?

ETHEL: I was an acrobat. And a soubrette. I was very versatile in those days.

The banter continues. Miriam catches Bill's eye, holds up her keys. Bill gets up from the chair arm. Miriam makes quiet, discreet goodbyes, barely interrupting the exchanges on the floor. Bill follows her out to the car.

Ext. Street. Miriam gets into the car, rolls down the window.

MIRIAM: I'm sorry ... it had to happen while you were away.

BRAND: Yeah. *(he sniffs, looks away up the street for a moment)*

MIRIAM: I read the papers. Are you in trouble?

BRAND: There's a censure move here this afternoon. Shaw. There are people who think it a bad show to vote against the Party when it's in power ... I also left the House on Thursday without the Whips' permission ...

MIRIAM: Christ!

BRAND: No no, just a distant relative. *(he grins; she returns the grin, chuckling. They're fond, momentarily)* I thought I'd come and see the kids tomorrow afternoon, if that's ... ok. *(she stares at the wheel, not answering)* I've these meetings, this afternoon ...

MIRIAM: Could you make it the morning?

BRAND: *(slowly)* If I must.

MIRIAM: I'm taking them out in the afternoon.

BRAND: P'raps I could come with you ...

MIRIAM: No. I'd sooner you came in the morning.

He stares at her a long while. Nods.

BRAND: *(stepping back)* Ten?

She nods. Starts the car. Looks at him once.

MIRIAM: I've taken the house off the market. *(pause. Remains impassive)* I think you should tell your mother soon ... when this is ...

She drives away. Brand watches a moment, then looks up at the curtained upstairs window before re-entering the house.

Int. Front bedroom. Mrs Brand stands by the small dressing table between the two narrow windows of the little room. On it, her husband's estate, laid out on a clean tea towel. She touches one or two things, with diffident fingers. Laughter, raised voice, from the room below.

BRAND: Hey. What happened to that tea, then?

MRS BRAND: *(turning)* You missed it, seeing Miriam off. I'll make another pot in a minute ...

BRAND: You all right?

MRS BRAND: I'm fine. I'm fine. Come and see what you want, while you're here.

BRAND: No, ma ...

MRS BRAND: Don't be daft. It's here to be had.

He joins her at the dressing table. Pan slowly over the articles: a pair of bowls in a bag; two individual chrome cups, with inscriptions; a gold wrist-watch, face down, with an inscription denoting long service; a union card; a post office savings book; a fancy brush and comb; a razor set; fourteen pounds in notes and a small pile of change; a sheaf of grubby policies and club books.

MRS BRAND: Eddie says he'd like the watch.

BRAND: *(uncomfortable)* Yeah, that's fine.

MRS BRAND: You take the money ...

BRAND: I don't *need* the money, ma ...

MRS BRAND: Take it anyway. Buy something for the children. From grandad. *(she presses the money into his hands)* He cared for you, our Bill. He didn't understand you, mebbe, but he'd not hear a word against you.

BRAND: Listen, how are you gonna manage?

MRS BRAND: *(dismissing it at once, moving to door)* Same as I've always done. Very badly. *(she's at the door)* I'll make the tea.

Eddie arrives in doorway, from stairs.

EDDIE: Oh, there you are. I thought you'd run off with the lodger.

MRS BRAND: *(caustic)* What, and leave you and Betty without a babysitter? I couldn't do such a thing. Get out of my way ...

She bustles off down the stairs. Eddie grins at Bill, who smiles back.

EDDIE: What about the watch, then?

BRAND: Yeah, that's fine.

EDDIE: *(advancing to dresser)* Great.

He picks up the watch, slips it on to his wrist. It's a simple, practical move, neither feeling nor callous. He looks at it, begins to wind it.

EDDIE: How's the job then?

BRAND: So so.

EDDIE: *(picking up policies, looking at them)* I'll get these cashed. There's about thirty quid there. I've sent off for the death grant. *(back to Brand)* At least you've got one. A job. Lynch's are closing next week and I'll be down to foreigners.

BRAND: Is there nowhere else?

EDDIE: You're joking. They're going down like ninepins. There won't be a shirt-shop in Manchester by the end of the year, Lynch says. *(he moves to a pile of cheap, cellophaned shirts on the floor, picks one up)* It's these. Look at that. A quid. A *quid.* Lynch does nowt under two twenty-five and he's at the cheap end. *(Brand takes it, examines it)* Hong Kong. Imagine *their* take-home pay. *(pause)* We'll be eating 'em soon. Cos they'll be cheaper than food. And more plentiful. *(pause)* You don't fancy a couple, do you? Thirty bob the pair. Eh?

BRAND: *(handing it back, knowing the routine)* I've got a shirt.

EDDIE: Really? Why didn't you wear it then? I thought you lot were elected to put the economy right. So here's your chance. Twentyfive bob. Go on.

Int. Agent's office. Day. Brand is signing mail left out by Irene on Friday night. A table has been cleared somehow for the meeting, and chairs set out. Jowett in, followed by Frank Hilton, Chairman of the Leighley CLP Executive Committee, and another man, Hughie Marsden, District Secretary of the AUEW and a member of the E.C.

JOWETT: Right, we're ready.

BRAND: *(standing)* Hello, Frank.

HILTON: Hello, Bill. Hughie Marsden, I think you've met.

BRAND: Yes. Hello, Hughie.

MARSDEN: *(early forties, hard)* Hi.

HILTON: *(sitting at top of table)* I've taken a few soundings. I'm reasonably sure he's on his own. I'd be glad if you'd leave it to me, Bill.

BRAND: *(terse-ish)* How do you mean, Frank?

HILTON: *(deliberately)* I think it's better if you're not put in the position of ... defending yourself.

BRAND: I don't mind ...

HILTON: Nevertheless.

A slightly tense moment. Jowett twitches a little.

JOWETT: Leave it to Frank. All right?

HILTON: OK Hughie?

MARSDEN: Fine.

Small committee room. Shaw and four others, E.C. members (one woman) sit at the table, agenda sheets before them.

Shaw wears a suede jacket, slacks, a polo-neck dove-grey sweater. Hilton at the head of the table. Brand sits to his right. Jowett sits on his left. Marsden, on Shaw's left at the bottom of the table, nods to two men to his left.

HILTON: Extraordinary meeting of the Leighley Executive Committee called at the request of comrade Shaw, to determine whether a vote of censure should be moved at the next formal meeting of the General Management Committee. Comrade Shaw.

SHAW: On a point of order, Chairman.

Hilton lays down his steel-rimmed spectacles, looks down the table at Shaw.

HILTON: Yes?

SHAW: This committee numbers twelve. We are only seven.

HILTON: We are a sufficiency, comrade. I think you'll find the rule-book quite specific on the matter ... *(he inquires of Jowett mutely. Jowett nods, emphatic)*

SHAW: That's not my point, Chairman. I think it's a pity such an important issue should be raised when only half the committee has been summoned ...

HILTON: *(deliberate, quiet)* I suspect that came out rather different from what you intended. Perhaps you'd care to rephrase it ...

SHAW: Yes, of course. *(looking round the table for support)* ... when only half the committee is ... present.

HILTON: *(deadpan, almost kindly)* Thank you. We'll have your regret minuted. Would you er ... *(he waves his hand for him to continue)*

SHAW: *(standing)* I have no personal axe to grind in this matter, none at all. Bill and I have known and worked with each other for years. And when *he* got the nomination, there was nobody happier than me that he had. *(pause)* But voting against our government, in these critical times, is not the way to do things. To me, it's a breach of the trust placed in our Member by all the loyal Party workers who helped to put him where he is. And I believe that we, as the Executive, should register our disapproval at his ... disastrous action.

He sits down, beginning to be marginally shaken by the impassive faces around him. Hilton looks around the table, as though inviting comment. Nobody accepts. His eyes finally reach Marsden's. Marsden stands.

MARSDEN: If I could say a word for the engineers, many of whom are loyal Party workers. Information arriving at my district office suggests that there is overwhelming support for our Member in his principled fight to secure jobs for working people. Mebbe ICI accountants feel differently, but my members – including the treasurer – will support Comrade Brand to the hilt. To the hilt. Let there be no mistake about that here today, comrades.

He sits down abruptly, the flinty tablets delivered. Hilton selects the man to Marsden's left. The man stands.

MAN: The T and G feel the same. And we'll resist all attempts to weaken his position in London by attacking him on his own doorstep. 'When is a socialist not a socialist? When he's in power' may apply to many down there, but it doesn't apply to Bill Brand. *(pause)* If you want my opinion, I think it's a bloody disgrace this meeting was ever called in the first place.

He sits down. Several people say 'Aye' or bang the table.

WOMAN: I've heard nothing but praise, on the knocker. *(looking at Shaw)* That's where it counts.

YOUTH: *(about 20, bearded)* We met last night. I'm asked to read you the following resolution, passed unanimously. *(reading from crumpled paper)* 'Leighley Young Socialists express total solidarity with Comrade Brand in his principled struggle against the forces of reformism within the Party, and against capitalism and imperialism in the wider arena. Smash the armed bourgeois state.'

HILTON: *(very dry)* Thank you.

He looks down the table at Shaw, whose frame concedes the trap is sprung.

HILTON: *(mild)* We could proceed at once to a vote, comrade. *(long pause)* Or ... you could simply ... withdraw the motion. You all know how excited the local press gets at the first sniff of ... disunity in our ranks ...

Close shot of Shaw, hard-eyed, annoyed.

Int. Agent's office. Brand in, followed by Jowett.

JOWETT: Right. That's them away.

BRAND: *(wondering more than angry)* It's worse than bloody Chicago. That was *rigged*, Alf.

JOWETT: *(on with his work at once, mild, uninterested)* Don't be wet, Bill. Shaw's a sodding menace, you know it, I know it, Frank knows it. Why doesn't he get wise and join the Liberals ...

BRAND: Look, notices of this meeting were sent out, weren't they ...

JOWETT: *(busy at desk)* It's on file. Check if you like.

BRAND: Tammany Hall.

JOWETT: Look, just think about the whips on Monday, they're the problem now. Hilton's asking the full E.C. Tuesday to pass a vote of confidence in you. Let's hope it's in time.

Hilton in, bus driver's cap and coat on.

HILTON: *(doorway)* All right?

Brand nods, smiles, shakes his head. Hilton leaves.

JOWETT: You've got the textile workers delegation Tuesday. Have you booked a room? *(Brand nods)* When do you see Bowers and the others?

BRAND: Monday.

JOWETT: Busy week.

He busies himself with papers, filing, traying, scratching odd notes to himself in pencil on a jotter. Brand watches him.

BRAND: *(finally)* Where do I stand with you, Alf?

Jowett sniffs, puts down pencil, lights a cigarette, draws on it.

JOWETT: *(smiling suddenly, generously)* I'll let you know.

Int. House of Commons Tea Room. *Brand, Bowers, Swinson and Wellburn (the textile MPs) sit round a table by a window. Each has a notebook before him. Bowers has been MP for Saddle for twenty two years, is close to 60, innocent still beneath the experience. Swinson, MP for Sowerdale, came in in 1972; a solicitor, around 40, ambitious, already PPS to a junior minister. Wellburn is Brand's age, smooth, bright, 'classless', MP for Rochdale Royton since February 1974, an advertising consultant with his hands on other things. They're all writing something down. Bowers, who's been talking, waits.*

BOWERS: OK? We're all agreed *I* put the question. Now, written or oral?

SWINSON: Well, perhaps we could use a supplementary. That way we could press for a promise of action ...

WELLBURN: What do you think, Wilf?

BOWERS: Star it. Definitely. They'll shunt it, else. *(they look to Brand, who shrugs his shoulders)* Meks the buggers work, if they have to write it down. And it's the only sure way you've got of getting an answer to the question you've asked 'em and not to a question they'd've preferred you to ask.

SWINSON: All right, star it then.

General agreement.

WELLBURN: I'll get Sandiford to put in a word with the Whips about speaking in the Trade and Aid debate. He owes me a favour or two.

BOWERS: Brand? I don't suppose you'll've found your feet yet, eh, lad?

BRAND: *(consulting book)* A few suggestions. I'd like to raise the whole issue of unemployment in my maiden speech. I expect to make that within the next week or so. It wouldn't be difficult to lay special emphasis on the threat to the jobs of textile workers that these increased yarn quotas represent. *(clucks of approval)* I'm ... er ... non grata just now in the Whips' Office, so there'll be few other chances to say anything at length in the Chamber for a while. *(pause)* I'm willing to raise it in the Trade and Aid Group, which I've just joined ...

WELLBURN: *(patronising, but only slightly)* Why not? Every little counts.

BRAND: Nobody mentioned approaching the Minister. *(he looks around. Silence)* Wouldn't it make sense to go to him direct and put it to him: reduce the level of imports or risk the irretrievable loss of thousands of jobs and the probable collapse of the industry?

A small silence.

BOWERS: *(patting his 'question' on the page before him)* Let's get the facts first, shall we? Time enough for ministers when we know the scale of the problem.

BRAND: We know the scale of the problem. Huge.

BOWERS: Mebbe. But *saying* it isn't gonna convince anyone. We have to show it. We put the question: what's the latest figure for processed yarn imports in the last six months; by what percentage is this greater than the same period last year; and to what extent can this be seen to be reflected in the loss of jobs in the textile industry in four constituencies? Let 'em answer *that* and we're armed for the fray.

BRAND: So how long will this take? I've a union delegation here tomorrow ...

BOWERS: A week. Two. Not longer.

WELLBURN: I'm meeting the Employers Federation early next week. *(to Brand)* There'll be people from your place there. Maybe you should come along.

BRAND: Fine. You'll let me know?

WELLBURN: Sure. *(looks at Bowers)* OK? *(Bowers takes the feeling, nods)* I'll have to dash. *(grinning)* Lunch with a merchant banker. *(masking neatly)* With a majority of 243, I can't afford to get too set in my ways.

He leaves. The others stand. Swinson says goodbye, leaves. Bowers zips his flat briefcase.

BOWERS: Word is, you went absent-without-leave.

BRAND: *(slight Bogart)* That's their story and they're sticking to it. I tell it differently.

BOWERS: *(smiling dryly)* You'd better look out, lad. It can be bloody lonely, a place like this.

Bowers leaves. Brand sits down to finish his drink. Sandiford arrives.

SANDIFORD: *(pleasant)* How are you? Settling in?

BRAND: Oh yes. Like a maggot in a bone.

SANDIFORD: I think you rather impressed the Boss last week ... *(Brand pebbles his eyes)* And others, apparently.

BRAND: Yeah?

SANDIFORD: *(silky, simple)* David Last, for example. *(Brand drains his cup, frowns)* I had a drink with him this Friday. Said he'd like to meet you.

BRAND: *(preparing to leave)* Is that so? *(ironic)* Well, I'll see if I can fit him in.

SANDIFORD: You'll fit the minister in. *(pause)* I'd wager on it. Word has it he'll be looking for a new PPS after Christmas.

BRAND: *(smiling faintly)* Only the voluntary blind need apply?

He leaves.

Int. House of Commons. Desk Room. Brand on phone, waiting for call to be answered. He's fiddling open a brown House of Commons envelope with his free hand.

BRAND: Irene? Bill. Look, put the machine on, will you, I want to do some letters.

He waits. Opens the letter out. It's on the Chief Whip's notepaper. 'Dear Mr Brand, You are summoned to attend this office on Wednesday April 20ᵗʰ at 2 pm.' He puts it down, sifts a couple of files from a large pile on the desk, opens them.

BRAND: *(starts dictating)* To: Housing Manager etc. Headed: Mrs Lilian Jeffreys, 293 Hillock Hall Road, Leighley. Dear Mr Benson, thank you for your letter, which still doesn't answer my original query. Was Mrs Jeffreys evicted from her flat for rent arrears (her rent book suggests not), for keeping pets (she has to my knowledge two goldfish and a tortoise, hardly a burden to the neighbours), or what? To claim that she was guilty of 'innumerable minor infractions over many years' smacks to me, I'm afraid, of grudge rather than social justice. Could you specify what these were, for instance? I should be grateful for an early reply, since I'm due to meet Mrs Jeffreys again on Saturday, when I shall have to decide whether to advise her to consult with a solicitor about possible wrongful eviction. Yours etc. To: Bro S Parfitt, TWU etc. Headed: Processed Yarn Quotas. Dear Bro Parfitt … *(studies file. Reg Starr in. Brand looks up at him)*

STARR: You're busy.

BRAND: Come in. *(he clicks the rest up and down a few times)* Irene? I'll ring back. Yeah. Fine. *(checking watch as he puts the phone down)*

STARR: *(standing by window, looking out)* We dropped you in it last week. I'm sorry. *(Brand silent, turning in his chair to face Starr's back)* We were so busy making our own minds up how to vote, nobody gave a thought to you. *(he turns to look at Brand)*

BRAND: I'll survive.

STARR: That's how it is with loners.

BRAND: A sort of … object lesson?

STARR: We'd like you in. *(pause)* Need you.

BRAND: *(slowly)* What would it entail?

STARR: One aim. To keep this … government of ours … on the rails. To fight for the realisation of the Manifesto. All of it. Root and branch. *Your* aim too, I take it.

BRAND: *(softly)* I didn't mean … aims … quite.

STARR: We're a group, a faction, within a democratic party. We argue, we reason, we persuade. We do it better as one voice, usually.

BRAND: *(still soft)* How's that achieved?

STARR: We formulate policy. As a group. You too. As a group, we ensure the policy is adhered to, in committees, divisions, whatever.

BRAND: Whips, you mean.

STARR: Not exactly ...

BRAND: *(fingering the Whip's letter)* I'm having trouble enough with the one I've got ...

STARR: You don't need to worry about Cedric Maddocks, I've had a word with him.

BRAND: How? I don't understand ...

STARR: He's prepared to put it down to ... inexperience. *(pause)* Now. *(pause)* I put it to him: feelings are running high in the Group as it is, singling you out for disciplinary action might just prove the flint to spark off wholesale rebellions ... *(pause)* Cedric's a reasonable man ... It was the least I could do. *(moving towards door)* Think it over. And let me know if there's anything I can do to help ...

BRAND: There is one thing.

STARR: Go on.

BRAND: I wondered if the Journal was planning anything on the textile industry ...

STARR: Why?

BRAND: We're losing jobs hand over fist in the north west. We're trying to get the yarn import quotas reduced to '75 levels at the very least.

STARR: Write something. We'll print it.

BRAND: Do you mean it? Just like that?

STARR: Say fifteen hundred words. Let me know.

BRAND: Are there ... strings?

Starr turns in the doorway. Stares at him for a long time.

STARR: *(slowly)* No strings, comrade. *(pause)* Roots.

Brand blinks, frowns, bites his lip, his unwitting insult already retracted. Starr leaves. Brand sits down, chastised. Puts his head to his steepled hands, rubs his eyes a moment, clears his face, staining with self-anger.

PART TWO

Int. Small Commons meeting room. Brand stands in the doorway, offering goodbye handshakes to the Textile Workers Mass Meeting Action Committee six-man delegation, who have just put their case. He shakes hands with a Pakistani worker, Patel, who leaves unsmilingly: turns to shake the hand of Wilkinson, the delegation leader.

BRAND: I'll do everything I can.

WILKINSON: *(short, stocky, 45, greying but young-looking)* Make it quick, won't you. We've taken all we're going to take. I didn't … burden you with the Action Committee's contingency plans … *(taps his flat document case)* … but we have 'em… and they won't be pleasant. I reckon there's two weeks at the most before closures begin …

BRAND: Right. I'll see if our meeting with the Employers Federation can't be brought forward.

WILKINSON: *(shaking head)* It's out of their hands now. We need government intervention or we'll be a disaster area.

BRAND: I'll be in touch. Are you going back up?

WILKINSON: Aye. After the march.

BRAND: Good luck, brother.

Wilkinson nods, crinkling his face, half-convinced the meeting has been useless. Leaves, calling to several of the others to wait for him.

Brand turns back into the smoke-filled room, surveys the littered table, picks up the cyclostyled sheets of data they've given him.

Patel returns: hesitates in the doorway. Brand sees him.

BRAND: Did you want something?

PATEL: I left a bag. Excuse me.

BRAND: Please.

Patel walks to his chair, picks up a crumpled duffel bag from beneath the table.

PATEL: Sandwiches.

BRAND: *(nodding)* You're from Bryant's aren't you?

PATEL: That's right.

BRAND: And where originally?

PATEL: Lahore.

BRAND: Do you still have family there?

PATEL: Many. Six brother, two sister. Uncles.

BRAND: What happens to them, if we halve these quotas?

PATEL: They lose job. *(Brand purses his lips)* You are socialist, Mr Brand. You know about the old bitch capitalism, you know way she work, worker against worker. I see it. *(pause)* I can't find way to change it.

BRAND: No. Have a good march.

PATEL: *(grave, courteous)* Thank you.

He leaves. Brand piles papers into attaché case.

*Int. **House of Commons bar**. About 9 pm. Brand pays for a bottle of Guinness, pours, pockets change, looks briefly round the half-filled room, walks past a table of well-heeled MPs deep in their cups to an empty table by a window. He's tired; slumps a little in the chair, draws heavily on the drink.*

VOICE: Brand, isn't it?

BRAND: That's right.

LAST: *(coming into shot)* David Last. Hello. *(hand out)*

BRAND: *(taking it)* Hello. Can I get you a drink?

LAST: *(indicating glass of pale ale)* No no, I'm fine. May I?

BRAND: Sure.

Last sits. Brand reassembles himself, studies Last. He's over 60, tall, angular, with a fine shock of white wavy hair, glasses. Wears a creased wool suit with leathered elbows, a mustard shirt and askew red wool tie.

LAST: *(not a question)* We've met before, haven't we.

BRAND: That's right. '64 election. I was one of your drivers. Shotton. Steel works.

LAST: That's right. And here you are. Are you making out?

BRAND: *(smiling)* You tell me.

LAST: Cecil Maddocks wanted us to withdraw the whip. *(pause)* Word has it he's still threatening to resign. *(pause. Mildly)* He won't, of course.

BRAND: How's life in the cabinet?

Last looks at him over his glass.

LAST: Bitter.

BRAND: Good.

LAST: Can I offer some advice?

BRAND: *(levelly)* So long as you don't mention boats the importance of not rocking them.

LAST: *(smiling, friendly)* Check my division record sometime. I had the whip withdrawn three times as a backbencher. I've never believed in rowing in the wrong direction. *(pause)* But I learnt early the crippling limitations of going it alone. *(pause. Softly)* The advice was: join the Journal Group. Be *effective*.

BRAND: *(surprised a little)* I'm having talks with Starr and one or two others.

LAST: Good. And make sure of your local party. What's the E.C. like?

BRAND: *(grinning, ironic)* Ferocious. They've got me eating out of their hand. They're ok.

A man approaches, whispers something in Last's ear. Last smiles, nods. The man leaves.

LAST: *(checking watch)* I've got to wind up this debate. That was Geoff Rennie, my PPS. I'm going to lose him Christmas. *(he studies Brand carefully. Brand says nothing)* Come over to the house and eat with us some time.

BRAND: Thank you. I'd like that.

Last leaves. The four drunks make some sneery comment sotto voce as he passes them, then burst into raucous brays.

Brand takes his empty glass back to the bar. Orders a packet of cheroots. Sandiford silks up to him.

SANDIFORD: *(innocent, knowing, ironic, eating a nut)* Did the Minister pop the question, then?

BRAND: I thought you knew everything. *(paying for cheroots)* Excuse me.

SANDIFORD: Guinness, is it?

BRAND: No, I'm off, thanks.

SANDIFORD: I suppose you know the Chief Whip's decided to … drop the charges.

BRAND: Yes.

SANDIFORD: *(smiling, ironic)* But he's … watching you.

BRAND: *(slowly, looking him up and down)* So I see. Goodnight.

Int. Textile Employers Federation offices. *A fine room, carpeted. Well lit by broad windows. A modern oval table, in teak, around which Brand, Walton (the Federation's Director-General, and Pearson (the Secretary) sit. A third man stands by the drinks cupboard, pouring gins. By the long window, a buffet lunch awaits them.*

WALTON: *(checking watch)* Not like Michael, this. Usually on the dot.

The drinks man – a personal assistant – carries a tray round, depositing gins and bottles of tonic by the Federation men. He leaves a light ale in front of Brand.

BRAND: Perhaps we should begin.

PEARSON: I think that might be a trifle irregular. It was Mr Wellburn who asked for the meeting …

WALTON: We're as anxious as you are to get on with things, Mr Brand, but I'd prefer Michael to be present, he knows our style … if you know what I mean.

A secretary in. She places a note and a telex before Walton, waits. Walton reads note first.

WALTON: Ah, he's arrived. *(reads telex)* This is from Bryant's … Another mass meeting called for four o'clock this afternoon … That's another two hours lost … *(to secretary)* See if you can get me Parfitt … Try union headquarters first, then his home, you have the number, I'll take it in … *(barely perceptible glance at Brand)* … doesn't matter, I'll take it here … *(he smiles)* … All right?

The secretary smiles, leaves. Wellburn passes her in doorway. He wears a fine suit, dark blue, with striped tie and white shirt.

WELLBURN: Apologies, gentlemen. My secretary gave me one meeting too many I'm afraid. *(to Walton)* Martin, *(to Pearson)* James ... Bill, you made it then. *(he pours himself a large gin and tonic)*

WALTON: *(light, ironic)* The Textile Employers Federation expects those on its payroll to be *punctual*, Michael, this won't do at all ...

WELLBURN: *(sitting down, drink poured)* You get your pound of flesh, Director-General. And more.

They grin mildly at each other. Brand takes it all in in silence.

WALTON: Well, shall we get started. Mr Pearson will give you the Federation's reading of the situation and then we'll have a spot to eat. All right.

PEARSON: *(from files)* Well, gentlemen, I think you've both had copies of the full emergency report on the industry drawn up by our research staff. I'd like to pick out here just a few of the more salient points ... First, in the last year alone, volume of work has decreased by no less than forty per cent. Second, in the same period, imports of cheap finished goods, principally from Asia, have risen – according to what figures we've been able to collect – somewhere in the region of seventy to eighty per cent. Third, finance capital has turned its back on us – £280 million withdrawn or withheld in the last year. Four, the textile industry is now permanently part-time. Five, without urgent government intervention – extensive but without 'strings' – you can expect a major series of closures involving perhaps thirty per cent of the work force, and a further shift to three or even two-day working for the remainder. *(he closes file, takes off glasses)* I don't suppose I need to tell you what that will mean for both of *you*, in your constituencies.

WELLBURN: *(lips pursing)* Yes, it's bad, it's bad.

WALTON: *(quiet, 'decisive')* What you won't find in the report is the fact that we have already had a private meeting with both the Chancellor and the Minister for Trade. *(pause)* Neither offered the slightest hope of a cut in the importation of processed yarn or finished goods ... or of any immediate financial intervention by the government to save the industry from collapse.

Pause. Wellburn looks at Brand.

WELLBURN: *(finally)* Well, I'd have expected that pretty well, Martin, given the state of the country generally ... We're working up some ... ammunition in the House that *could* set a bomb under that position ...

BRAND: *(interjecting)* You talk about a 'major series of closures involving thirty per cent of the work-force'. What's that figure based on?

PEARSON: *(frowning slightly)* Largely upon members' forecasts and projections for investment strategies. We collect them each year and ...

BRAND: ... You mean, they think they can't make money ...

PEARSON: *(patiently)* The industry is on the brink of bankruptcy, Mr Brand ... I can show you the figures, believe me ... Talk to a shareholder some time ... to whom we are all responsible ...

The phone rings on the long table by the buffet, the secretary enters, walks down the room to gather the phone and bring it to Walton.

BRAND: *(through all this)* It isn't shareholders who'll be losing their jobs, Mr Pearson. What about your employers' responsibility to the work force. What happened to earlier profits then? You didn't make them on your own and you shouldn't have disposed of them on your own ...

PEARSON: *Profits*, Mr Brand ...?

WALTON: *(intervening, taking the phone)* Excuse me, gentlemen. *(covering mouthpiece)* Parfitt? *(the secretary nods, leaves. He keeps hand on mouthpiece. To Wellburn principally)* Another mass meeting this afternoon, at Bryant's. I put a call in to the union man. *(to phone)* Hello Reg, how are you? ... What? Oh dear, never mind, get the wife to put it in the oven, it shouldn't take long ... *(listens)* Ahunh. Ahunh. Yes, I did, that's really why I'm ringing, Reg. Go ahead.

He listens, looking briefly at Brand, offers him a small vacant smile. Brand looks away. Walton gestures Pearson to push him the ashtray, stubs his half-smoked king-size, smiles his thanks.

Int. Small Commons meeting room. *Wellburn, Bowers and Winson sit (backs to the door) in front of a large desk. Behind it, a small, dapper man, Browning, a department lawyer. Bowers turns as Brand closes the door behind him. Browning suspends his address. A secretary, young, bored, takes notes at the side of the desk.*

BRAND: *(frowning at man behind desk)* Sorry I'm late ... I lost my way.

BOWERS: Come in, Bill. Thought you'd gone AWOL again, sit yourself down. *(to Browning)* The member for Leighley, Mr Brand.

BROWNING: How do you do. *(Brand nods. It's a question)* My name's Browning. I'm a lawyer working in the Department ... I was just explaining to your colleagues some of the difficulties inherent in your request for reductions in yarn imports ...

BRAND: I see. *(deadpan)* Weren't we supposed to meet the Secretary of State?

BROWNING: *(bland)* Unfortunately the Secretary of State has urgent business elsewhere. *(he smiles, the matter closed)* ... He's asked *me* ...

BRAND: Might one ask *where*?

Silence. Wellburn frowns, uncomfortable. Swinson looks at Bowers. Bowers stares at the far window, lips pursed, non-committal.

BROWNING: I'm not sure I can answer that. As I understand it, something cropped up last evening ... the 'brief' was on my desk when I arrived this morning ... I've already conveyed his regrets to your colleagues.

BRAND: Is this meeting minuted?

BROWNING: *(pointing to secretary)* It can be, if you wish it ...

BRAND: *(very cool)* Could it be minuted then that I consider the Secretary of State's failure to be present at this meeting without adequate explanation for his absence to be not only discourteous but also, lacking other pointers, an alarming indication of the dismally low priority he accords the issues we seek to raise with him.

The secretary blinks, wide awake, at Browning.

BROWNING: *(finally)* If you wish it, Mr Brand. *(to secretary)* Do you have it? *(she nods)*

WELLBURN: Come on, Billy boy, you know as well as I do where he is ...

BRAND: *(tough)* Then why the hell doesn't he *say* so? If he thinks a junket in the City's more important than closures and redundancies, let him say so and we'll know where we stand.

BROWNING: Gentlemen, I don't see anything to be gained by this, I really don't ...

BOWERS: *(mildly)* All right, Bill? *(he winks, friendly)* We'll hear him out, shall we?

BRAND: *(yielding slowly)* All right.

BROWNING: *(thumbing files)* Well ... er ... gentlemen ... The ... er ... Secretary of State ... has asked me to put you in the picture about the importations of processed yarn ... a picture, I should add at once, by no means drawn by this Department only, but by several others of ... shall we say, somewhat more decisive influence than the Department of Trade. I refer to the Treasury, the Foreign Office and Defence. *(pause)* ... I think you'll all agree that the speed and manner in which your question in the Chamber was answered give some indication of the seriousness with which the Minister regards your case. It's because he concedes the urgency that he agreed to ... er ... meet with you. *(the room listens to the clang of the last phrase. Brand stares at papers in a file)* However, *(longish pause)* he wants you to understand the ... complexity of the issue and interests involved ... and their sensitivity in the present state of play. *(pause)* Broadly speaking, the Government accepts the view of this Department and of the Treasury that the greatest threat to our economic survival is a world recession in trade. That is, to bring it to cases, any act on our part to protect home markets by the erection of tariff barriers would inevitably result in reprisal measures abroad, with the prospect of incalculable escalations sucking other economies into the vacuum created. And obviously, the Treasury is adamant that nothing should be done to damage our prospects of securing an export-led revival of our economic fortunes by the early '80s. *(pause)* The defence interest specifically centres on Pakistan, from which, as we said in our answer, some sixty per cent of the total importation of processed yarn currently originates. The Government is currently seeking to negotiate a sizeable arms deal with that country. Clearly, a reduction in import quotas *now* could seriously threaten those negotiations and deal a further blow to the balance of payments. *(pause)* The

Minister also asked me to remind you all ... as socialist members, of our responsibility to assist, however we can, the growth of developing countries. Any reduction in quotas would inevitably result in chaos in those exporting countries of the third world. He adds that any attempt to cut back on imports from Asia would meet with the bitterest resentment by his colleagues in Overseas Development. *(he takes up another file)* I turn now to the new issue you raised, in your letter seeking this meeting with the Minister: namely, the question of Government intervention in the industry in the form of loans or grants, or by taking equity in the industry, or by taking the industry, in whole or in part, into public ownership. He's asked me to say that while these decisions do not, strictly speaking, fall within the scope of this department, he will refer the matter to the Cabinet Study Committee for Trade and Industry, where he will be able to secure the views of other ministers and departments. He asks me to add that, from discussions recently held in that committee with the Chancellor, he seriously doubts whether the capital required for compensation following nationalisation could actually be raised, in the present critical state of the economy. *(he stops, dabs his mouth with a handkerchief)* I do hope I have accurately conveyed the real nature of the Minister's concern in this matter ... *(he looks finally at Brand)*

Close shot of Brand, tight-lipped, clicking his attaché case to.

Int. Clapham bedroom. *Warmed a fraction (as is the whole) flat since we saw it first. Evening. Brand stands at the window, in old sweat shirt and underpants, looking down at some kids at play in the passage below. They're mainly Asians, playing a sort of makeshift cricket. A thirteen-year-old Sikh does a marvellously accurate rendering of Bishan Bedi and is hammered without mercy by the ten-year-old slasher at the crease. Their voices carry faintly into the room. From his living room, Archie Shepp and Jeanne Lee do 'Blasé' on the turntable.*

Brand watches, intent, absorbed. The phone buzzes four times, his internal signal. He strides across the floor bed to answer it.

BRAND: Yes. Hello, Winnie. *(listens)* Sure, help yourself. Fine.

He puts the receiver back, crosses to his trousers, drying on a chair before the electric fire, inspects the damp right leg, wrinkles his nose, opens a wall cupboard, selects a pair of dark blue underpants, removes the ones he wears to put them on.

Living room, rearranged into functional areas. The desk now has files, typewriter, a cassette tape-recorder on it. A Sasco year planner on the wall. Etc.

Winnie Scoular in, in smart boots, mid-calf flared and tucked trousers and shirt. She carries an armful of books, papers, magazines, 8mm films and tape cassettes.

SCOULAR: *(calling from doorway)* Hi, I'm here.

Brand appears from bedroom.

SCOULAR: *(laughing, putting load on desk)* Ah, is this some sort of proposal, Mr Brand?

BRAND: *(grinning)* Touché, comrade. There's a simple explanation actually.

SCOULAR: Glad to hear it.

BRAND: *(taking record off turntable)* I er ... I met a delegation from the Mothers Union this afternoon. They're worried about violence on tv, law and order, the absence of discipline in schools, rising prices, metrication, premarital sex and dogs fouling the pavements. *(pause)* I promised to look into it. *(pause)* Anyroad ... one of them had her daughter with her, about three. And I suddenly got this image of myself as a real politician, you know? So, I picked her up and gave her a kiss and sat her down on my knee. And then I felt her pissing down my leg. *(Scoular laughs)* And, since I have only one pair of trousers with me in the metropolis ... *(he gestures at his legs)* you gain ... unearned, I might add, this unexpected first glimpse of my legs ...

SCOULAR: *(dry)* Very nice. Where is it?

BRAND: Here. *(he takes the tape recorder out of its case, checks the batteries)* Do you want to record?

SCOULAR: No no, just playback. You think you've got problems ...

Brand picks up a couple of magazines, flicks the pages, disbelief crescent on his face.

BRAND: Amazing. Mmm. *(expels air through half-whistling lips. Innocent)* I thought women didn't go in much for this sort of thing, Winnie ...

SCOULAR: *(fitting a cassette)* You'd be surprised.

BRAND: What's it about, then?

SCOULAR: Sh. Listen.

She clicks the tape on. We hear the beginning of a badly recorded porn tape, fairly uncomplicated, very artificial fuck talk and simulated orgasm. They catch each other's eyes several times as they listen. At length she clicks it off.

BRAND: Mmm. Sounds like a quiet day in the Chamber.

SCOULAR: *(indicating the heap)* I've got a roomful downstairs. Compliments of a new Festival of Light detachment just formed in my neck of the woods. *(she thumbs a magazine, face enigmatic)* Some of them must do nothing else but collect this ...

BRAND: Pressure, is it?

SCOULAR: Could be, I suppose. They know my position, I think. They're flooding the House with it, I'm surprised you haven't had yours ...

BRAND: Mine's probably been stopped by the Whips ... How do you feel about that?

He nods at the page she's opened at. It's a picture of two women, naked save for brief see-through knickers, kneeling in the corner of a suburban living room, arses in the air. Scoular studies it, unconcerned.

SCOULAR: It degrades women, that's for sure. Still, I'm not too keen on morphine, but I can see its uses. *(pause)* Poor buggers.

BRAND: Do you want a drink?

SCOULAR: No thanks. Have you eaten?

BRAND: No, I got something in...

SCOULAR: Come on, I'll treat you to a Chinese on the corner.

BRAND: Well, I should do some phoning about these textile closures ...

SCOULAR: Oh yes, you saw the Minister ...

BRAND: Like hell we did. He didn't show.

SCOULAR: It'll wait an hour, won't it?

BRAND: *(smiling)* Sure.

He walks into the bedroom, comes out immediately, trousers in hand.

BRAND: I've no trousers.

SCOULAR: Bring them down. I'll put an iron over them. Get your things ...

He puts on his jacket, socks, shoes. Scoular winds the tape back, boxes it, tidies the pile. Mapson knocks, enters. Half backs out, as he see's Brand's legs.

BRAND: Evening, Tom.

MAPSON: *(looking at his bare legs, impassive)* Evening, Bill. Winnie.

BRAND: Can't stop, Tom. Going for a meal.

MAPSON: Aye, well ... *(a look at Scoular)* ... Go easy ... *(twinkling)*

SCOULAR: *(ready)* OK?

BRAND: *(smiling)* Oh yes.

He follows her out, trousers over arm.

PART THREE

Int. House of Commons. Desk room. Waverley at his desk, working on the Telegraph crossword.

Brand in, carrying internal mail, files and attaché case. He's angry. Chucks his things onto his desk, re-reads a memo, which he has taken from his pocket. Throws it onto the table. Stares at it, white-faced. Begins to look through internal phone book.

WAVERLEY: 'A turn for the worse'. Ten letters.

BRAND: Revolution?

WAVERLEY: Mmm. Ugly but right. *(he begins writing it in)* You're wasted here, my boy. Enjoyed your speech. Good turn of phrase. *(still at crossword)* You'll have to learn to speak up, though. You're a long way back. *(Brand sits down, still looking through the internal phone book)* Don't fret. They'll be forced to put the money up, if it comes to the crunch. Napoleon called us a nation of shopkeepers ... Now he'd call us a nation a lame ducks, I shouldn't wonder.

Bowers in.

BOWERS: Great speech, Bill. Really good. You can always tell a good speech by watching the front bench. Not a flicker. Frear looked as if he'd swallowed a shuttle. We've got him on the run, lad.

BRAND: Like hell we have, Wilf. *(he hands him the memo)* I asked for another meeting ... with him *there*, I mean.

BOWERS: *(reading)* Shoulda left it a week or so, lad. He's got his face too, you know.

BRAND: *(furious)* Sod *face*, Wilf. We're talking about men's *jobs*.

BOWERS: All right, keep calm, keep calm. *(he looks in Waverley's direction. Nods. Waverley acknowledges with a wave of his Parker)* They know we mean business. And we've a card or two left up our sleeves. I shall be seeing the Chief Whip early next week ...

Brand looks at him; sees the weakness, the impotence, candid and unmaskable.

BRAND: You've *seen* the papers, have you?

He pushes a copy of the Leighley Recorder across the desk. We take in the huge 'Closures' headline, the 'Three Day Week' crosshead.

BOWERS: Aye. The Settle Advertiser's full of it too.

BRAND: This is only the beginning, Wilf.

BOWERS: Aye. *(pause. He's leaving)* We'll think of something. *(turns in doorway)* Fine speech.

He leaves. Brand returns to the number he's isolated, picks up phone, waits, asks for it, waits.

BRAND: Yes. I'd like to speak to the Secretary of State for Trade, please. Brand, member for Leighley. *(he waits. Looks across at Waverley, who fills in another word, laughing to himself)* He's what? *(pause)* I see. Thank you.

He clouts the phone down. Sits very tense for a moment. Reads the memo again. Leaves it on his desk. Pockets the Leighley Recorder. Leaves, quite fast, decisive.

The phone rings again. Waverley stands, removes his half-glasses, crosses to answer.

WAVERLEY: Yes... Who? ... No, he's just left ... No idea.

He returns the receiver to its rest. Picks up memo. It reads: 'Dear Mr Brand, the Secretary of State for Trade has asked me to thank you for your letter of the 19th and to tell you that, in his opinion, no useful purpose would be served by meeting you again on the subject of imported yarn quotas ...'

Int. Commons bar. *Brand in, tense, a little wild about the eyes. It's tiny, crowded. He searches for his man. Sights him. Moves in. Winnie Scoular catches his arm as he passes her table.*

SCOULAR: Bill. Join us.

Brand takes in the table. David Last, Reg Starr, Tom Mapson.

SCOULAR: I think you know David ...

BRAND: Yeah. Hello. No thanks, there's er ... there's someone I've got to see ...

He stares up the bar, where Frear, the Secretary of State for Trade, is standing with a group of PPSs. They laugh at something he says. Scoular follows his look.

STARR: Nice article. Sorry we had to cut it a bit.

BRAND: Thanks.

SCOULAR: *(sensing the danger now)* Can't it wait?

BRAND: *(shaking head)* It's waited. Excuse me.

She releases his sleeve. He continues to the bar, approaches Frear's group, stands on its edge, watching the man. Frear is around 45, thin, rather distinguished, in an academic's sort of way.

BRAND: *(finally)* Excuse me.

Frear turns to look at him.

FREAR: Yes?

BRAND: Brand.

FREAR: Oh yes.

BRAND: I wrote to you.

FREAR: Yes?

BRAND: I'd like to talk to you ...

FREAR: I'm sorry, I'm ... *(he indicates the group)*

BRAND: *(very quiet)* Fine. I'll wait.

He turns, walks towards door, leaves. Winnie Scoular watches him go, concern on her face. Up the bar, the PPSs are pulling faces at each other.

SCOULAR: It's just possible Comrade Brand is about to sort out the Right single-handed. Starting with friend Frear.

LAST: *(sardonic)* I hope he does nothing foolish. *(pause. Staring at Frear's profile with distaste)* Well, not too foolish.

STARR: *(smiling)* What can he do to Frear? How do you attack a swamp?

LAST: *(standing)* Can I get you drinks, while we all ponder that last ... extraordinarily gnomic utterance?

He approaches the bar. Frear drains his gin. Checks watch, says his goodnights, begins to leave, passing Last on way to door.

FREAR: *(cool, formal, en passant)* David.

LAST: Malcolm.

Frear sees Brand standing in the poorly lit, partly recessed doorway, half checks his stride, goes on. Reaches Brand, who holds the Recorder in his hands.

FREAR: *(not blustering; reasonable)* Look, Brand, you've had my answer ...

BRAND: *(handing him the paper)* And you've had yours. *(pause)* So what are you going to do?

Frear studies the headline carefully.

FREAR: Look, man, you're a new member ... these are complex issues, as I think my department explained ... Nothing's simple in this world ... It's a contracting industry. Some redundancies are inevitable.

BRAND: Have you ever been made redundant ...?

FREAR: *(starting to move off, twitching with impatience)* I haven't time for this ...

Brand grabs him by the lapel and pushes him against the wall.

BRAND: *Listen,* will you. Jesus Christ, there's mebbe four thousand men and women going down the road. They need *help.* From *us.* *(he releases Frear suddenly, half-embarrassed by his lack of control)* The least you could do is *talk* ...

FREAR: *(straightening his jacket and tie, iced)* What are you, some sort of fascist ...?

BRAND: All right, I'm sorry.

FREAR: If you want to make yourself useful, you could do worse than catch the next train north and start cooling things down at that end ... *(he catches Brand's frowning enquiry)* ... You haven't heard ... Workers at Bryant's occupied the factory at five o'clock today. More occupations are promised. *(Brand absorbs the news slowly, stepping back a pace. Frear gathers himself together)* Take a message from the Government with you. We sympathise. We're doing everything we can to help. But occupying the factories is the surest formula for economic suicide. Tell them.

He hands the paper back to Brand, pushes through door, unhurried. Brand stares at the paper again. Scoular approaches.

SCOULAR: You all right?

Brand sees her: gathers himself.

BRAND: Yes. Any three-lines for tomorrow?

SCOULAR: No, I don"t think so.

BRAND: *(checking watch)* Good. I'll see you.

SCOULAR: Wait, we'll share a cab home, eh?

BRAND: No, I'm going north. *(bleakly)* Trouble at t'mill.

SCOULAR: *(stopping him going)* Bill. *(he turns. She half wants to say something tender: can't or won't)* Journal Group meets Monday. Will you be there?

BRAND: I might. By Monday the Group might not want me … See you.

He leaves. Scoular returns to the table, where Last has returned with the drinks.

STARR: *(pleased)* Is he going to settle, do you think?

Close shot of Scoular, drinking her scotch, somewhere else.

LAST: Settle, Reg?

Ext. Bryant's Factory. *Day. Brand, Parfitt and Jowett drive in Jowett's van up to the gate of Bryant's. Pickets line the perimeter. Beyond, the gaunt red structure of a 19th century mill.*

Brand gets out of the van, looks over it to speak to the others.

BRAND: *(to Jowett, who's locking the door)* Will there be press?

JOWETT: I've no idea. But *act* as though there are, for Christ's sake.

PARFITT: *(short, squat, fattening, late 50s)* Last I heard they were keeping press out. But they tell the bloody union nothing, these buggers.

BRAND: *(deliberately)* Maybe they know a thing or two then.

PARFITT: What's that supposed to mean?

BRAND: *(hard)* Which word is giving you trouble, Brother Parfitt?

JOWETT: Hey, right, come on, let's get in there.

Jowett and Brand walk off towards the gate. Parfitt stumbles after them. They pass two parked police cars, two men in each.

They reach the padlocked main gate. The Bryant's has scrawled under it 'Under New Management'. Several workers stand inside. A tall, thin man around 30, balding, wiry, steps out of the gate house. Watches their approach. Recognises Parfitt.

MAN: *(at Parfitt)* What do *you* want?

BRAND: Bill Brand. MP. I want to see what's going on.

MAN: *(pointing at Jowett)* Who's he?

BRAND: He's my agent.

The man stares at them a moment longer.

MAN: Wait a minute.

He re-enters the gate house. The pickets stare through the bars at the visitors.

PARFITT: *(under breath)* Bloody madness, this. Destroy the bloody industry. Spent all my bloody life ...

Silence again. The man reappears, gives the signal for the gate to be opened; pins a red disc on Brand's lapel, another on Jowett's; bars Parfitt's path. Nod for the gate to be closed.

PARFITT: *(shrill)* Eh, what's going on? I'm the union representative here ... *(he takes out some papers from a wallet)* You know me ... Every one of you ...

MAN: Precisely, Brother Parfitt. We know you only too well. Now piss off. Go and phone a boss or something ... *(to Brand)* Welcome. You'll find the Works Committee in the main block. George'll take you ...

They walk off across the cobbled yard. Behind them, Parfitt scowls and gesticulates, locked out.

Int. Spinning shed, at full hum and clatter. Brand, Jowett and Wilkinson view it from a tiny gantry leading to a suite of managerial offices.

BRAND: *(shouting)* How long can you keep this up?

WILKINSON: As long as we have to.

BRAND: Producing, I mean.

WILKINSON: A week, mebbe more. We're on to the banks for credit ... No dice so far. But they're gonna have to burn it down to get us out.

BRAND: How can I help?

WILKINSON: I don't know. *(pause)* You could address the men.

JOWETT: *(listening intently)* Hey, now wait a minute, brother ...

WILKINSON: *(ignoring him)* What do you say?

BRAND: *(a fraction of a hesitation)* Fine.

Jowett blows in disgust.

Factory dining hall. Brand stands on a table in the large dining hall, packed with workers drinking after-dinner tea. He nears his conclusion. We see him first in long shot, and track slowly in.

BRAND: ... Let me finish on this, then. I offer my 100% support for the action you have taken, 100% solidarity, as a trade unionist, with your principled fight to secure the right to work. *(cheering, stamping, whistling)* And I will do everything I can to see that that fight is represented in Parliament. *(cheers*

again, then silence) Because I can offer no allegiance – no allegiance – to a
government or party that will allow these closures and redundancies to occur,
when they have pledged themselves, as they have repeatedly, not to use
unemployment as a means of solving the economic crisis. *(loud cheering and
stamping. Close shot of Jowett, eyes closed as if in pain. Brand stands,
impassive, waiting for the noise to die)* A final word of advice, brothers. *(long
pause)* Make sure you win.

*Whistling and stamping. Brand stands on, waving, uneasy in the role of
demagogue. A light flashes suddenly, surprises him. Jowett stands, muttering
'Shit' several times. Brand looks for its source. Another flash.*

Close shot of the pic of Brand, front page, Sunday Express.

Int. The Boathouse Café, *a smallish wooden structure, perched twenty or so feet
above a small river.*

*Brand stares at the picture. The headline reads: 'Rebel MP lashes government
inertia'. 'I support sit-ins 100%'.*

He looks over the paper at Jane, who fiddles with her pizza.

BRAND: Where's *he* gone?

JANE: Lavatory. *(picking still)* There's meat in this.

BRAND: There can't be, you heard me order it. *(seeing Michael at the fruit
machine, fiddling)* Mike. Mike. *(the boy turns, stares)* Come and finish your
food … *(to Jane)* Here, let me look. *(he looks. It's meat)* I'll get you another.

JANE: It's all right. I don't want one.

MICHAEL: *(arriving)* Can we have ice-cream soda, dad?

BRAND: *(pointing to plate)* You've not finished that.

MICHAEL: Can I have a go on the machine?

BRAND: Sit down, eh.

Michael sits opposite Brand. Jane stares out of the window, at the river.

JANE: There's those swans. *(Michael looks, uninterestedly. Brand asks the waitress
for two ice-cream sodas and a cup of tea)* Mummy says swans are vicious.

BRAND: Only when they're attacked. Or threatened.

MICHAEL: *(showing several 2ps)* I've got my own money …

*The waitress brings the ice-cream sodas – big ones, packed with ice-cream – and
the tea. They tuck in at once. Brand watches them.*

JANE: What's yarn, father?

BRAND: *(cup to lip)* What?

JANE: *(pointing to the strap head over his story in the paper)* Yarn.

BRAND: It's fibre. Spun. Prepared for weaving – cotton, silk, wool, flax.

MICHAEL: Is it boring?

BRAND: How do you mean?

MICHAEL: Sounds like yawn. *(he grins suddenly, pleased with his joke. Brand pulls a face at him)*

JANE: I thought it meant a story. Gran said Grandad always told a good yarn.

BRAND: Yeah, it means that too.

JANE: It's a funny word. Yarn. Yarn.

BRAND: Originally it was the word for gut. That's the long tube in your stomach that food passes down. If you saw one outside the body, see, it'd look like a long piece of rope. And then later it became a story ... Shall I tell you how? ... *(Jane nods, absorbed)* You see, sailors used to have to make thick ropes to hold the sails and lash things down with. And they made these thick ropes by winding lots and lots of thinner ropes together. And this was probably very boring. So, they would tell each other stories, to pass the time. And they called it spinning a yarn. Telling a tale while making a rope.

Long silence. Brand finishes his tea. Michael stares at the fruit machine doggedly, his ice-cream soda finished.

JANE: *(finally)* And which have you been doing, father? *(she points to his picture)*

BRAND: *(standing, picking up bill)* I wish I could answer that, brown eyes. Come on, let's get you home ...

He shepherds them towards the till desk and the door. Michael lingers around the fruit machine. Brand collars him.

Pull back slowly, through the virtually empty room, to the table again. Close on Brand's pic.

- *end* -

Episode 4

Now and in England

was broadcast on Monday 28th June 1976

The cast was as follows:

Bill Brand   Jack Shepherd

Miriam Brand   Lynn Farleigh

Mr Hollins   Bernard Atha

Alf Jowett   Allan Surtees

Hughie Marsden   James Garbutt

Mrs Pilling   Anne Raitt

Alex Ferguson   Cherie Lunghi

David Last   Alan Badel

Waitress   Louise Jervis

Police Inspector   Geoff Tomlinson

Wilkinson   Gary Roberts

Pakistani   Albert Moses

Geoff   Peter Martin

Mrs Marples   Rona Anderson

Mr Marples   Robert Hardy

Wellburn   Richard Ireson

Cedric Maddocks   Peter Copley

Designers: David Ferris, Harry Clark

Executive Producer: Stella Richman

Producer: Stuart Burge

Director: Michael Lindsay-Hogg

PART ONE

Solicitor's office, late afternoon. Early summer. The tidy desk is untenanted. Before it, separated by its length, sit Brand and Miriam. Brand still wears his outdoor coat – a battered parka; Miriam's light mac hangs from a coatstand in the corner.

They sit in silence. An old wall clock tocks remorselessly. Brand checks its time against his watch. Studies Miriam from behind steepled fingers. She sits quite upright; quiet, pale, a little tense; looks straight ahead of her.

BRAND: *(eventually; barely disturbing the silence)* Who's got the kids?

MIRIAM: They're at my mother's.

Silence again. The phone rings twice; is cut from another office.

BRAND: This is ridiculous.

A secretary enters, carries files and letters for signature to the desk, lays them on the leather-cased blotter, smiles at them. She switches on the Anglepoise, though it's not needed, leaves.

BRAND: *(sotto)* Look, why can't we just talk? … Without all this bloody pantomime.

MIRIAM: *(quiet, tense)* Because I know you.

Silence. He fiddles inside his canvas grip by the chair leg, removes a pack of cheroots, opens it, lights one, looks for an ashtray around the room, finds one, returns to his chair.

BRAND: *(on the move, matter-of-fact)* I'm not having adultery, Mim. If you go for adultery, I'll contest, all the way. *(she says nothing. He sits down wearily)* And I want access. Those kids need me.

She turns to look at him, contempt and bitterness flecking the eyes. Brand studies her, impassive.

BRAND: *(tight, low)* You've stewed me in guilt for long enough, lovey. I'm done. Now you turn off the heat or I'm gonna stick to the sides …

MIRIAM: Don't be more melodramatic than you can help, will you …

She looks away towards the large window. Brand stares at her, then throws his head back in a dry, soundless laugh, wholly without mirth.

MIRIAM: Don't go on. You can say what you have to say when the solicitor comes.

Brand gets up, studies framed articles and Law Society certificates on the wall.

BRAND: *(casually, over shoulder)* Is it anyone I know? *(nothing. He turns to look at her. She's looking at him)* I know, Mim. The kids have talked about him … and I can tell, anyway … *(he gestures at her)* … And I'm glad. Honest.

MIRIAM: *(distinct, spaced, cold)* You're glad. Of what?

BRAND: *(softly, continuing)* But it *is* … adultery too. Have you told our friend here …? *(hand towards desk)* You'll have to, if I contest.

MIRIAM: *(hard)* Were you a bastard when I met you? I can't make up my mind.

BRAND: Show me how I can behave *well* then, here, in all this. *(she ices over, half turning in her seat, spraying her face with distaste, disdain. He grimaces, angry, fights for control, returns to his chair)* Look … Look I stopped loving you. I'm sorry. I'm sorry. Here, *(he touches his brow)* here *(he touches his genitals)* I hope I never have to say anything uglier, because God knows it's the ugliest thing one person can say to another. But *that's* the reality. That's what we have to work with. Not whether I sleep with A or you with B. *(long pause. She shows no sign of hearing him)* I've signed the house over. I've promised you half my salary for as long as you decide you need it. Now, please Mim, tell me what you want.

MIRIAM: *(returning to him)* You. Or not-you. I don't want anything in between.

He sits back in his chair, defeated. Closes his eyes. Silence again, for a long time. Long shot of the room, the two of them, perfect strangers.

Hollins in, old, smooth, with thick whorled bifocals, three-piece rather upright suit.

HOLLINS: Forgive me, that took longer than I'd bargained for. You'll be Mr Brand. *(hand out)* Hollins.

Brand stands to take the hand. Hollins smiles at Miriam.

HOLLINS: *(sitting at desk, removing glasses, wiping weak eyes)* This is slightly irregular, as you're no doubt aware, but er … your refusal to fee a solicitor to act for you does make normal process rather difficult, Mr Brand …

BRAND: Yes. I think I explained why in my letter.

HOLLINS: Yes. *(he returns his glasses, sees the letters for signature, takes out a fountain pen, begins to sign)* Well, you have something to say to your wife … Would you care to … er …?

He signs on. Eventually becomes aware of Brand's non-response. Squints at him.

BRAND: *(quiet; neutral; controlled)* Wouldn't it be better if you signed those first?

Hollins blinks. The brain's smiling message arrives on his lips, as a stiff and solitary rictus.

HOLLINS: Yes of course.

Agent's office. *Evening. A rock group is setting up in the hall beyond for the Friday night Young Socialists' dance. Brand sits at Jowett's desk, writing letters, a mound of files before him. His grip is open on the floor, files, papers, letters and pamphlets bursting from it. The phone rings. Brand looks at it with considerable venom; doesn't budge,*

Jowett in, in shirt sleeves, pullover, two brown mugs of instant in his hands. He places one on the desk by Brand's arm.

JOWETT: *(nodding towards phone)* What's wrong, you paralysed?

BRAND: Numbed. I spend half my working hours on the bloody thing.

JOWETT: *(lifting it, mouthpiece covered)* Christ. Get some in sonny. *(to phone)* Leighley Labour Party. *(he listens, picks up pencil, scrawls something on pad)* I see. Well, I suggest you bring it along to the Member's surgery tomorrow morning ... Ten. ... Well, there's usually a fair few ... As early as you can. Adelphi Hall, 12 John Street, just behind the Town Hall ... You know it, good ... Not at all. Good night.

He puts the phone down, drinks from mug, stares at Brand, who's thrown down his pen and is staring at his paper, very tired.

JOWETT: You look knackered, lad.

BRAND: *(recovering)* What was that?

JOWETT: Another council eviction. They're coming tomorrow.

Small silence.

BRAND: *(checking watch)* What time do you have, Alf?

JOWETT: *(checking)* Twenty to. Minute after.

BRAND: I've got to be in Manchester, nine at the latest. What're the buses like?

JOWETT: Twenty two, every twelve minutes, if they're running. They've been refusing to go out after nine, weekends, since that stabbing ...

BRAND: *(picking up pen)* Better get my skates on ...

Jowett strips a postal packet, takes out a dozen posters for a jumble sale, studies them.

JOWETT: What happened to the car?

BRAND: *(carefully)* My wife has it.

JOWETT: You need one.

Hughie Marsden in. He stays in doorway, hand on handle.

MARSDEN: Alf. *(seeing Brand)* Bill.

JOWETT: How'd it go, Hughie?

MARSDEN: Fine. We got the South African thing through. It'll go to Council next week.

JOWETT: Good. I'll watch out for it.

MARSDEN: *(in Brand's direction)* What time's Last arriving?

BRAND: Midday, thereabouts. I'm picking him up at Victoria. He's speaking in Liverpool tonight.

MARSDEN: You did well, getting him up here. The men at Bryant's are grateful, though they won't let on they are. *(pause. Brand shrugs)* Still taking stick, are you?

BRAND: I wouldn't say that. *(grinning)* Though I'm bound to say I'm not exactly scooping popularity plaques in the Parliamentary Labour Party either.

MARSDEN: Never mind, we can't all be Lenin. *(pause)* But we can try. *(a hard grin. Brand winces silently at the pretension)* Oh, on the subject of Bryant's and the occupation ... don't expect too much from it ... All right?

He's preparing to leave. Brand gets up, frowning.

BRAND: No, hang on Hughie, how do you mean?

MARSDEN: I've over fifty engineering lads out there, I'm in touch daily. See for yourself tomorrow. It's not good, they've no leverage ... they've got problems ... mm? It could just ... *(he blows his lips out)* ... you know? All I'm saying is: think ahead a step or two. Mmm?

He nods at Jowett, leaves, closing the door behind him. Brand works on Marsden's message, frowning more deeply. Looks at Jowett, who's returned to his posters, checking one against his draft.

BRAND: *(worried)* I spoke to Wilkinson this morning by phone. He gave no hint ...

JOWETT: He wouldn't, would he. *(pause)* There's half a dozen other mills meeting this weekend with the Action Committee at Bryant's. If they can pull only one of them – two mebbe – it could snowball. *(screwing face up, unhappy with some of the lettering)* Wi'out support ... they're in dead trouble.

Knock at door, light yet noticeable.

JOWETT: It's open.

A woman of about 34 enters. She carries a baby of maybe five months in one arm; has two others – boys, of 4 and 2 – in tow. She has a toughish, angular face, light wispy hair, dark coat, platform shoes.

WOMAN: Is this the Labour Party?

JOWETT: That's right, what can I do for you?

WOMAN: I wanna see me MP.

She looks from an impassive Jowett to a frowning Brand.

JOWETT: What about?

WOMAN: Are you him?

JOWETT: No ...

WOMAN: Well, mind your own bloody business ... *(looking round room)* Is he here?

JOWETT: He'll be here tomorrow, ten o'clock in t'morning.

BRAND: *(standing)* All right, Alf, I'll look after it.

JOWETT: *(under breath)* I thought you said you had to get off ...

BRAND: *(gently)* All right. Mmm? *(he smiles at Jowett, who sniffs, resigned; leaves)* Sit down, Mrs ...?

WOMAN: Pilling. *(to kids)* Now you sit there and sit still or I'll crack you one ...

The kids sit, unconcerned, unalarmed at her familiar aggression. She sits at the chair by the desk, Brand sits to face her.

BRAND: I'm Bill Brand. Your MP. What can I do for you?

MRS PILLING: Me husband's pissed off and left me.

BRAND: *(slowly)* Ahunh?

MRS PILLING: Left me with this lot ... And another, she's seven, she's at home. *(pause)* I've no one as'll help. I'm from Hull, you see. All mine're over there, what's left of 'em. Dad were killed on t'boats, me ma went off wi' someone else ... Anyroad.

Brand writes her name on a piece of paper.

BRAND: Where do you live, Mrs Pilling?

MRS PILLING: 29 Milton Street, Leighley.

He copies it down.

BRAND: I'll talk to the Social Services people first thing Monday morning. They'll probably send somebody round ...

MRS PILLING: I've seen them, they're not interested ... *(to be baby, brusque)* Sh. Sh.

Brand sits back, puts down the pen, studies her.

BRAND: Mrs Pilling, what exactly is it you're wanting?

MRS PILLING: I'm up the spout again, aren't I? I want an abortion, what do you think I want?

BRAND: Shouldn't you see ... your doct-

MRS PILLING: I've seen 'em all. I've been up to Boothroyd. They won't give us one. *(Brand picks up pen, writes on the pad before him. The woman watches him. The aggression and assertion slowly drain from her tired face)* I've four already. I can't do with another. Not without him ...

Pause. Brand stares at his notes blankly, then looks at her.

BRAND: *(quiet)* OK, Mrs Pilling. *(pause)* I'll do what I can.

She gets up, oddly crushed, the wind gone. Brand stands with her.

BRAND: I'll be in touch. *(she doesn't believe him)* It's a promise.

She leaves, herding kids ahead of her.

He returns to the notes briefly. Stands, very pale, collects his parka, puts it on. Behind him, through the door, the rock band has begun its exploratory first number. Jowett comes in.

JOWETT: OK?

BRAND: Yeah.

JOWETT: Pity you can't stay. The Young Socialists can't be ignored, you know.

BRAND: No, I know, Alf, I've just er ... got things to do. Personal.

Jowett purses his lips.

JOWETT: *(for him, gentle)* Listen, we're gonna have to talk, you know.

BRAND: Yeah, I know.

JOWETT: I'll back you, Bill. You know that. But I have to know ...

Brand fastens his parka for a moment.

BRAND: *(not looking at him)* She's divorcing me.

JOWETT: Ahunh. Grounds?

BRAND: We're working on it.

JOWETT: Well, work hard. It's important. We've enough problems ...

BRAND: *(sharp)* I *know* that. Alf. All right?

Silence. Jowett stands on his cigarette end.

JOWETT: *(quiet but distinct)* I don't make the rules, Bill.

Brand turns to look at him. Smiles.

BRAND: Sorry.

JOWETT: Shouldn't you be looking for your own place? *(Brand closes over again)*

BRAND: I have a place ...

JOWETT: Think about it. *(he turns back to his files on the desk)*

Close shot of Brand, tense, sharp, as he turns to leave.

Lobby, Friends Meeting House. *Brand browses in front of Diary of Events board.*

ALEX'S VOICE: *(addressing meeting in nearby room)* ... the pressure upon societies like this to admit into their repertoire of possible behaviours the things we've been discussing and ... bearing witness to tonight ... will of course continue ...

Brand checks watch. A man in fairly fetching make-up, perhaps an ear-ring, comes out of door leaving it partly open. Brand moves until he can glimpse Alex standing at head of table, past heads of one or two listeners. He watches intently.

ALEX: ... But it would be wrong, in my view anyway, for Gay Lib and the rest to conduct separate and secular struggles against the structures that oppress them. Because – again in my view – the problems that face the deviant are not finally separable from the problems of those many others in society who are exploited and oppressed from the cradle to the grave. When we come to see what is to be *done*, that is, we inevitably discover that the issue is not sexual but political. I repeat: 100,000 families – responsible for 300,000 children – below the official state poverty line. Three million dependent on supplementary benefit. Three and a half million heads of households too poor to pay the full fair rent on their houses. While at the other end, over twenty five per cent of total personal wealth is in the hands of just one per cent of the population. And while in England and Wales 100,000 people *underneath* live in just over 30,000 rooms, 100,000 *above* live in no less than 750,000 rooms ... and beneath them all, perhaps 50,000 lacking any rooms at all ... I repeat, while a million people face unemployment, upwards of a hundred currently report an average investment income of £196,000, and assets worth at least £4 million *each*. We live in a *barbarous* society. There are, all around us, greater indignities inflicted on the human spirit than the oppression of sexual predilection. It's foolish to imagine you can win your rights without changing the whole map of inequity and injustice that even the most cursory reading of official government statistics – the General Household Survey, the Inland Revenue Reports and so on – will show up. *(pause)* And even if it were possible ...

The man in the make-up returns and closes door behind him. Alex's voice is now indistinct. Brand stares at the door.

ALEX'S VOICE: ... No rights so gained could ever be secure, on the shifting sand of that sort of inequality.

Int. Alex's bedroom.

Mute.

Alex's bed. Lit by gasfire and streetlamp. Brand and Alex fuck, long, strong, occasionally savage, under a sheet. The fuck is good but not complacent: glints of struggle, competition, as they thresh towards separate orgasm. Alex's arrives as he takes her nipple in his mouth: Yes, yes, yes, she mouths, mute, over and over, spills quickly on last, extended affirmation. Brand drives on, excited by her excitement, his climax traceable in rigid clusters of muscle on his back and shoulders.

Close shot of alarm clock, with bells, on bedside table. Three minutes past two. Sound up: it ticks heavily, rather fast. Sounds of breath being reined in from the gallop.

ALEX'S VOICE: *(over)* You never make a sound. You should read some Reich ...

BRAND'S VOICE: *(over)* Why, what did he do, yodel?

A little later. Alex in from bathroom, in short white bathrobe. Sounds of lavatory flushing. She enters bedsitting room, crosses to stove, turns off pan of milk, pours onto prepared cups of cocoa, stirs and sugars, carries them over to the bed area, now lit by bedside lamp. She puts one down by Brand, who snuggles down beneath the sheet, protected from the light.

ALEX: Here's the cocoa you requested.

She returns to her own side, squats, places her cup on a table, takes a strip of pills from her handbag, removes one, swallows it, washing it down with cocoa.

Brand emerges, feels for his cup, sips from it, props himself up against the wall, cup in hands. They sit for a moment, caught inside their own separate moments of vacancy.

ALEX: *(eventually)* It was a good meeting. Gay Lib had a dozen or more there. And a lot of women's organisations. I wish you could have got there ...

BRAND: You doing more of that now ...?

ALEX: Mmm. *(pause)* With my own ... particular emphasis, of course ...

BRAND: Yeah, I gathered. *(Alex looks at him)* I heard you winding up.

ALEX: You think I've got it wrong?

BRAND: *(glancing at clock)* Well, I thought it sounded a mite ... opportunist. I mean, you might actually persuade the sexual deviant to see his oppression in terms of the more general oppression of the exploited classes ... But will you persuade those classes that the sexual deviant is an ally in the struggle.

Alex puts down her mug, climbs on and into the bed.

ALEX: Listen ... Christ, you should've been there ... This guy in drag started telling us about a dance at Stockport Trades Council Club, three hundred trade unionists, with their husbands and wives ... and eight transvestites from Gay Lib ... affiliated members ... and not a voice raised in protest all evening. Not a murmur. Guy said ... that's his name ... Guy said ... he went to the Gents and stood between two miners, skirt in his hand ... mm? ... and one of 'em looked at him and said ... It's better out than in, eh ... You're losing touch, Mr Brand, down there in that House of Wind of yours ...

BRAND: *(setting mug down, checking alarm)* Probably. Probably.

They lie down together, her head on his arm. He clicks the light off.

ALEX: You're a puritan. Down below you think it's all ... pretty distasteful, don't you?

BRAND: *(mildly)* Meaning ... you find it pretty attractive. At last. All that crap about 'particular emphasis' ... It turns you on ...

ALEX: It's not *crap.* So what if it does?

Silence. He removes his arm, turns towards her, looks down at her face on the pillow.

BRAND: Does it?

ALEX: Sort of. In the head, maybe.

Brand puts his hand on her temple, strokes it gently.

BRAND: Since when?

ALEX: I don't know. They force you to … reconsider yourself. Stop suppressing. *(pause)* I think I could make love with a woman, given the right circumstances.

BRAND: *(ironic)* Well, I'll go to the foot of the stairs.

ALEX: Do you find that unpleasant?

BRAND: *(after thought)* No. *(pause. Serious)* On … reconsideration.

ALEX: What about you?

He lies back on the pillow, stares at the ceiling.

BRAND: I'm a puritan, remember?

ALEX: So answer the question, Bill.

BRAND: *(simple, unforced)* I actually did sleep with a guy once. Nineteen. Second year at university. Stranded at a party, mile from anywhere. The guy giving it – I didn't know him, met him that night – offered me a bunk-down. There was one bed. I'd just settled down when I felt his hand reaching for me. I couldn't believe it. I was paralysed for a minute. *(pause)* Just … long enough.

ALEX: *(eventually)* You … came?

BRAND: *(finally, still gravely matter-of-fact)* Most emphatically.

ALEX: *(soft)* Jesus.

BRAND: I was thirty before I told anyone. For years my arse'd go tight just … thinking about it. Pathetic. But finally … it forced me … to reconsider myself. *(he turns on his side again, to face her. Smiles)* Shall we sleep?

She kisses him gently on the lips.

ALEX: You've turned me on again.

BRAND: *(grinning)* Me and my big mouth.

She kisses him again.

ALEX: My. *(kiss)* Honourable. *(kiss)* Member. *(kiss)*

PART TWO

Just after noon. Outside Victoria Station, Manchester. Brand slings a bag into the boot of his borrowed car, bangs it to. On the back window, a strip poster says 'Labour Cares'. He returns to the open driver's door. Streams of football supporters pour from the station.

Interior, car. David Last, in the passenger seat, studies a small notebook as he waits. He wears a faded green combat jacket, old brown cords, the red wool tie. Brand rejoins him.

BRAND: Thanks for coming.

LAST: Hiding to nothing, I suppose.

BRAND: Where are you staying?

LAST: *(checking book)* Midland?

BRAND: *(mock-disgust)* Right. I said we'd be there for two.

Car. Outskirts of Leighley. Last works on some papers on his knee, Brand drives.

BRAND: *(finally)* What are you gonna say?

Last looks up and around him, disengaging from the work.

LAST: I don't know. *(pause)* Officially ... *(long pause)* ... I'm here to tell them the government ... 'has the matter in hand'. *(he looks at Brand)* Maybe I'll just listen. *(pause)* I don't enjoy your ... freedom, Bill.

Brand says nothing. Last looks down at his papers, back at Brand.

LAST: *(without conviction)* The PM's ... listening. We could get some sort of a move by the summer recess ... *(Brand honks at something ahead)* ... Word has it you've been written to the Chief Whip threatening a vote-strike. *(not ironic)* Very daring.

BRAND: A slight exaggeration. I've simply ... let it be known ... I'm considering one. *(pause)* I'll see what support there is among the others.

LAST: Take care. Don't push Maddocks too far. *(pause)* Did you join the Group?

BRAND: Yes.

LAST: Well. It's something. You've made a few enemies. The Sunday Express piece didn't help.

BRAND: *(grinning)* I don't suppose it'll worry the Sunday Express over much. There she is.

Bryant's factory. Bryant's gate and wall loom up through the windscreen. Two policemen – a constable and an inspector – wave the car down. The Inspector approaches the driving door. Brand rolls down the window.

INSPECTOR: Do you have business here?

BRAND: Yeah, I'm the MP. *(the Inspector's eyes screw inwards. Silence)* This is David Last, Minister for Employment.

INSPECTOR: *(gloved hand to cap peak)* I see. Thank you, sir.

The car drives up to the gate. Long shot. Brand gets out, talks to the men on the gate. Gates open. He drives the car through.

Managing Director's office. Large, airy, though an old room. Last and Brand, red tabs in lapels, sit at the middle of the long conference table. Around them sit the occupation committee, Wilkinson prominent, directly opposite Last and Brand. Patel (from episode 3) sits on his left hand. About six other senior representatives present.

Last has just spoken. The men are grim, unimpressed. Wilkinson looks at each of them in turn before speaking.

WILKINSON: *(slowly)* Not much of a message, comrade.

LAST: No. But it's the best I can do. I'm not here to con you with promises we can't keep. The PM's ordered an urgent review of the whole industry. We've set time aside for an all-party debate in the Chamber. And the Chancellor's agreed to meet the Employers' Federation again. *(pause)* I'd like to say more but I can't.

MAN: *('Communications' armband. Top of table)* You've said next to nowt up to now, comrade.

LAST: *(quiet, distinct)* I'm aware of that, comrade.

WILKINSON: What's your ... What's your own opinion of all this then?

Last looks around the table very steadily.

LAST: I'd like to think you could win.

WILKINSON: *(pausing)* But you ... don't think we will.

LAST: *(carefully)* I think you've got problems. Finance, access, transportation, morale ... *(he leaves his accurate intelligence to seep in)*

WILKINSON: *(toughening)* You might have a few problems of your own, come tomorrow, if we can spread the sit-ins. It wouldn't take much to bring the whole bloody shoot to a halt.

LAST: I know.

Pause.

WILKINSON: So what will you say to the men?

LAST: I'm here to tell them ... we understand their anger and frustration ... and we want to help. *(pause)* Principally, I'm here to listen.

Wilkinson looks round the table. The committee signals diffident assent, save for the man at the top of the table.

WILKINSON: Geoff?

MAN: *(unyielding)* OK. I think we should have some assurance that our comrade isn't proposing to hand out ... advice. *(beat)* If only for his own sake ... It's a fair while since they've seen red meat ...

Some mutters, tough grins, around the table. Last taps the table with his biro, cool, held in. Wilkinson studies him.

BRAND: *(quietly)* Wouldn't it be more ... fraternal ... to allow the comrade to take his chances?

Silence. A shimmer of resistance, in the consideration, but not more.

LAST: *(at last)* I'm not here to advise. *(he looks round the table, careful, deliberate)* The Government wants you out; of that there can be no doubt. But those are not the terms I agreed to come on, I'm not here as an emissary, I'm here to learn. *(pause)* If anyone here imagines I've abandoned a lifelong belief in the efficacy of militancy since I joined the Cabinet ... maybe he should say so.

Nobody speaks. He pockets his biro, looks at his watch, then at Wilkinson.

WILKINSON: *(standing)* We'll go down, then. *(things are gathered, chairs scrape. To Last)* We've got some things for you to take back to London, when you go ... Files on 'troublemakers', 'deals' with Parfitt and the union, stuff like that, tapes of telephone conversations ... We've had some copies made ... A regular little Watergate, all tucked away in the Managing Director's safe. *(pause)* They've *always* been on a war footing. Might help some of your less 'militant' colleagues in Cabinet to see the *real* situation in industry today ... *(to others)* Right. We'll go. *(to Geoff, checking watch)* Hang on for the Lycro call for a bit, will you Geoff ... *(Geoff nods)*

BRAND: *(to Last; sotto)* OK?

LAST: Hiding to nothing. Yes.

Factory corridor, leading to canteen stage area. Last, tall, bony, stooped, untidy, leads, flanked by Patel and Geoff. Wilkinson and Brand follow, six or seven paces behind.

BRAND: I spoke with Hughie Marsden yesterday. *(Wilkinson looks at him, keen-faced, says nothing)* I need to know how things stand, Tom.

Wilkinson looks over his shoulder at the men following, measuring his volume.

WILKINSON: *(monotone; eventually)* Production stopped Wednesday. The banks have turned us down. The engineers are getting sucked off into other jobs. The men are getting bored. The union won't back us, so we're living on donations, hand to mouth. Parfitt's floating a redundancy scheme fed him by the employers that aims to drop night-shifts. That hits the Asians. You can imagine what the National Front are doing with all that. *(sniff)* We need Hall's and Lycro to follow us this weekend, or we'll split apart at the seams. *(mild)* I think that just about covers it, Bill.

He walks ahead as they reach the doors, says something to Last. Two men with armbands stand with hands on door bars. From within, the sounds of a large, packed hall. Wilkinson nods, the doors are opened, Last walks through and onto the stage. Patel and Geoff follow him. Sudden storm of booing and stamping erupts. Doors close again.

WILKINSON: *(to Brand)* You in or what?

BRAND: Sure.

He passes through the doors. Some applause, thin but sustained. Wilkinson notes it.

WILKINSON: *(to door man)* Seen Geoff?

*The door man nods over Wilkinson's shoulder. Wilkinson turns. Geoff,
straightening his armband, clops towards them, a piece of paper in his hand.*

GEOFF: Lycro. *(hands Wilkinson the paper)* Just phoned through.

Wilkinson studies the paper briefly, impassive.

WILKINSON: All right, Geoff. We'll wait for Hall's and the others before we say
out, OK?

*Geoff nods, leaves. Wilkinson nods to the door men, who let him through. Within,
Last taking his hiding well. The doors close. The door men relax, alone again.
One takes out a ten pack of Park Drive, offers one to his Asian mate. The Asian
takes it, provides the match.*

Int. Night. Midland Hotel. *Last's en-suite bathroom. Brand, in shirt sleeves, is
bowed over the washbasin, sousing his face in water. He kecks once or twice but
isn't sick. On the glass ledge below the mirror, his Russian watch has almost
midnight. His head, face, appear in the mirror. He blinks, trying to focus. Grins at
himself, finally.*

BRAND: This is nice.

*Last's room. Six floors up. Last stands at the window, looking out over St Peter's
Square. He holds a half glass of whisky in his hand. The room is a chaos of
clothes, files, papers. Brand's parka is on the floor by his empty chair. Knock at
door.*

LAST: *(turning)* Come in. *(a uniformed waitress pushes a trolley in)* Oh thank you,
here if you would.

*The waitress smiles, lifts a tray from the trolley, places it on a table, begins to
strip it of huge open sandwiches, salad, celery and a bottle of Scotch. Last
empties the bottle they're on, allows her to take it.*

WAITRESS: *(handing him her book)* If you'd just sign here, sir.

Last signs, smiles at her.

LAST: Thanks.

WAITRESS: *(shyish)* You're in the government, aren't you?

LAST: Yes, that's right.

WAITRESS: I thought you were. *(pulling trolley towards the door, stopping,
grinning suddenly)* Never mind, eh.

Last chuckles. Brand opens the bathroom door, steps out behind her.

BRAND: Don't look now, but you're surrounded. Here you are ... *(he opens the
door for her. She looks back up the room at Last)*

WAITRESS: *(mock disdain)* Who's your friend, then?

Brand closes the door with exaggerated gallantry after her, turns back into the room.

BRAND: Welcome to the Lead Balloon Club. Listen, I ought to go ...

LAST: Rubbish, sit down, eat your sandwich. How are you feeling?

BRAND: *(dry)* Grand. *(pause. Lifting glass)* Considering. How about you?

Last picks up the new bottle of White Horse, strips the cap.

LAST: If past experience is anything to go by, round about there ... *(he fingers a spot about halfway down the bottle)* I should begin to feel ... fine.

Brand sits, picks at salad.

BRAND: *(Bogart)* That's a lot of red-eye.

Last joins him at the low table, pours Brand's, his own.

LAST: *(mild up to 'shit', then a tiny explosion)* Well, maybe you didn't notice, Mr Brand, but I ate an awful lot of shit this afternoon. *(pause)* But. *(glass up)* We make our own beds.

They drink in silence. Brand picks up a celery stick, dips it in the scotch, bites it. Last looks around the alien room.

BRAND: *(finally)* I noticed.

LAST: I spent my whole life on the back benches. Thirty two years of principled refusal. It took me two hours to say yes, when Arthur offered. I had lunch with my wife, she put all the arguments against, I agreed, went back and said yes. Was I wrong?

BRAND: *(noncommittal)* Depends what you want.

LAST: You *know* what I want. I want to build socialism. But *this* way. Because here, now, for us, there is no other ...

Brand gets up, walks around the room, rather suddenly, fumed rather than drunk, oddly up.

BRAND: I don't know. I don't know. *(he stops at window, looks down over the Square)* That's where I studied, when I were a kid, school, then university. The Library, Central Ref. I'd sit in there. Rediscovering the world in a poem. Donne probably. The Metaphysicals were back in, after centuries of neglect. 'I wonder by my troth what thou and I *did*' ... Leavis's unforgettable *did* ... 'till we loved. Were we not weaned till then, but sucked on country pleasures childishly? ... Twas so ...' And opposite, down the desk maybe, there'd be a downer, a tramp, a layabout, with newspapers sticking out of his boots, matted hair, sleeping, trying to sleep, in out of the wet. They were always there, six or eight maybe, different ones. And I got to thinking, why are they them and I me? I never spoke to them, except once, one asked me for the price of a cup of tea, and I said I hadn't got it, a reflex, it couldn't have been true, and he said: 'I've been to China ... and I'm back now'. *(pause. He takes a drink)* I started looking ... for the reasons, him him, me me. *(he turns back into the room, resumes his seat)* I read your book on Morris when I was seventeen, your book on Tom Mann a bit later. *(pause)* I've always seen you as in the tradition, a fixity, part of an earlier Great Refusal. *(pause. It's harder now)* Now ... there's nobody where you were ... and there's nobody where you are.

He looks at his glass, then at Last, then back at his glass. Last sits, lips pursed, silent. No sound, no movement.

LAST: *(slow, distinct)* You see this ... as a sell-out, then.

BRAND: No. *(pause)* I don't know what I see it as. *(pause)* The scourge of the Right, they used to call you. After Nye died. CND. Clause Four. Rights of immigrants. *(pause)* You were ... greatly admired. *(pause)* What do *you* see it as?

Last pours more scotch, moves a sandwich, chews the lettuce frill.

LAST: Well, I'll tell you. *(a long sip)* All those years I sat there, watched all those dull and slippery men work their way through the machine, get their departments, pull real levers, make decisions, see them enacted, driven largely by ego and a sort of adolescent lust for recognition ... all the Tonys, the Bobs, the Georges, the Peters, the Jacks ... and I was sixty. Suddenly. Thirty years, like a week, all of it touchable, bound together by what? By a sort of rhetoric. Words. Precept, argument, ire. Air on air. Not ... enough, I thought. I thought, if our party *is* the real agent of socialist transformation – here, now, I mean – and that's been a bedrock of political faith for me, all my adult life – why doesn't it happen? I thought: if parliament *is* the seat of real political power in this society, why, when we're in office, do we slide and squelch about like shysters and milksops when it comes to translating our programmes into realities? A month later I got the invitation from Arthur to join the government. *(pause)* And I just felt ... I no longer had the right to say no. It doesn't ... ever ... just happen; it has to be made; and it has to be led.

BRAND: *(absorbing it; soft)* Couldn't it be argued that they've simply ... muzzled you ... inside their collective responsibility?

LAST: Perhaps. I've lost some freedom, certainly. You saw me this afternoon. It's not pleasant. *(long pause)* Yet it's not wholly inconceivable ... now ... I might make leader of the Party, even PM.

He says this mildly, as one might crease a piece of paper, thinking. Brand sharpens, blinks, shifted from his critical slouch. Last smiles dryly, diffident as ever.

LAST: I have a base, in the House, in the country. Arthur could well retire before this Parliament's through. And the Right's grip on this party is not God-given.

Silence. Brand takes a drink, puts the glass down on the table.

BRAND: *(without animus)* Mebbe not. The question is: will you still be able to tell the difference, by the time you get there?

LAST: I was in Venice with Phyllida in the early sixties, holidaying. We'd bumped
into Dick Crossman – he was there on a British Council lecture tour – and we
arranged to meet for drinks. I'd just helped persuade Conference to the
unilateralist programme. Dick was highly amused by it all, in that
characteristically classical way he had of refusing to commit to the major
issues of the time. The leadership ... the Right, that is ... was very far from
amused. Suddenly, Gaitskell appeared, Dora on his arm, from nowhere it
seemed ... It turned out later Dick had a lunch date with him ... just part of his
amusement, to confront us with each other. Gaitskell approached the table on
the terrace, Dick greeted him, he stopped, stood and talked a minute, then left.
(pause) He never addressed me once. Never looked at me. *(pause)* I'll know
the difference, comrade.

*He gets up. Walks into the bathroom, closes the door behind him. Brand sits there
for a moment, saddened somehow. Finally, he leans across to the colour tv,
switches it on, rather idly. Switches off again. Last returns from the bathroom.*

BRAND: Listen, I should go ...

LAST: Yes, I know. One for the road.

Last pours again.

BRAND: I can't drive with this lot inside me. I'll have to get a cab.

LAST: I'm sorry.

BRAND: *(softly)* Get away with you. It's been ... a pleasure.

LAST: I had these lines running round my head ... in there. Haven't read them in
... twenty years; and there they were, sharp as foxes, as I peed. *(he thinks; not
drunk, more loosened)*
    'If you came this way,
    Taking the route you would be likely to take
    From the place you would be likely to come from ...
    It would be the same at the end of the journey ...
    If you came at night like a broken king,
    If you came by day not knowing what you came for,
    It would be the same, when you leave the rough road
    And turn behind the pig-sty to the dull façade
    And the tombstone. And what you thought you came for
    Is only a shell, a husk of meaning
    From which the purpose breaks only when it is fulfilled
    If at all. Either you had no purpose ...
    Or the purpose is beyond the end you figured
    And is altered in fulfilment ...'

*He stops, deep inside the lines still. Brand stands, picks up his parka, puts it over
his arm, walks, a little unsteady, towards the door, turns.*

BRAND: *(half-fierce, sudden)*

'There are other places
Which also are the world's end, some at the sea jaws,
Or over a dark lake, in a desert, a city –'

LAST: *(shaking his head twice)*
'But this is the nearest, in place and time,
Now in England.'

Brand dwells a moment longer. They study each other's faces.

Brand leaves.

PART THREE

Alex's flat. Brand works at the table by the window. The curtains are drawn, though it's a bright day already outside; he works in the light of an angle-poise. He's writing letters on House of Commons notepaper. His face is pale, unshaven, the pocket-alarm in front of him says 8.20. He's in vest, trousers and shoes.

Alex sleeps on her back, an arm thrown over her head. She stirs a little; he looks at her, works on a moment, gets up to stop the kettle whistling, pours the water into a coffee pot, stirs, puts on the lid, takes out two cups, pours milk and sugar in each.

He crosses to the phone. Checks his watch. Dials. Waits.

BRAND: Hi, it's me. *(little or nothing from the other end)* How are you? *(pause)* Are the kids up? *(pause)* Could I have a word with them …? *(he waits)* Hi, son, how are you? … Yeah? When d'you do that? *(he listens, smiling)* So what did *you* do? … Ahunh. Great. And did he give it to you back? … What? Go on, try me. *(listens)* I don't know, what *is* white, swings through the trees and beats its chest? *(listens, laughs)* A meringue-utang! Brilliant. Who told you that? … You never, get away with you. Listen, Mike, I'll see you next week, Friday, all right? *(listens)* Well, we'll see, no promises. And we'll do some reading, see how you're getting on. OK. Big kiss. See you. *(he waits again)* Hi, babe … What? No, I couldn't make it this weekend. *(listens to her complaints)* I know, sweetheart, and I'm sorry. Next weekend, we'll drive out somewhere, mm? Have lunch at the boathouse. … All right, we'll go swimming … Yes … Yes. *(listens)* Listen, I'm sorry. A promise. Yes. All right. Listen, don't go away … I love you, baby. All right. And I miss you very much. And I think about you. Give me a kiss then … Mmm. That was a good one … Yes. All right. Is mummy still there …? *(listens)* All right. Goodbye.

He returns receiver to rest. Turns. Alex sits up in bed, wide awake, watching him.

BRAND: Hi.

ALEX: *(gravely)* Hi.

He crosses to the kitchen-area, pours the coffees, stirs, brings them to the bed.

BRAND: Toast?

ALEX: No, I'm fine. How'd it go yesterday?

BRAND: OK. We took the expected hammering out at Bryant's and got drunk together.

ALEX: We? What do they have against you?

BRAND: All right, Last took a hammering. *(pause)* I remain ... popular but impotent. And actually, I think they do resent it.

He gets up, moves back to the table, takes his discarded shirt from the chairback.

ALEX: There are clean shirts ...

BRAND: *(looking at her; beat)* Thanks.

He crosses to wardrobe, selects a shirt from a hanger, puts it on.

BRAND: I got so sodden I had to leave Jowett's car down there. That's why I was so late.

ALEX: How did you get on with him?

BRAND: Fine. *(tucking shirt into waistband)* Fine.

ALEX: Did he mention the job again?

BRAND: No.

ALEX: Will you take it if he offers?

He crosses to the table, searching for a tie.

BRAND: I don't know.

Alex gets out of bed, walks, naked, to the bathroom. Brand gathers a few things together at the table, ticks matters dealt with from his surgery pad.

ALEX: *(calling, matter-of-fact)* I've been offered a job in London ...

He stops his process to absorb it, suddenly a little taut. Sound of lavatory flushing. Alex reappears, stands in doorway; she's put on a pair of faded white knickers.

ALEX: I'm tempted.

BRAND: *(back to process)* What's the job?

ALEX: Community project, Hackney. *(she lies down on the bed, begins a routine investigation of her breasts, left, right, very functional, for lumps)* I like the sound of it.

BRAND: Do you know any of the people?

ALEX: One or two. I'd be assistant to the leader.

BRAND: Sounds good. When would it be?

ALEX: September, I think.

Small silence. He puts some files into his briefcase.

ALEX: So what do you think?

BRAND: *(facing her at last)* I think you should decide on the merits of the job. What I want's irrelevant.

ALEX: *(getting up)* I'd still like to know.

She begins to dress, jeans, sweater, bumpers.

BRAND: I've got at least a thousand reasons for wanting you with me ... all of them probably deeply male chauvinist. Shirts, socks, order, food, emotional succour, sexual convenience, whipping girl, butt, the whole ancient repertoire of use ... You know me. *(pause)* Come ... because *you* want to come. Come because you have something to come for. I don't want you to come for me. OK?

She begins straightening the bed. Brand watches her.

BRAND: *(finally, as though remembering)* Oh ... and I love you. I forgot to mention it. The ultimate blackmail.

ALEX: Actually, I was thinking on more practical lines. If I do take it, I could keep this place on for you and maybe get somewhere for both of us down there ... How does that sound?

BRAND: *(smiling, dry)* Sounds very practical.

He puts on his parka, fastens his briefcase.

ALEX: You got to go?

BRAND: Yeah, I've got to pick up the car and drive over to Alderley Edge ...

ALEX: Oh yeah? Who do you know in the stockbroker belt then?

BRAND: It's a gynaecologist. He's refusing an abortion for a constituent *(he winces at the word. Checking in a notebook)* His name's ... Marples, do you know anything about him?

ALEX: Yeah, he's new; from Birmingham ... *(Birmingham has immediate meaning for him)* We've picked up a few shock waves already, down at the Advice Centre. Catholic. Hysterically anti-abortion. Part of the Birmingham ring ... Talk to Joe Fitton, he'll fill you in, he's doing a pamphlet on them ...

Brand stares at the notebook, oppressed again.

BRAND: Christ, that's just what I need.

ALEX: *(kind but tough)* Hey. It's *her* who's got the real problem ...

BRAND: *(taking it)* Touché. *(he salutes her with his sword)* See you next week.

ALEX: Yeah. Take care.

He kisses his finger, flicks it across the room. She winks, familiar. He leaves.

Living room of a large country cottage. The room is on two levels. Brand sits in the well area by the large fireplace (no fire). The feel is pleasant, airy, light, effortlessly comfortable, lived in. He feels the old leather of his armchair, clocks discrete items around the room: scold's bridle on the wall; a calendar bearing a picture of St Joseph and the Infant Jesus; a tiny holy-water finger-font by the door; a colour tv; a Hacker stereo record-player; books.

Calls at the back of the house: 'Stephen, Stephen' – a woman's voice, unurgent, gracious.

The woman appears – Mrs Marples – carrying a silver tea tray. She's fadedly pretty, mid-forties, strong, composed, with some plain elegance about her dress. Brand makes to stand up.

MRS MARPLES: Please sit down, Mr Brand. I'll pour the tea.

She places the tray on a long desk-table. Over her shoulder:

MRS MARPLES: I've called my husband. He's in the orchard … tying back or … clipping … or whatever it is one does with pear trees. He has the least green fingers of anyone I know. Sugar?

BRAND: One.

She hands him the cup, carries a plate of currant cake, half sliced, places it on a low table by his chair.

MRS MARPLES: You seem quite young, for a member of parliament. I met the Health Minister once, what was his name?… He was opening a new hospital in Birmingham … Godber, was it? … I can't remember … nice man … He seemed very old. *(she smiles him, half-mocking her own lack of memory)*

BRAND: It's a lovely house.

MRS MARPLES: Isn't it? Wasted on us, I'm afraid. Imagine what a few children could do in a garden like that.

BRAND: *(probe under charm)* I can't believe yours are all grown up, Mrs Marples …

Marples in through french window, a small man, wiry, alert, dressed casually for the garden. He strips off his gloves, lays down secateurs, descends the two steps into the room proper.

MARPLES: Sorry, couldn't leave it …

BRAND: *(standing)* It's good of you to see me.

MARPLES: *(hand out)* Stephen Marples.

BRAND: Bill Brand.

MARPLES: Any of that for me?

MRS MARPLES: Sit down, I'll pour it.

Marples sits down in the second armchair, to face Brand. Bird song from outside. A relaxed, easy day in the country.

MRS MARPLES: *(pouring etc)* I was remarking how ... young Mr Brand seemed, for a Member of Parliament.

MARPLES: *(dry, not unfriendly, yet dismissive)* First signs of incipient ageing, darling, when you start to find your MPs looking young suddenly ...

MRS MARPLES: *(handing him cup)* Or my consultants ... I'll be in the studio, if I'm wanted ...

She smiles sweetly at Brand, leaves the room,

MARPLES: She pots, you know. *(Brand doesn't quite understand)* You know, the wheel ... she makes things. She's quite good. *(he offers Brand a cigar: Brand refuses. He takes one, begins lighting it)* Well now, this ... Pilling woman ... I've looked up the file since we spoke on the telephone ... What can I tell you about her?

BRAND: *(steadily)* I understand she's been refused an abortion.

MARPLES: That's right.

BRAND: By you.

MARPLES: That's right.

BRAND: May I ask on what grounds?

MARPLES: Mr Brand. The doctor does not have to offer grounds for refusing an abortion. The patient has to offer grounds why she should have one.

BRAND: *(quiet, contained)* Which, in the case of Mrs Pilling, you presumably reject?

MARPLES: Yes. Medically, she's as sound as a bell.

BRAND: Psychologically?

MARPLES: She seems quite capable, level-headed, realistic. Nothing there.

BRAND: Socially?

Marples hesitates a moment, relights the cigar.

MARPLES: *(deliberately)* She has a life not significantly harder than tens of thousands of women who bear their children quite happily without a thought of ... abortion.

BRAND: Mr Marples, I have spoken with the Social Services Department, Mr Pilling *has* left her and has no intention of returning. She is currently having great difficulty finding the rent for that four-room hovel she calls home, and could soon be evicted and have her children taken into care. In the view of the Social Services Department, unless she is given an abortion soon, Mrs Pilling will find herself a backstreet artist, with possible consequences you're doubtless aware of ... *(pause)* I beg you to think again.

MARPLES: That's a little hysterical, don't you think? Just a touch? In any case, you can't remedy one evil by perpetuating another. *(he stops, aware the ice has thinned dramatically)*

BRAND: 'Evil', Mr Marples? It is the law of the land, *this* land, now, that in certain conditions and with proper medical safeguards, pregnancies may be terminated ...

MARPLES: I am well aware what the law is, Mr Brand ... If Mrs Pilling is not satisfied, she is entitled to go elsewhere, I have only one hospital ...

BRAND: Yes, that will be my advice to her, Mr Marples. I'm now beginning to worry about all the others ... *(he stands, preparing to leave)* You do ... terminate pregnancies, don't you ... I mean, circumstances do exist in which you have decided to abort the foetus rather than risk irreparable damage to the mother's health ...?

MARPLES: *(calm)* Mr Brand, I suspect we have concluded our business ...

BRAND: Mr Marples, I suspect we've only just begun it ... Please say goodbye to your wife for me.

Brand leaves, placing his hand in the finger-font, checking it's in use.

Marples follows to the window, watches as the car drives off. Mrs Marples in behind him.

MRS MARPLES: Oh, has he gone? What a pity. I liked him. What did he want?

Marples turns, crosses the fine long room, picks up his gloves and secateurs, moves out into the garden.

MARPLES: Nothing much, darling. He just wanted to involve me in a little gentle murder ...

Int. House of Commons. *Desk room. Brand on phone.*

BRAND: *(file open: angering)* ... I don't care what his status is in the profession, he's denying women in my constituency their fundamental rights in law ... *(listening against his will)* ... Yes, I know that, yes, yes, ahunh ... Look, excuse me, the *real* question is whether you're going to do anything about it ...I don't know, it's your bloody department ... *(listening briefly)* What do you mean, electoral embarrassment? I haven't met a constituent yet who doesn't believe she should have the right ... *(forced to listen)* ... Oh sure, men, yes, they don't have the bloody problem ... *(listening again)* ... All right, I give you warning, I'm going to raise it ... and if that doesn't get us anywhere I'll go to the papers ... Right.

He slams the phone down, seething. Bangs the file closed. Sits. Wellburn in, suave, good wool suit, smiling but uncomfortable, already looking at his watch.

WELLBURN: Bill. You wanted to talk. Can't stay, got a lunch appointment.

BRAND: *(terse)* Thanks for coming. I wanted to know what you thought about the idea of a vote-strike?

WELLBURN: a vote-strike? How do you mean?

BRAND: There's a two-line whip tomorrow on the education things. We threaten to vote *against* unless they promise immediate action on textile import quotas.

WELLBURN: Against? Oh come on now ...

BRAND: What?

WELLBURN: I'm a parliamentary private secretary, Bill. I'm a member of the government for Christ's sake ...

BRAND: You're a Member of Parliament. For a constituency that will lose five hundred jobs in the next three months unless something is *done*, Michael.

WELLBURN: *(freezing)* Why don't you leave my constituency to me, old chap, mm?

BRAND: *(tight)* Sure.

WELLBURN: What do the others say? Swinson, Bowers ...?

BRAND: Why don't you ask them?

WELLBURN: No, you mean? I'm not surprised ...

A Commons messenger in, places telegram on Brand's desk. Brand picks it up, doesn't open it.

WELLBURN: *(tastefully vicious)* You're a sententious bastard, Brand, do you know that?

He leaves, high on hauteur. Brand nods several times, as though agreeing, lips furl. Opens telegram with one hand, very slowly, straightens it to read it. We stay on his face as he reads it. It remains impassive, but gradually drains of all vitality. Finally, blinks, blinks again. Stands. Folds telegram up without looking at it, places it in pocket, walks out of the room.

House of Commons, corridor. Brand walks it, very slowly, hands in trouser pockets, shoulders bowed.

He stops by a tea-trolley. Joins small queue. Buys a coffee. Sits on a small bench to drink it. Close shot of Brand, absorbing his news, grim, dispirited.

He gets up eventually, places his cup on the stand, moves off, turns into a room on the right, knocking once.

Int. Chief Whip's Office. Maddocks sits at his large desk, reading The Times. He looks up as Brand enters. Stands, waves him in.

MADDOCKS: *(genial)* Come in, brother, come in, thank you for coming. Grab a chair.

BRAND: *(sitting)* You wanted to see me?

MADDOCKS: That's right, that's right. Just wanted a chat really. Not seen a lot of you since that little ... misunderstanding, shall we call it ... over the Finance Bill. Wondered how you were getting along?

BRAND: Yeah? *(long pause)* I'm getting along famously. Or in the words of one or two of our honourable friends, it beats working any day.

Silence. Maddocks chooses to laugh.

MADDOCKS: Good. Good. Like to keep the troops happy, that's what I'm here for. *(pause, to look for words)* Look, about the fracas we had ... it's not important, an honest difference, all right? I want you to know, as far as we're concerned, it's forgotten. OK?

Brand puts his palms on his chair arms, raises them, puts them down again to push himself to his feet.

BRAND: Fine. *(pause. About to leave)* Is that all?

MADDOCKS: *(standing too)* Let's have a drink sometime, get to know each other a bit. A Chief Whip can't afford to get out of touch ...

BRAND: Sure thing.

MADDOCKS: *(confidential)* I heard a whisper David Last had got his eye on you to follow Renshaw. *(he winks)* Nice one.

BRAND: *(reflective, mild)* You didn't also pick up a whisper I was trying to organise a vote-strike, did you, Mr Maddocks?

MADDOCKS: *(a beat to adjust; half laughing)* A ... what?

BRAND: It doesn't matter. Just a rumour. You know what this place is like ...

He leaves.

Int. Front hallway, Clapham flat. *Night. Brand in from street, bushed. A heap of letters in his pigeon hole. He sorts them mechanically, opens one marked Hollins & John, Solicitors and Commissioners for Oaths, 82 Market Street, Leighley, Reads. Close shot of letter:*

'Dear Mr Brand,

I have to inform you that my client, Mrs Miriam Brand, has now decided to institute proceedings for divorce on grounds of irretrievable breakdown of marriage due to mental cruelty and not, as previously indicated, adultery ...'

He folds the paper, walks slowly up the stairs.

Brand's living room. Dark, chill. Brand in. Walks to desk, puts on Anglepoise, slumps into chair, throwing mail onto his in-tray.

He sits for a long time, hands to face, rubbing eyes, forehead, very slowly, otherwise inert. Finally he takes out the telegram, opens it, places it on the desk.

Close shot telegram. 'BRAND, HOUSE OF COMMONS, SW1. OCCUPATION OVER STOP FACTORY CLOSED STOP NOBODY WANTED TO KNOW STOP THANKS ANYWAY WILKINSON'

- end -

Episode 5

August for the Party

was broadcast on Monday 5th July 1976

The cast was as follows:

Bill Brand   Jack Shepherd

Reg Starr   Douglas Campbell

Mapson   Richard Butler

Venables   Peter Howell

Winnie Scoular   Rosemary Martin

Miriam Brand   Lynn Farleigh

Jane Brand   Karen Silver

Michael Brand   Philip Cox

Alex Ferguson   Cherie Lunghi

Alf Jowett   Allan Surtees

M.C.   Don Hawkins

Bernard Shaw   Colin Jeavons

Angie Shaw   Carole Hayman

Pru   Peter Ellis

Martin   Alan Luxton

Peter Malone   David Bradley

Woman Interviewer   Jan Harvey

Secretary   Lynne Verrall

Maidstone   Peter Jeffrey

Pat   Carol Drinkwater

Bonny Clark   Helen Rappaport

Christine Waite   Jane Briers

Designers: David Ferris, Harry Clark

Executive Producer: Stella Richman

Producer: Stuart Burge

Director: Roland Joffé

PART ONE

House of Commons bar, noisy, filled with members just in from the division lobby, among them Venables, the Home Secretary, Maddocks, the Chief Whip, several senior Liberals.

VENABLES: *(on his way through with someone)* A quiet word with you ...

Brand joins Reg Starr and Tom Mapson

BRAND: Hey ... what was all that nonsense about? I thought we just adjourned and that was it. I was tidying my desk up.

STARR: I hope you went through the right lobby, didn't vote against ...

BRAND: There was no shortage of guidance. Great. Into the breach, out of the muzzle, guaranteed painless.

STARR: It was the Liberals playing silly buggers, last day of term and all that. They forced a division.

MAPSON: *(watching Venables in a corner of the bar)* What 'quiet word' has the Home Secretary got for the Liberal Chief Whip, do you imagine?

Starr laughs.

BRAND: Shall I get them in, then?

MAPSON: Not for me, I've got to get off. We've got a Group meeting tonight, we're talking Conference ... will you be there?

BRAND: No, I've promised to get back to Leighley.

STARR: Well, enjoy yourself. See you in Blackpool.

He leaves.

BRAND: Tom, I was ... sorry to hear about your wife.

MAPSON: Thanks, Bill. She's better off, believe me.

BRAND: I don't suppose there's owt I can do ... *(Mapson declines gratefully)* Let me know if there is, eh?

MAPSON: Good of you to offer, lad. I'm sorry you can't make the meeting. There's no point in joining if you're not going to *join* ... Think about it.

Mapson leaves. Brand drinks his pint thoughtfully.

Clapham flat. Brand's living room. Winnie Scoular sitting in an armchair. Sounds of taxi drawing up outside, the front door slamming. She gets up as Brand runs upstairs whistling cheerfully. He enters the room.

BRAND: Hi!

SCOULAR: *(brightly)* Hello.

BRAND: How are you?

SCOULAR: I'm fine. I er ... thought I'd let you have the books back before you went off. Thanks.

BRAND: How did you find them?

SCOULAR: Well, they helped pass the time ... The pamphlet was a bit heavy.

BRAND: *(taking the books, turning the pamphlet over: a picture of Alex on the back of it. pause)* Yeah.

BRAND: I didn't expect you, otherwise I'd ...

SCOULAR: That's all right.

BRAND: Tom said it might be another week ...

SCOULAR: No ...

BRAND: *(busy clearing the kitchen area ready to leave; turning the gas tap off under the sink, rinsing a milk bottle)* Did you get the flowers?

SCOULAR: Mmm. Thanks.

BRAND: *(still busy in kitchen area)* I'd've come to see you, but Tom said you didn't want visitors ... *(turns back to her)* It's nothing serious, is it, Winnie?

SCOULAR: No. Nothing like that. So, what's been happening this week?

BRAND: Not a lot.

SCOULAR: What about Last's Unemployment Bill?

BRAND: *(packing last few things into his suitcase)* Disappeared Wednesday. It appears our ... beloved leader is having second thoughts ... It's being reworked for next session. Ha ha ha ha ha ... I shan't be sorry to be shot of it for a couple of months ... Jim McNab keeps telling me, it's the first fifteen years are the worst.

He turns into the room, glooming slightly now the sun's gone. Winnie sits as before. Her face is greasy with soft, inexplicable tears. She stares at the fireplace, remote, wholly self-absorbed.

Brand moves a pace or two towards her, dwells.

BRAND: Hey. Hey.

She blinks suddenly, begins wiping her face with a handkerchief in her right hand.

SCOULAR: Shit. It's ridiculous. I'm sorry, it just happens.

BRAND: What is it, Winnie?

SCOULAR: I'm *fine*, Bill. I've been in hospital and now I'm out ...

BRAND: ... So what are those, tears of joy ...?

SCOULAR: ... I told you, it just happens, it's a nervous reaction ...

BRAND: ... Reaction to *what*, Winnie ...?

SCOULAR: ... To the termination of a very slight, rather inconvenient pregnancy. All right?

Brand has nowhere to go; takes it between the eyes; rubs his forehead, as though to undaze them. The front door bell rings loudly. He peers through the window.

BRAND: That's my taxi. Erm ... I'll send him away and phone for another.

SCOULAR: No, you'll never get one. Go on, get off. Enjoy recess. I'll see you at Conference, mm?

BRAND: Look, if you give me the number I'll phone your husband, he should drive up for ...

SCOULAR: Richard thinks I've just been in for a check-up. It has ... *(she leaves it hanging)* ... nothing to do with him. *(doorbell again. Gently)* Taxi.

Brand moves towards the door, unwilling yet anxious to leave.

SCOULAR: I don't have to ask you to ...

BRAND: No of course not. *(he turns back, moves towards her, cups the backs of her upper arms in his hands)* Now you take good care, eh?

SCOULAR: *(smiling; much better)* I'm really glad you were here ... I felt ... bloody frightful ...

Brand picks his bags up, moves towards the door.

SCOULAR: See you in Blackpool.

BRAND: You're on, comrade. Go well.

He leaves.

Miriam's living room. *A match sputters in the dark, lights a ten-candle cake. Sounds of young children being quiet. The lit candles light up the faces around the table, Jane, Michael, others. Miriam's voice leads the birthday song. Jane blows out the candles, pleased yet faintly embarrassed to be so much at the centre. A whoosh of cheering as the flames subside into smoke.*

Kitchen. Party noises carry through from the front room, party dishes litter surfaces. Brand is sitting at the table, pouring two mugs of tea. Miriam in

BRAND: Sugar?

MIRIAM: No. I'm trying to give it up.

She sits down at the table, in profile. He pushes the mug over slowly. She takes it, drinks a little.

BRAND: Nice party.

MIRIAM: Mmm.

BRAND: Jane seems fine. *(pause)* The House is in recess. So ... I'll be available ... if there's anything you want me to do.

MIRIAM: Like what?

BRAND: I don't know. Look after the children mebbe. Or whatever.

MIRIAM: No, I've an arrangement with my mother. It's this summer she retires.

Silence. He stirs his tea.

BRAND: *(finally)* Have you fixed a holiday?

MIRIAM: I've booked the cottage in Mull again.

BRAND: Oh. *(pause)* What, a fortnight?

MIRIAM: Ahunh.

BRAND: *(patient, patient)* Mmm. *(pause)* When?

MIRIAM: August. *(he waits. She straightens wisps of hair about her ears, forehead)* First two weeks. *(pause)* Pour one for mother, will you, I'll take it through.

Brand pours another mug.

BRAND: I'm er ... I'm doing a summer school at Ruskin, last two weeks. I'd ... I'd like to take them with me, if that's OK.

MIRIAM: I'll have to think about it. I'll ask mother, she may have made other arrangements.

BRAND: *(mild but deliberate)* You might try consulting the children while you're about it. They're people too. With rights and ... preferences.

MIRIAM: I can manage quite well, thank you, without your advice on the handling of the children ...

BRAND: ... Handling? What're you talking about, *handling*? What do you think they are, some sort of putty? Jesus God!

MIRIAM: *(cold)* I don't want to argue, all right? I'll let you know.

BRAND: Jesus Christ, you're *shrivelling*, do you know that. You're wrinkling up into nothing, into a, into a little sack ... a little bag of pus. There's no joy left in you, no warmth, no largeness ... no generosity ... For Christ's sake *see* yourself Miriam. It's not pleasant. And while you're about it you can tell your mother those children aren't about to 'lose a father', divorce or no divorce.

Jane appears in the doorway.

JANE: Geoffrey Raines wants Michael for his partner.

MIRIAM: Michael ought to go to bed. I'll come and see him ...

JANE: Is that tea, dad? Can I have some?

She advances to the table, feels the teapot, reaches a rabbit cup from the cupboard. Miriam looks hard, contemptuous, at Brand, leaves with her mother's cup.

BRAND: *(with teapot)* Here we go then ... Still got old Rabbit eh ... he's almost as old as you.

JANE: He's nine and a half. Mummy told me. You bought him in Oldham Market one Saturday afternoon. And I was in the carrycot.

She sits on a stool to drink her tea and nibble a biscuit. Brand watches her, remembering fragments of the historic purchase. Reaches out to touch the dark straight hair about her ears. Jane flicks her head, self-reliant rather than dismissive.

Alex's flat, morning light filtering through drawn curtains. Brand and Alex sleep naked, Brand on his stomach, on the edge of the bed, Alex on her side, her hand on his shoulder.

The phone by the bed rings, two feet from Brand's head. He reaches for it, still half-asleep.

BRAND: Hello... Hi. What time is it? ... What? ... Fine, I was coming in anyway ... I've been busy. That's right. ... OK. Anything special? Fine. ... Oh, ten? Right.

He puts the phone down, sinks back down onto the pillow.

ALEX: Don't settle.

BRAND: *(still half asleep)* Mmm.

ALEX: Who was it?

BRAND: Jowett.

ALEX: *(peering at clock)* At half past eight?

BRAND: Mmm.

Jowett's office. Brand sits by the desk, reading a letter in a file before him. Jowett pours boiling water onto instant coffee in a corner of the littered room. Brand finishes reading, rubs his nose. Jowett returns with the cracked white mugs, sits at the desk facing Brand.

BRAND: *(tapping letter)* So?

JOWETT: Maybe it's too early. Think about it a bit.

BRAND: *(studying letter again)* What is this, Alf, my starter for ten? So the General Secretary of the Party wants a pre-Conference session on organisation with his agents?

JOWETT: *(deliberately)* Red. Alert.

BRAND: *(mystified)* How's that?

JOWETT: It's happened three times before, in the twenty some years I've spent in the job. And each time it's turned out to be a stand-by operation for a snap election.

Brand reads the letter yet again, brows furled.

BRAND: God almighty.

JOWETT: Keep calling, we'll need all the help we can get. *(Brand closes the file, sips his coffee)* Nowt's certain, of course. After the 1970 fiasco, Arthur'll be in no hurry. You've heard nothing, I take it? *(Brand shakes his head)* No, you wouldn't. You'll hear when you need to, not before. *(pause)* We had a caucus meeting Thursday. The general view is that our leader's keen to improve his majority in the House so that he can shake off his 'image' as a prisoner of the left.

BRAND: *(mirthless)* That's very nearly funny, Alf.

JOWETT: Very nearly.

Brand stands, walks around the cramped room a little, mug in hand.

BRAND: So what's the feeling? Will he risk it or not?

JOWETT: It's doubtful. Not as things stand. But if he can lose a couple of hundred thousand unemployed and cook up a few decent trade figures this summer, he just might give it a whirl in November. Might.

Brand returns to his chair.

BRAND: OK. Let's have the *bad* news.

JOWETT: *(opening a large file)* Did you have plans for the summer?

BRAND: Yes. Last two weeks in August. Ruskin Summer School. Otherwise I'm here.

Jowett nods several times, checking the August dates on a year planner on his desk. Brand waits, patient but frowning.

JOWETT: *(scratching something out)* That should ... be ... all right, I think. Got your diary handy.

BRAND: Yeah, I have my diary, Alf.

Jowett looks up at him, blinking, neutral.

BRAND: But *I'll* fill it, OK?

Jowett pushes back in his chair, opens a drawer, props a leg on it, rubs his eyes, tilts his battered trilby back from his forehead, putters his lips for a moment.

JOWETT: *(patient beyond enduring)* Bill ... If you're not going to listen you might as well leave right now. Either you take it from me ... or you take it from the GMC Thursday. You please yourself.

BRAND: Take what, Alf? Orders?

JOWETT: *(toughening beneath the mildness)* Tell you what, if you like 'em, we'll call 'em suggestions. If you don't, they'll just have to be orders.

Brand pushes his lips out, thinking. Jowett watches him, quiet, still, hard.

BRAND: *(taking diary and biro out)* OK. Let's go.

Jowett sighs deeply. Checks the year planner for the first date.

JOWETT: 27th, this month. Afternoon.

BRAND: *(checking)* Free.

JOWETT: *(top letter in file; fastish)* Leighley Sporting Club are running a beauty contest at the swimming baths. They want you to judge it. *(back to planner)* 28th. Evening.

BRAND: *(not writing)* Free.

JOWETT: Masonic Lodge Banquet, guest of honour. 30th. Evening.

BRAND: Free.

JOWETT: Junior Chamber of Commerce, Young Executive of the Year award. 2nd August.

Brand puts his pen down on the table carefully. Jowett stares at him.

JOWETT: What's wrong, am I going too fast for you?

BRAND: Not too fast, Alf. Just too far. *(pause. Jowett gives nothing)* Alf, beauty contests *degrade*. Masons are petit-bourgeois *buffoons*. The only thing I would consent to give the Leighley Young Executive of the Year is an illuminated scroll containing the names of all those he's declared redundant over the last twelve months. What *is* this shit, Alf?

JOWETT: *(clouting file with palm)* I'll tell you what this shit is, Bill. It's your bread and butter. Iron rations. For the duration. And I don't give a monkey's tosser what your personal views on masons and beauty contests are, because the object of the exercise is not to set you at ease with your sodding conscience but to get you a platform and win a few votes if there's an election this autumn. As far as I'm concerned, the honeymoon's over ... *(checking watch)* ... and I've got *work* to do. 5th August. Evening.

Pause. Jowett keeps stolid eyes on the year planner.

BRAND: *(quietly)* Say it all, Alf.

JOWETT: *(quick)* Look, you've had a free hand, we've gone all the way with you, you can't say we haven't. *(picks them off on his fingers)* Voting against the government, motions of censure here, the occupation at Bryant's, the 'communist' tag, the smears, your private life, the lot. All the way.

BRAND: If there are any objections to my politics ...

JOWETT: *(fast)* There aren't. It's your social ... image ... there are objections to.

BRAND: I'm the same man that won last April...

JOWETT: Shite! Same man. You're being sued for *divorce*, man, you're living with a young girl in Wordsworth Avenue, you're going around procuring abortions for constituents ...

BRAND: *(tight)* What?

JOWETT: Don't *what* me, comrade. I've spent the last week keeping it out of the Recorder. I've had the Society for the Protection of the Unborn Child round, I've had three parish priests, I've had that birk at Radio Manchester on the phone every day, so don't come the what with me, right? As far as I'm concerned, it hasn't happened.

BRAND: *(slowly)* Even if it did?

JOWETT: *(hard)* Especially if it did. There were 23,000 catholics in Leighley at the last count, and most of 'em vote Labour. *Especially* if it did.

BRAND: There was nothing illegal ...

JOWETT: I'm glad to hear it. Do you get my drift?

They stare at each other, a solid, hard, unloving contact. Brand finally re-opens his diary, picks up the biro, clicks it ready.

BRAND: Yeah, I get the drift, Alf.

JOWETT: August the 5th. Evening.

BRAND: That's Trades Council.

JOWETT: Scrap it. Shaw's throwing a fundraising cheese and wine do in South Ward. Be there. OK?

Brand's pen hovers over the Trades Council entry. Scratches it out.

PART TWO

Montage sequence.

Leighley swimming centre, a year old, a huge glass and concrete complex. The pool, arranged for a beauty contest. The audience basks in refracted afternoon sun, awaiting the main event. The girls, fifteen of them, in swimsuits, wait at the bottom end of the pool. The MC takes the microphone. Behind him, at a long table, sit the panel of judges.

M.C.: Ladies and gentlemen, Leighley Sporting Club in conjunction with Mecca proudly presents the election of Miss Leighley 1976 ... *(some ironic cheering from the youths present)* ... to represent the town in the forthcoming National Contest in London in the autumn. Before I call in those very important and very delectable young ladies down there, it gives me great pleasure to introduce to you Mr William Brand, MP, the chairman of the panel you see before you ... Mr William Brand.

Some rippled applause. Brand stands, takes the mic.

BRAND: Ladies and gentlemen, I'm ... er ... I'm delighted to be here today to help
    ... officiate at this ... function. *(pause)* Let me ... introduce to you now my
    fellow judges. On my left, Miss Angela Belway ...

Cut to

Brand, hair whipped by wind.

BRAND: *(shouting into mic to be heard)* ... I now take pleasure in declaring the St
    Aloysius Women's Sodality Fete open ... Enjoy yourselves, won't you.

*A light squall of rain splatters his face. The lightest tremble of applause, as
people scatter to get out of the rain.*

Cut to

*Brand, in track suit, hounded by Cubs, on a charity walk. A cruising car carries a
banner (232nd cub troop (Leighley) 5th annual charity walk.) Open out to show
deserted countryside, through which their B-road gently dawdles.*

Bernard and Angie Shaw's modern Georgian detached house. *In close shot, a
hand dunks a cob of French bread into a pan of hot cheese; another fills four
glasses with Spanish red. Noise, chat, banter, greetings.*

*The Shaws' house is two years old, on the grandest estate in their area, where
their membership of the Labour Party (Shaw is on the Executive Committee)
probably earns him the nickname red or bolshie. He is, as a matter of fact, at the
professional-meritocratic centre of the party, an ultra-empiricist with a distaste
for both history and ideology. Tonight he is in one of his social elements,
democratically mixing, without a trace of condescension, with people mainly his
inferiors in terms of brain, earning power and occupational status. His wife is
cooler, more detached, easier, quietly blatant in her long blue dress.*

*A long table, half the length of the rustic wall, is laden party nothings and cheap
plonk. The mood is restrained, the big house muzzling many of the paying guests
a little, trapping them inside their best suits and half-sleeve sensible dresses. A
spattering of professionals – doctors, teachers, social workers – gives it an
occasional though by no means decisive lift in confidence.*

*Early Bob Dylan on the good hi-fi. Paintings by respected local painters – Derek
Wilkinson, Peter Shore – on the walls; landscapes, sombre, remote, uninvolving,
well made,*

*Brand stands against the wall, a glass of wine in his hand, taking people's
greetings, smiling. Shaw pours wine.*

SHAW: Any more while I'm at it? Celia, what about you, we can squeeze a drop in
    there, surely. *(he squeezes the drop, emptying the bottle)* Ah, Spain, thou art
    dead. I'll away and get the rest in.

He threads his way towards the door, encountering Brand on the way.

SHAW: Now then, Bill. How's the glass, all right?

BRAND: *(showing him)* Fine, Bernard

SHAW: Glad you could come.

BRAND: *(evenly)* Wouldn't have missed it for worlds.

SHAW: Well, you've got the summer ahead of you, eh. Nice one.

BRAND: Oh yes.

The doorbell chimes, once, twice, three times.

SHAW: *(surveying room)* Seventy quid this little lot's made. One of these every week and the Party'd be in clover. *(intercepting his wife, who's on her way to the door)* All right, loved one, I'll see to it. *(holds up bottle, smiling, leaves)*

Angie Shaw stares at Brand, measuring him against some interior image. Brand sips from his glass, returns the look levelly.

ANGIE: You've got taller.

BRAND: It's just the way I hold myself. *(she smiles. He shows her his lifts)* Changed my life.

ANGIE: Can you ... dance in them?

BRAND: I can manage a passable Fronkensteen Shuffle. *(he shows her minimally. She laughs)*

ANGIE: Great movie.

BRAND: Terrific.

Pause. She fixes him again. Holds her arms out, an odd, ambiguous movement.

ANGIE: Well?

A burst of noise in the doorway draws his eyes. Several newcomers vigorously cluster in, many beers to the good. They are substantially the group Brand met in the Nelson in episode 1: Pru, Martin and others from the revolutionary left in Leighley, with three or four more massing behind them.

PRU: *(small boy's voice, a deliberate quote)* 'Excuse me, is this where they're going to have the revolution?' *(sees Brand)* Eh up, it's the Man of the People himself, how goes it comrade?

BRAND: Grand. Makes all the difference, knowing you're among us, Pru.

PRU: And I'm very far from alone, William ... As you will no doubt ... *(searching for the drinks. Spotting them)* ... see for yourself.

They filter after him, throwing their greetings at Brand, who smiles patiently. Sees Alex at the tail. Turns away. Back again. She dwells a moment, uncertain, smiles vaguely, follows others to the groaning board.

ANGIE: *(missing nothing)* Later, perhaps.

He nods, smiles. She moves away, round the inside angle of the L-shaped room. Brand stares at Alex's back, as she pours herself wine. Pru and the others squat in a corner, in a half circle, begin rolling some grass. Brand looks around the room once. Crosses to stand behind Alex at the table.

BRAND: I think I'm off.

ALEX: *(not turning)* What a cock-up. They suddenly took it into their heads to come here ... *(some laughter from Pru's corner)* ... I'd completely forgotten ...

He places his glass on the table, depressed, frustrated.

BRAND: Anyway ...

ALEX: *(selecting a cold savoury)* I'll have to stay on a bit ...

BRAND: *(glancing at the corner, spreading its joint)* Yeah.

He wanders away. She turns, watches him, as he moves into the hallway.

Hallway. Shaw in from kitchen, carrying four large bottle of plonk.

SHAW: *(meanings below the meaning)* Not off already, are we?

BRAND: 'Fraid so. Hard day tomorrow. Is Angie about?

SHAW: Kitchen. OK?

He moves back into the room. Brand takes the passage and door into the spacious, handsomely equipped kitchen. Angie stands by the stainless steel double sink, staring out into the dark of the garden, or simply at her own reflected image. She smokes a long cigarette, cradles a glass in her hand; is very still, private.

BRAND: *(finally)* I'm away. *(she turns, sees him)* Thanks for the ... *(he leaves it)*

ANGIE: Coffee's on. *(she points to the percolator)* Two minutes.

BRAND: I should go.

ANGIE: How's Miriam?

BRAND: *(slowly)* She's all right.

ANGIE: She's divorcing you, isn't she?

BRAND: Is she?

Angie smiles, begins to pour coffee. Brand dwells, uneasy, uncertain.

ANGIE: Sugar?

BRAND: One.

ANGIE: Bernard told me about it weeks ago. *(pause)* You take things so gravely.

BRAND: It's in hand. I'm enrolled for a course in Flippancy four days a week ... at Westminster.

She smiles again, over her coffee.

ANGIE: Oh. Already.

BRAND: No, not really.

ANGIE: You didn't imagine it would be easy, did you?

BRAND: No. I just thought it would be possible.

Shaw in, with more dead bottles.

SHAW: Shan't disturb you ... just establishing a little order. *(to Angie)* That I.S. crowd are pushing grass around ... you might keep an eye on them ... they're in the far corner ... *(he's finished stacking the bottles in a cardboard box)* Back to the fray. *(to Brand)* Oh, there's a fellow from the Recorder here, says he'd like a word with you before you go ... OK? *(to Angie)* On you go then with your ... conversazione ...

He leaves. Brand drains his cup.

ANGIE: At least half of him would really like you to screw me, you know. *(Brand says nothing, screening the discomfiture)* Save him having you himself. *(long pause)* And what is truly pathetic is, if he heard me say that, he wouldn't know what I was talking about ... *(pause)* Do *you*?

BRAND: *(carefully)* Yes, I think so. *(hand on door)* I just can't quite figure out ... how *I* got in there ...

He spreads his hand as goodnight. She begins to laugh, suggesting, though not winningly, amusement.

Brand pushes through the people standing in the hall towards the front door, saying goodnight to those he knows who notice him. A man watches from the living room doorway, approaches him as he passes. He's Brand's age, rather modishly dressed, faintly louche.

MALONE: Mr Brand? *(Brand stops, sees him)* Peter Malone, Recorder.

BRAND: How do you do.

MALONE: Sorry to bother you in the middle of a party ...

BRAND: No bother. What's the problem?

MALONE: Can we er ...

He indicates a quieter spot by the stairs. The living room door opens. Brand catches a glimpse of Alex dancing with Pru, her hands on his leather jacket.

BRAND: *(following Malone with reluctance)* Actually I have to be somewhere else rather soon ... *(checking watch)*

MALONE: Won't take a minute, promise. I just wondered if we could fix a time some time in the week when we could do an interview. I'll tell you what it is, I've been given free run of the features pages and I want to put some life in them. And what better way of starting than with a feature on you ...

BRAND: *(slowly)* What sort of ... feature ... did you have in mind?

MALONE: Up to you. It would be good to have a piece on the problems of your constituents and how you deal with them – you know, housing, marriage, abortion ... whatever turns you on ... I'm a great admirer ...

BRAND: *(checking watch)* Look, I've got ... two minutes, Mr Malone. Why don't you just say what it is you really want?

MALONE: I'm sorry, I'm not quite with you ...

BRAND: Quite. But you do have my meaning.

MALONE: *(stiffer now)* Look, I've told you quite clearly what I'd like to do. If you're not interested in being interviewed, we won't press you, we'll lose a good article, you'll lose the publicity. Besides, there's more than one way to skin a cat.

BRAND: Try telling a cat that. Look, in four months your ... greasy rag you call a paper hasn't had a single good word to say about me. Not a syllable. You've smeared and sneered at everything I've said and done. It was *your* office that sold the picture of me at Bryant's to Fleet Street ... don't deny it, I have the proof, right? At the same time you've printed *nothing* that might indicate, however vaguely, that I was doing anything at all that might serve the interests of the people of Leighley. So what's all this about, eh? Suddenly you want to do an in-depth, sympathetic profile? Pull the other one, Malone, it plays a passable version of Who do you think you're kidding Mr Hitler in 6/8 time. *(he's on his way, turns back, a slim fury pushing him)* I'll tell you something. You go for me, you start scratching, you'd better make it stick, because if you don't you and your miserable employers are about to discover ways of skinning a cat you've never even dreamt of.

He's gone. The door clouts to behind him.

Alex's flat. *Early morning light through curtains. Brand lies awake in the double bed. Sounds of door as Alex enters the house. He reaches down to the phone on the floor beside the bed and replaces the receiver. She enters the room, dressed as for the party (jeans, boots, etc). She's pale from a sleepless night, but tension keeps her lively.*

ALEX: Hi.

BRAND: *(cool)* Hi.

ALEX: I tried to call but I couldn't get through.

BRAND: *(out of bed now, crossing to bathroom to wash his face and clean his teeth)* Ahunh.

ALEX: We went on to the Y.S. thing at the Adelphi. *(pause, watching him)* OK?

BRAND: Sure.

ALEX: *(angering)* Look, if it's my being at Shaw's party last night, I've said I'm sorry once already, and that was probably once too often. *(he spits into the basin, wipes his mouth with a facecloth) I* have an existence too. I have a right to exist ... And I'm not prepared to go on being only where you're *not,* when you're up here.

BRAND: *(cool, walking past her into the room)* Fine.

ALEX: Oh, for God's sake, don't go into that Man of Stone routine! *Talk.*

BRAND: *(putting shirt on, turning slowly, growing decisive)* OK. I think I'm going to have to find a new place. Here, I mean. I need a separate, I need an *independent* base ... I don't think I can do the job well enough from here. And I think it'd be better for both of us.

ALEX: *(even, unflurried)* Fine. Shall I help you to look? There's always something going down at the Advice Centre.

BRAND: No thanks, I'll manage.

ALEX: OK.

She crosses to the kitchen area, fills kettle, sets it to boil. Brand begins dressing. They remain fairly separate, during the ensuing exchange.

ALEX: *(over shoulder)* What about Ruskin? Shall I come or what?

BRAND: Well, it looks as if I'm going to be allowed to take the kids, and I owe them time ... so ...

ALEX: Yeah. *(tea into pot, busy)* I might spend a few days with my mother ... Did Joe Fitton get in touch?

BRAND: No. What about?

ALEX: I told you, he's doing a pamphlet on medical attitudes to abortion in the area ... he's keen to put something in about Marples and the Mrs Pilling case. I said he should call you.

BRAND: *(careful, slow)* Well, he didn't.

ALEX: Maybe he rang when the phone was off the hook. *(pause)* You could give him a ring at the Advice Centre. He's anxious to see you before you go off to Oxford ...

BRAND: I'm doing something at Radio Manchester today. ... In any case, I don't know how I can help him.

ALEX: *(facing him at last)* How do you mean?

BRAND: I've been advised to keep a low profile on the abortion issue.

ALEX: What does that mean?

BRAND: It means not airing my views ... and practice ... in right wing weeklies or left wing occasional pamphlets.

ALEX: Advised ... by whom?

BRAND: By the party ... here.

ALEX: Why? I thought they were with you?

BRAND: *(unselfpitying, spare)* There's an autumn election scare brewing. The Leighley Party want a Labour member. Principles have therefore to be suspended for the duration. I'm promised full use of them again when the matter's been resolved one way or the other. In the meantime, I behave.

Alex nods, turns back to the stove.

ALEX: Do you want toast?

BRAND: No thanks.

Pause. She takes bread from a bin, places a slice under the grill.

ALEX: Is that why you're moving house?

Brand fastens his tie in front of the mirror; fixes her reflection; waits for her to follow the question with her face, his hands poised about the tie-ends. She turns at last. He looks at her, hard-eyed, minatory.

Local radio station studio. *Brand and the woman interviewer sit opposite each other, headphones, listening to a Lennon piece, almost over. The interviewer's cue-light reddens as the track fades.*

INTERVIEWER: A Working Class Hero, John Lennon, the second choice of our studio guest this beautiful Monday morning, Mr Bill Brand, the Labour MP for Leighley. And remember, if you want to talk to our guest or ask him questions, the number to ring is 061 – if you're outside Manchester – 137 4433.

Cut to Alf Jowett in his office, tuning in his small portable radio.

INTERVIEWER: *(radio)* ... and let's hope you get your mortgage in time for the baby. Thank you for calling.

Back to radio studio.

INTERVIEWER: *(handing slip of paper across the desk to Brand)* This is Monday Choice, and our next caller is ... Mrs McDermott, I think ...?

WOMAN'S VOICE: *(phone)* Mrs McDermott, that's right.

INTERVIEWER: Do you think you could turn your radio down, Mrs McDermott, we can hear it in the background there. Lovely, thank you. You have a question, I think.

Cut to close up of a hand adjusting a tape recorder and microphone, pressing the 'record' button. We see the young woman who is speaking on the phone.

WOMAN: Yes, I'd like to ask Mr Brand his views on the abortion question. As a member of the Society for the Protection of the Unborn Child, I feel that last

year's Bill amending the law on abortion didn't go far enough, and I'd like to
see the law strengthened so as to eliminate the thousands of unnecessary
abortions we still see permitted every year in this country. Could I ask Mr
Brand whether he agrees with me that the abortion laws are still far too
permissive ...?

*Cut to radio studio. Brand's pen puts a question mark against the 'food prices'
written on the slip of paper, pushes it back to the interviewer, whose face
frowningly questions the producer in the box.*

BRAND: *(to mic; slowly, but working like mercury in his head)* Thank you, Mrs ...
McDermott. The whole abortion issue is, of course, a highly ... complex one
...

*Cut to Jowett's office. Jowett stares stonily at his transistor, as the Brand position
unfolds. Drops his head onto his propping hand, finger and thumb on closed eyes,
finding it all a little hard to believe.*

BRAND: *(via Jowett's radio)* ... I know, of course, that there are many women
who, for religious or other reasons, cannot accept the idea of abortion in any
shape or form. What I say to them is: they have the right to reject the
termination of pregnancy in their own case, but by what right do they seek to
harrass those many more women who have different principles ...

*Cut to Recorder office. Close shot of secretary, phone in hand. Camera moves
down and round, through her following question, to pick it up, in Malone's
writing, on the desk before her.*

SECRETARY: ... Are you saying, Mr Brand, that it is a woman's right to kill her
unborn children? Is that what you're saying ...? Would *you* help a perfectly
healthy woman –

BRAND: *(on their radio; low; a calculated interruption)* ... I'm not sure I accept
your somewhat emotive terminology, Mrs McDermott ... In what sense can we
talk of *children* being unborn ...?

INTERVIEWER: *(interrupting)* ... I must butt in here, because we're coming up to
news time very soon ... If you could hold on, Mrs McDermott, I'm sure we
can find time after the break to deal with the points you've raised ... You're
listening to Radio Manchester, ten thirty and news time.

Cut to Malone's office. The secretary holds the phone up.

SECRETARY: I've been cut off ...

MALONE: *(fast, urgent)* Ring again.

Radio studio. Brand, cans off, standing, tense.

INTERVIEWER: *(via mic, to producer)* What's happening, Mike? *(listens)* OK.
Clever, eh? *(turns to Brand. Not labouring her meaning, but clear nevertheless)*
We've lost her. Sorry about that. Bit fishy eh: food prices to foetuses ...

Brand turns away, hiding his self-anger, lights a cheroot.

INTERVIEWER: I'm right in thinking you don't … want to go on with that?

BRAND: *(finally)* Whatever you say. *(pause)* I fancy a bit of music myself.

PART THREE

Brand driving through the centre of Oxford, the children in the back. The colleges, the spires; bells.

BRAND: Oxford. What do you think?

JANE: Great.

MICHAEL: I like all the scaffolding on the churches.

College room. The kids pillow-fight on their bed in the ante-room adjoining Brand's room. Bags on floor etc.

BRAND: Hey, hey. Cool it. *(they stop)*

He moves into his own room, where Maidstone, the course organiser, waits by the door to the landing.

MAIDSTONE: I'll show you the crèche later. It's quite professional.

BRAND: Terrific. Thanks.

MAIDSTONE: *(looking in file, handing Brand some duplicated papers)* So here's the revised schedule … There's a third seminar now, on Women in Literature, Bonny will be taking that, but you might like to be involved …

BRAND: Fine.

MAIDSTONE: Good. You'll see we've had to change the title yet again … it's now called Women and Politics … *(self-critical yet easy)* … How bland can you get …! We've thirty two enrolled, slightly more women than men but no more than is usual at these things … Oh, and you'll see that we've given over the last day to reporting back and general free-for-all. You can stay for that, can you? *(Brand nods)* Oh good, good. Yes, well, I think that's everything. Do you know Oxford at all?

BRAND: No, not really.

MAIDSTONE: *(smiling)* It's really lovely at this time of year … with the students gone … *(leaving)* Bonny Clark and Chris Waite arrive this evening, John Venables later in the week, Friday probably … Do you know the Home Secretary?

BRAND: No. Know *of* him.

MAIDSTONE: Used to be a Fellow of All Souls. *(offering a layered meaning)* I thought you might have … encountered him …

BRAND: *(taking it)* No. I don't read Encounter. Never got the habit.

They smile drily.

MAIDSTONE: Well. You'll hear the gong for dinner. Enjoy yourself.

He shuts the door behind him. Brand becomes aware of the silence from the children's room. Goes into it quietly. They sit on the bed, playing chess, engrossed. Brand watches them. Michael tries shifting a knight. They continue a discussion as they play.

JANE: Not *that* way, silly. See ... *(she shows him)* ... *three* squares ... *(Michael breathes out once, through clenched teeth, his eyes narrowed)* Anyway ... women *can* drive trains. They do it in China, I've seen them.

MICHAEL: *(finally)* There's one thing women can't do that men can do.

JANE: *(straightening her back row)* What?

MICHAEL: I'm not telling you.

A brilliant summer day. Brand plays cricket with the children on the grass outside the college. Jane catches the ball and runs away with it. Brand chases her.

BRAND: Jane ... give me the ball ... give me the ball ...

He catches her, swings her round. The children scream and laugh.

Through an upstairs window we see Jane and Michael in a gaggle of six or eight other children and a couple of minders, a man and a woman. Fun is had. Pull back into the room. Brand is opening the window, talking over his shoulder. Turns back into the room, perches on the edge of a desk in front of the small circle of mature students, four women, three men.

BRAND: *(developing the idea)* ... What I'm carefully *not* saying, you'll have noticed, is that the political left is, in terms of actual *practice*, markedly different from the political right, in this respect. Free women – women who exist in their own right, as persons, persons before women – are pretty hard to find any place, in political parties as elsewhere. Of course, the left can lay claim to a *different* tradition, philosophically speaking, from the right. In very crude terms, it's the difference between *comrades* and *ladies*, if you like. But, beneath the ideologies, remarkable correspondences cluster ... *(he reaches down for his books, takes a pamphlet from the pile. On his way up, he sees a plump brown girl next to him recross her bare legs)* ... I looked this out before I came down here, some of you may know it ... it's Clara Zetkin's 'Reminiscences of Lenin' ... Here's Lenin on sexuality: '... You must be aware of the famous theory that in communist society the satisfaction of sexual desires, of love, will be as simple and unimportant as drinking a glass of water ... I think this glass of water theory is completely un-Marxist ... Of course, thirst must be satisfied. But will the normal man in normal circumstances lie down in the gutter and drink out of a puddle, or out of a glass with a rim greasy from many lips?' *(he pauses, scans the group, face by face)* Now, we can pick up the main strands of the *argument* in that passage this afternoon, but for now I'd like you to consider that final sentence ... Because you see, when it comes down to it, for Lenin as for any other ... patriarch, communist or capitalist, things ultimately turn on what is good for the normal *man* ... Mmm?

PLUMP GIRL (PAT): *(pad in hand)* What's that pamphlet again?

Brand hands it to her. Others copy the title. A bell sounds. Maidstone in.

MAIDSTONE: Phone, Bill.

BRAND: Can it wait?

MAIDSTONE: Says not. From your constituency.

Brand stands apologetically.

BRAND: *(to group generally)* I'll see you at lunch. Help yourselves to the books.

Cowled phone in nondescript corridor. Brand places receiver to ear.

BRAND: Bill Brand. Hello, Alf. *(listens for some moments)* The Sunday what? ... I
  wouldn't know, I don't read it. ... No, no-one's been in touch ... *(listens again)*
  Oh Christ. So how did they ... never mind, it doesn't matter, probably that weevil
  from the Recorder put them onto it, like last time ... What? *(brief pause)* Look, I
  can't give you details over the phone ... *(Jowett goes daft on the other end. Brand
  listens stonily, interrupts him finally)* Alf ... Alf ... All right, Alf. The
  gynaecologist said no, I asked around, the ring held, I fixed her up at a private
  clinic. *(brief pause)* Never *mind* where the money came from, the bill was paid, an
  unwanted pregnancy was terminated, no law was broken ... Alf, I don't care what
  it looks like to the vermin who make the news, that's what happened ... Well, too
  bad. *(listening, then terse)* So fire me. *(listens again)* All right, I'll see you when I
  get back ... Oh, by the way, I think I've got a house ... Ahunh ... We try to
  please, Alf ... Right. *(replaces phone. Stares at his whitening face in the mirror)*

*He returns to the seminar room. The plump girl is still there, reading the
pamphlet, the sun glinting on her strong bare thighs.*

BRAND: Hi.

PAT: Hi.

College Common Room. *Brand, Bonny Clark, Christine Waite and several
students sit in relaxed groups drinking wine and talking. Outside, the children
play with a frisby on the lawn. A large chauffered car skirts the lawn, stops at the
front entrance. Venables steps out, is met by Maidstone, who shakes him
attentively by the hand.*

BONNY: *(35, thickset, shortsighted academic from Oxford, in long dress and
  sandals)* That's whatsisname.

CHRISTINE: *(drinking)* Yeah.

BONNY: *(to Brand)* Friend of yours?

BRAND: We vote in the same lobby ... usually.

CHRISTINE: *(late 30s, feminist, novelist)* Labour Leaders. Historian, wasn't he?

BONNY: Of sorts. All Souls sorts.

BRAND: Would it be too much to ask if he was ever Liquorice All Souls Sorts?

They both turn to look at him.

BRAND: Sorry. I couldn't resist it.

Bonny begins to laugh. Christine follows suit, the inexplicable laughter rising in waves. It has barely subsided when Maidstone arrives with Venables.

MAIDSTONE: *(on the walk)* Did you have a good journey?

VENABLES: Yes, yes, it was fine, thank you.

MAIDSTONE: Good, good. I must say it's marvellous of you to spare us the time ... Well, come along and meet everyone ... This is Bonny Clark ... teaches literature here ... Chris Waite, who writes novels ... And er ... Bill Brand ... John Venables, who I'm sure you all recognise ...

VENABLES: How do you do? *(he shakes each hand in turn, charming, deferential with the women, pleasant and open with Brand. To Brand)* We've never met, have we ... How are you?

BRAND: *(taking his hand)* Fine, thanks.

VENABLES: Good. Isn't this wonderful? I only wish I could have spent the week with you ... *(staring at distant college spires)* I taught here once, you know, Oxford. All Souls. *(the two women turn away, fighting their laughter. Brand watches Venables in profile, studies the keen face, the sticky jaw)* I sometimes wonder why I ever left.

Seminar room. *The thirty students are gathered for the final plenary session, sitting in ragged rows around the 'platform' of Clark, Venables, Chairman Maidstone, Waite and Brand.*

VENABLES: *(serious face above serious steepled fingers)* ... I do think the lady there has touched on something very central and very important ... Namely, in a democracy such as ours, is it not fitting that all voices, all opinions, should be heard ... I'll answer this way ... and hope you won't find it too casuistically 'political'. You say important voices are missing from our – colloquium – Tories, Liberals, Nationalists and so on. Well, yes and no. Yes, for the obvious reasons you've indicated. No ... and this is where I might become shall we say controversial ... no, because at this particular moment in our political life, it's perfectly possible to argue that the present Labour Party, both in the House and in the country, includes and subsumes every kind of opinion and value *within* that spectrum you've just described. Because the Labour Party is, and in a sense always has been, a consortium, an alliance of necessary and fruitful contradictions expressive of the *whole* of a society, not just of a segment or a class. And as I say, this has always been so, ever since the Party formed, out of its diverse beginnings, at the turn of the last century. But what makes it *crucially* representative today, as I read it, is that those historic differences, between hand and brain, between wealth and labour, between position and equality, are sensed and expressed, inside our Party, *at a higher intensity* than anywhere else, certainly within any of the other historical political parties. Labour has, if you follow me, taken the main ground. The real debate, as I now see it, *can* only take place there. And so long as we comport ourselves as responsible, mature, balanced people, we will continue to hold that main, vital ground that is the road to the future.

He smiles apologetically at the lady, suggesting he had not meant to speak at such length. Brand has his hand up, for Maidstone's attention. Maidstone nods.

BRAND: The one 'historic difference' John Venables fails to mention is, of course, that between men and women. And in my own seminars ... as in the others' too ... we've seen that the domination of the one by the other has been as characteristic of the parties of the left, including my own party, as of parties of the right.

VENABLES: Oh, come now, Brand, you can't mean that. What about our Equality for Women Act?

BRAND: *(calm, factual)* Mistitled, in my view. We'd've been better calling it what it plainly is: a Less Inequality for Women Act. I don't argue it's unimportant, far from it. But historically it was the Party responding to forces outside itself, to a largely autonomous movement of women who are no longer prepared to lie back and think of England. *(pause)* On the 'political spectrum' issue ... it seems to me that the Minister ... *(correcting himself)* ... John Venables has a point. If anybody doubts the width and scope of action and belief in that Party, I have here *(thumbing a paperback open at a marker)* ... I have here a few lines from a book called 'The Future of Socialism', which some of you may have read. *(quoting)* 'I am sure that a definite limit exists to the degree of equality which is desirable. We do not want equality of incomes, since extra responsibility and exceptional talent require and deserve a differential reward ... I do not myself want to see *all* private education disappear: nor the Queen riding a bicycle ... nor the manufacture of Rolls Royces banned; nor the Brigade of Guards, nor Oxford and Cambridge, nor Boodles nor the Royal Yacht Squadron ... nor anything so dull and colourless as this.' *(he closes the book quietly in the silence)* Not Ian Macleod, not Keith Joseph, not Edward Boyle. Tony Crosland. The Future of Socialism ...

Evening. Bryant's Mill perimeter: large 'For Sale/To Let' sign on wall. Brand's car drawing to a halt. His view of the padlocked gates and deserted yard. Brand just sits, staring at the place. Michael stirs in the back seat.

MICHAEL: Daddy ...

BRAND: Soon be home, son.

He starts the car, draws away.

A terraced working class house in Leighley, small, old but sturdy. A 'Sold' sign in the ground floor window. Sounds of life all around – babies, children, dogs, radios.

Brand raises an upstairs window, looks out, is joined by Jowett. Jowett waves his hand in general disgust and incomprehension. Brand shakes his head, drives home his point. They disappear from view.

The front door opens. Jowett is out first, staring up and down the street, then back at the house. Brand closes the door, locks it, pockets the key.

JOWETT: You're out of your bloody mind, do you know that?

BRAND: *(calm)* Alf ... You said I should get a house of my own. I got one.

Jowett takes in the street again, up, down.

JOWETT: I give up. *(looking at Brand, the faintest gleam in his granite-chip eyes)* You're just not bloody corrigible, are you. Come on, let's get this Sunday People thing sorted ...

He pecks his sinewy way off up the street, Brand behind him, dodging kids and dogs on the way.

- *end* -

Episode 6

Resolution

was broadcast on Monday 12th July 1976

The cast was as follows:

Bill Brand   Jack Shepherd

Television Director   Robert East

Winnie Scoular   Rosemary Martin

Wilkinson   Gary Roberts

Alf Jowett   Allan Surtees

Morgan   Gerald James

Garner   Clifford Cox

Lane   James Walker

Parfitt   Fred Feast

Robert   James Maxwell

Jim   Don McKillop

David Last   Alan Badel

Renshaw   Peter Davidson

Moores   Ray Smith

Wiltshire   George Waring

Frear   Geoffrey Palmer

Watson   Arthur Lowe

Designers: David Ferris, Harry Clark

Executive Producer: Stella Richman

Producer: Stuart Burge

Director: Stuart Burge

PART ONE

Outside Broadcast van. A bank of four tv monitors, showing aspects of the empty Conference Hall in Blackpool. As the camera pans slowly across the monitors and then back again the director talks a casual way through the rehearsal.

DIRECTOR'S VOICE: ... Loosen a bit, George. Yes, try and lose the column. Fine. No, that's OK Geoff. Plenty. Can you get tighter, Mick? Fine, I'll buy that. All right, super five and ... cue music ... *(over the long shot of the hall a caption: 76ᵗʰ Annual Conference of the Labour Party) ...* Where's the bloody music then ...? ... *(music up, part of a general introductory glob that might usher It's a Knock-Out, Test Match Special, Golf Highlights or outdoor politics onto our screens) ...* OK. Lose caption ... lose music ... Mmm. Right. All we need now is a few bodies and we're away ... Thanks chaps.

Brand's hotel room. Portable radio, spouting, on bed table. Gradually the hotel attic room is established: clean, sparse, orderly. On the bed, six Saturday newspapers, headlining the Blackpool Conference, and linking it up with a possible snap autumn election. A bag, half-emptied, on a case rack; shoes; a suit hung on the wardrobe door.

SCOULAR'S VOICE: *(radio)* ... You seem to have got it into your head that the Labour Party Annual Conference has been especially convened to hear whether the Prime Minister is or is not about to call a general election ...

INTERVIEWER: ... But surely, Mrs Scoular, as a member of the National Executive, you're aware of the intense speculation that surrounds –

SCOULAR: ... As a member of the NEC I'm here in Blackpool, along with several thousand grassroots delegates, to hammer out party policy for the coming year ...

INTERVIEWER: I'm sorry, Mrs Scoular, I have to stop you there. We take a break now. Join us in two minutes for more of The North West at the Weekend.

A station advertising ident. The first ad starts, as we pan slowly back to the radio.

RUGGED MAN'S VOICE: *(radio. Sounds of speedboat in background)* Crisis? What crisis? Take a tip, get a boat, get away from it all. *(phone in room rings. Brand answers it)* Rule the waves with Waverley's, the boat for all seasons and all pockets –

Brand turns off radio. He stands by the bed, naked save for a bath towel tucked at the waist, his hair still dripping from the shower.

BRAND: *(phone)* Brand. Hello, Alf. Yeah. Come on up. 27. *(checking watch)* Half an hour yet ... Ahunh.

Puts phone down, begins to towel his hair, slip into shirt, y-fronts, trousers, socks. Rejects a tie finally, stares at his reflection in the wardrobe mirror. Begins to comb his damp hair.

Knock at door.

BRAND: S'open.

Wilkinson in. He wears light cotton jeans, thin windjammer.

BRAND: *(surprised)* Hello.

WILKINSON: Hello. I met your agent in the foyer place. We're here too.

BRAND: Come in. *(he clears files from a chair)* What're you up to? Fancy a beer? *(he indicates a six-can box of Guinness on the dressing table)*

WILKINSON: *(half declining)* I've gotta see some of the lads at four ... Go on then.

Brand splits a couple of cans, smiling, hands him one. Wilkinson takes the proffered chair.

WILKINSON: We've got this demo, Tuesday ... the Textile Workers Action Committee, I mean.

BRAND: Yeah, I heard. Timed for Watson's arrival, right?

WILKINSON: Right. We thought you might join us.

Brand crosses to his diary, delaying an answer until he has the page.

BRAND: What time Tuesday?

WILKINSON: Eleven. Outside the main entrance.

BRAND: All right. I'm the CLP delegate but I should be able to manage it. *(he puts diary away, slips jacket on)*

WILKINSON: I saw the Leighley resolution in the final agenda. Your idea?

BRAND: Not really. Came up through the party. I approve it though.

WILKINSON: Will it be called, do you know?

BRAND: *Some*thing'll be called. I'm due at a compositing meeting in half an hour. *(pause)* Along with your union delegate.

WILKINSON: Yeah. That's what I wanted to talk to you about ... There's no future for textiles under private capital. None whatever. The union, not surprisingly, believes differently. Which is why they stick to quota reduction. We favour *your* resolution.

Knock at door.

BRAND: Come in.

Alf Jowett in. Sees Wilkinson, who has stood to place his can on the table. Stands in doorway, his face questioning Brand.

BRAND: Come in, Alf.

WILKINSON: Right, I'll be off. Good luck with it.

BRAND: Fine. Let me know if there's anything in the pipeline.

WILKINSON: Sure. Look, we've had delegations out at the major docks recently, seeing if there's anything can be done about dumping. There's a lot happening in the docks just now ... A national dock strike of any length of time could go some way to settling the import quota issue at a stroke. No dockers, no imports.

JOWETT: It's been in the air all summer. Maybe it's why Watson's playing with a snap election, to head it off.

WILKINSON: *(grim)* Ironic, eh? See you Tuesday.

He nods to both men, leaves. Brand offers Jowett a can of Guinness. Jowett shakes his head, closes the door.

JOWETT: What's Tuesday?

BRAND: They've called a demonstration. They'll be lobbying the PM when he arrives at Conference.

JOWETT: They'd better get there early, there's likely to be a queue ... *(pause)* You joining them?

BRAND: *(factual)* Of course.

Jowett sniffs. Brand searches for shoes, sits on bed to put them on. Jowett crosses to the window.

JOWETT: No trouble with the credentials?

BRAND: No. They'd had your letter about Frank being ill ...

JOWETT: And you're clear about the resolution?

BRAND: *(patient)* Perfectly.

JOWETT: There'll be pressure. Especially with the union in there ... For God's sake don't go alienating the other delegates ...

BRAND: Right, Alf. It's a promise. *(he looks at Jowett, who stares moodily, rather down, out of the window)* Anything up, Alf?

JOWETT: *(turns, stares at him, frowning. Finally)* Up? No. *(he takes a can of Guinness from the table, pierces it, takes a deep accurate swig)* I never liked Blackpool. *(he turns back to the window)* Toytown.

Brand watches him carefully.

BRAND: What time are the agents meeting then?

JOWETT: Five. It's been put back.

BRAND: *(standing)* Let us know how it goes, will you.

JOWETT: They'll tell us nowt, don't worry. It's got too delicate. The fact is, Watson doesn't know what the *hell* to do.

BRAND: *(sardonic)* He'll think of something.

JOWETT: Oh yes. He'll do that.

BRAND: A bigger majority would 'free his hands' ... 'prisoner of the left' and that.

JOWETT: Mmm. Or he could simply ... retire, make way for someone else to start with a clean slate.

BRAND: A Government of National Unity, you mean?

JOWETT: Our leader is, without doubt, the Littlest Englander of them all ...

(the phone rings. Brand answers it)

BRAND: Brand. Sure. *(off phone, to Jowett)* Last. *(to phone)* David, how are you. Fine. *(listens)* Tuesday, yes, sounds good. Where? ... Imperial, ahunh. About eight? ... OK, thank you. *(listens for some time)* I see. Well, if you think so ... No, no, I'm game ... Ahunh. Ahunh. I'll leave it to you. Probably see you tomorrow anyway. Thanks again. Bye.

He puts receiver down, wrinkles nose reflectively. Jowett picks up Brand's conference file.

JOWETT: Don't forget this.

BRAND: *(taking it)* Thanks. *(casual, ironic, looking round room)* I'm invited to Last's hotel for a private supper Tuesday evening.

JOWETT: That's nice.

BRAND: Along with one or two Cabinet Ministers, the General Secretary of the Party, the General Secretary of the National Union of Transport Workers ... and the Right Honourable Arthur Watson, Prime Minister of this parish and wizard of the realm.

(Jowett opens the door)

JOWETT: I hope the *food's* good.

BRAND: Do you think I'm being groomed for office?

JOWETT: Groomed or gelded. I'll talk to you later ...

He leaves. Brand smiles at his chippy sourness. Checks the file for his credentials. Close shot of his card.

Compositing room. *Close shot of card, being pushed back across the table. Brand takes it, replaces it in his file. The man who has just checked it (Ellis Morgan) writes something in an exercise book.*

MORGAN: Anywhere you like, Mr Brand. *(checking watch)* We're one short.

Brand smiles at the two men who sit around the table, removes his jacket, places it over the chair at the end of the table, sits down. The man on his right, about 40, extends a hand.

GARNER: Gerry Garner, Saddle. Wilf Bowers sends regards.

BRAND: *(taking hand)* Bill Brand. How are you. *(he looks at the man on his left)*

LANE: Lane, Sowerdale. How do you do.

Brand smiles. The door at the top of the dingy room opens and Parfitt, Regional Secretary, Textile Workers Union, enters. He carries a good briefcase. He does not see Brand immediately.

PARFITT: Sorry, I had a caucus meeting. *(places briefcase on table, takes out credentials. Morgan checks them, hands them back)*

MORGAN: Thank you, that's fine.

Parfitt looks confidently down the table, a big gun among peashooters. Sees Brand. The barrel wilts a little. Brand nods coolly up the table. Parfitt's is curter.

MORGAN: *(about 50, North Welsh)* Well, gentlemen, good afternoon. My name's Morgan, of the Conference Arrangements Committee, and I'll be chairing this meeting. As you know, there are four resolutions tabled on textiles for the Industry debate on Wednesday. Bearing in mind the pressures on Conference time, the Committee wants to see whether you can't agree to arrive at a single composite resolution embodying the substance, if not the detail, of the four. So that's what we're here to do. I should point out that if a composite were to be worked out, it would pretty well automatically be called. *(pause)* No such guarantee exists for separate resolutions falling outside a composite. *(pause)* But the choice is entirely yours, I want to emphasise that. I'm not here to influence you one way or the other. *(looks around the table for signs of initiative. Opens his final agenda)* Any suggestions?

PARFITT: Point of order, chairman. It was my understanding that the Leighley resolution was to be put by Councillor Frank Hilton ...

MORGAN: Mr Brand's credentials are in order, Mr Parfitt. Councillor Hilton has been taken ill. Mr Brand replaces.

Silence. Parfitt retires into his agenda.

GARNER: It seems to me there's two alternatives ...

MORGAN: Would you mind identifying yourselves, just so we all know who we are.

GARNER: Garner. Saddle Constituency Labour Party. *(clears throat)* Resolution 181 ... *(throat again)* ... I think er I think our resolution could go either way. I mean, there's quotas and there's public ownership. Of course, we'd like action on both ...

LANE: I think that'd go for us too. *(catching Morgan's sharp, demanding eye)* Lane, Sowerdale CLP. Resolution 182.

Morgan scans from Brand to Parfitt, waiting for movement. Parfitt studies Brand. Brand reads his agenda, scribbles notes in the margin with a biro.

PARFITT: Parfitt, Textile Workers Union. Resolution 184. Representing 60,000
affiliated members. Now let me tell you, my Executive, on behalf of those
members, all working in the industry under discussion, thought very hard about
this resolution. The battle lines are very clearly drawn. The issue is not whether
to take the textile industry into public ownership. Because even assuming the
government were willing or able to do it, it would take the best part of another
year to get it through Parliament. By which time there would be no textile
industry to take over. Now those are the facts. *(pause)* The *issue*, the only issue,
is how to save our members' jobs and secure their livelihoods. And the answer
is, and will remain, by getting Conference to instruct the government to impose
a further reduction on imports of unprocessed and semi-processed fibres, i.e., to
provide a bulwark against unfair foreign competition until such time as we can
defend ourselves again in world markets. Now that's the union position. And I
think it behoves this ... gathering ... to pay it both attention and respect.

Pause. Morgan, then Garner and Lane, look towards Brand.

MORGAN: *(eventually)* Mr Brand?

*Outside Broadcast van. We see the three shots of the hall as before, then, on the
fourth (transmission) monitor, we watch them mixing one shot through to the next,
ending on the long shot of the empty conference hall.*

DIRECTOR'S VOICE: *(over)* ... And ... super caption. *(the music starts up, stops
abruptly)* Caption, caption. *(the caption zooms unsteadily up, holds finally.
Under breath)* ... Shit. And ... cue music. *(nothing. His pencil taps on the
desk)* Do you have some music for us down there? *(silky)* No no, when you're
ready ... *(sweet)* Let's go back shall we ...?

*Compositing room. Morgan switches on the lights. Brand sits obdurate in his
place. Lane stretches his legs by the bare window. Parfitt sits on a long table by
the door, talking on the phone. Garner in, carrying plastic cups of coffee on a
beer tray.*

GARNER: Sorry it took so long. Queue halfway round the building.

*He places the tray on the table. Brand and Lane reach for theirs. Morgan stares
frowningly at Parfitt on the phone, checks his watch against the wall clock, which
has 5.25.*

MORGAN: *(in Parfitt's direction)* Well, can we go on, gentlemen?

*Parfitt half turns, sees them waiting, ends the conversation. Returns to his seat.
Sugars his coffee.*

PARFITT: So where do we stand?

Morgan looks down the table at Brand, eyebrow raised.

BRAND: *(the concession tactical, calculated)* All right. I'm prepared to consider a
wording that would avoid direct criticism of the government's record to date.

GARNER: Well, that's a good half of the battle as far as I'm concerned.

LANE: Aye, that throws a new light on things. I reckon I'd support most of what's left in the Leighley resolution, that gone.

PARFITT: And quotas? Leighley's makes no mention, yours do. What about that?

GARNER: That's true.

MORGAN: Look, this thing is very simple. Either Mr Parfitt must accept the idea of public ownership, or Mr Brand must agree reference to quota reductions, or there's no composite. *(pause)* Now what's it to be?

BRAND: I'd accept reference to quotas if it didn't crucially contradict the basic thinking behind the demand for public ownership, as I've already explained, at least to the satisfaction of my CLP colleagues. Reducing import quotas for six months will offer just enough protection to fatten the industry up for its next recession. Besides which, there's not a cat in hell's chance of persuading the Cabinet to go any further on quotas. There's GATT, there's the MFA, there's the EEC ...

PARFITT: *(barking laugh)* And what chance is there of getting them to nationalise, eh? Where've *you* been living, on the moon? *(to Garner and Lane)* Listen, I think you two had better think again. *(mounting his concession)* Now er ... I'm quite prepared to include a request for public ownership somewhere, if you'll agree quotas as the main thrust of the resolution. But I am not trucking with the Leighley wording. Because it won't stand an earthly with the National Executive, let alone the government. *(pause)* I mean, you know, you might have an ... amateur interest in these matters, to me it's my living, right?

GARNER: *(quietly)* Mine too, brother. I've worked in mills sin' I were fifteen.

PARFITT: Then you should know enough to see the sense of it.

GARNER: *(unimpressed)* Maybe.

PARFITT: *(to Lane)* What about you?

LANE: I think we can find something in the Leighley resolution.

Parfitt breathes heavily, pushes chair back, draws briefcase onto his knees.

PARFITT: *(putting file in bag)* All right. I've taken advice *(pointing to phone)* and I propose to withdraw from this compositing conference. The Textile Workers Union resolution will stand. *(to Morgan)* In the circumstances, I must ask you to see to it that it's called.

MORGAN: Well, as I said at the outset, Mr Parfitt, resolutions that fail to find a place in composites ...

PARFITT: ... Nevertheless, Mr Morgan, I think you can assume that my General Secretary will have something unpleasant to say if his union is denied a voice at this Conference. *(fastening bag, standing)* As for the composite you propose lashing together, I think you can take it that my union – *and* others – will cast our votes against it.

He nods tersely, leaves. Morgan drains his coffee, makes a note in his book.

Brand works away at the final agenda, crossing out, inserting, rerouting.

GARNER: *(mild, deadly)* Always liked Brother Parfitt. Salt of the earth.

Lane grins, suddenly relaxed. Offers fags round the table.

BRAND: *(declining)* OK, what about something like this: 'This Conference deplores the indifference shown by ...' *(he becomes aware of their resistance)* Yeah, OK. 'This Conference demands the following socialist policies be implemented by the Labour Government to secure the future of a textile industry currently losing upwards of five hundred jobs a month: one, immediate nationalisation of the industry, under full workers' control, complete access to information, and minimum compensation to shareholders; two, the immediate short-term strengthening of procedures aimed at ending the practice of dumping goods on the home market; three, the securing of long-term fibre agreements with the countries of the developing world and the replacing of exploitative with genuinely reciprocal and mutually beneficial trade arrangements; four, the immediate release of finance via the National Enterprise Board to enable these policies to be implemented.' *(he looks in turn at the three)* Not great literature exactly, but it might do.

GARNER: Yeah, could I have a look?

Brand shows it to him. He studies it, then hands it to Lane. Meanwhile,

BRAND: *(to Morgan)* Sound all right?

MORGAN: *(checking watch)* At five forty five on the eve of a Conference, Shakespeare himself could not have sounded sweeter.

Brand smiles, relaxing, lights a cheroot.

LANE: Yeah. Mmm.

BRAND: We can tug it about a bit if you like.

GARNER: I'll buy it as it stands, I reckon.

LANE: Ahunh.

MORGAN: All right, can we agree on a mover and a seconder? I suppose it'd make sense for Leighley to move and one of you two to second.

Brand searches for consent; gets it.

BRAND: Fine by me.

GARNER: *(spinning coin)* Go on then.

LANE: Heads.

GARNER: *(looking)* Tails. Me. Bloody hell.

MORGAN: *(writing it up, reaching for Brand's composite)* Good. Thank God for that. Thank you gentlemen. I'll get this to the print room, if you'll excuse me. Have a good Conference, won't you.

He leaves quickly, cogs whirring. Lane and Garner get up to go.

BRAND: One thing. The National Executive may ask to remit it ... for further study etc. *(Lane and Garner halt blankly)*

GARNER: You think so?

BRAND: *(ironic)* It has been known.

LANE: Well what do you think?

BRAND: I think we say no.

Lane and Garner look at each other, nod, turn to Brand.

BRAND: Fine. Thanks.

Brand's hotel room. *Brand lies reading on his bed, moves a little into the small pool of light from the bedside lamp. A clock striking eleven. Knock at door.*

BRAND: *(sitting up)* Yeah?

Jowett in, mac over shoulder, hat pushed back.

JOWETT: Any of that beer left?

BRAND: *(pointing)* Help yourself.

Jowett tackles the trip to the table carefully, sodden rather than drunk.

JOWETT: *(at table)* Want one?

BRAND: No thanks. I've just had my cocoa.

JOWETT: I'll take the rest, if you don't mind.

BRAND: Be my guest.

JOWETT: Let you have 'em back.

BRAND: How was the meeting?

JOWETT: Oh yeah. *(pause)* Not ... spectacularly informative. *(pause)* Options were ... explored. Yours?

BRAND: No problem.

JOWETT: Good. Good. You were lucky, they can be sticky. I've done a fair few in my time.

He sits down in the armchair in the dark, lost suddenly. Takes short, almost continuous sips from the can until it's empty. Brand sits on the side of the bed, watches Jowett with care, concern.

BRAND: How about some coffee?

JOWETT: You know what? Twenty years ago I came here, Blackpool, my first Conference. And I stayed here, this place, I've always stayed here, it's cheap, it's clean, it's handy ... You know what? I'm in the same room I had first time I came. '56. I remember it 'cos it was the same as the year, you see, 56, it helped me to remember the room number when I asked for the key at the desk. *(he opens another can)* And what have we done, eh? What have we actually done, this great Party of ours? Come on, teacher, what have we achieved? Mmm? *(Brand says nothing, saddened by this unexpected descent into incertitude)* Y'ever met my kids, Bill? *(Brand shakes his head)* Me neither. Off I'd go and up they'd grow. And the wife? You'd love the wife. I did. The kindest of strangers. *(pause. He stuffs two cans into his mac pocket)* So what have we achieved, eh? Twenty years of struggling and arguing and wheedling and bullying and hustling and chiselling and promising and welching and offering and not delivering ... Jesus Christ. The same sodding room, Bill. Can you credit it? *(he stands heavily)* Do they know a thing or two! *(he begins searching for the cans)*

BRAND: *(gently)* Mac pocket.

Jowett feels for them, finds them.

JOWETT: How was your thing?

BRAND: Fine. No problem.

JOWETT: *(leaving)* Nice to get an easy one, first time. They *can* be a bugger ...

He's gone. Brand crosses to the door, watches him up the stairs, closes it. Returns to the bed, picks up the book. Close shot of its title: 'Running Elections, by Alfred S. Jowett'.

PART TWO

Outside broadcast van. We watch this scene on the transmission monitor. Hum of hall filling up with conference delegates on the first morning. Organist playing 'I do like to be beside the seaside'. We're on the establishing long shot of the hall. When it comes, the introductory sequence works beautifully.

DIRECTOR'S VOICE: Ten seconds. Stand by ... And mix ... and mix ... Sound up ... Cue caption ... Cue music ... and cue Robert ...

ROBERT: *(commentary, as cameras search the hall's geography)* Good morning from Blackpool, at this the 76th Annual Conference of the Labour Party, where, in four or five minutes time, the delegates will have assembled, the leadership will have taken the platform, and proceedings will be under way. A Conference which many people more ... percipient and expert than myself feel may well prove to be as er dramatic and er historic an event as any we have seen in recent years. Jim, what are the key things to watch out for this week here in Blackpool?

JIM: Well, it's a fascinating prospect, though by no means unique in the long and often torrid history of Labour Party conferences. It's anybody's guess what will happen, but already the battle-lines are well and truly drawn, with all the signs of yet another contest of strength between Conference and Government as to whose shall be the decisive voice in the shaping of policy for the country as a whole. That's nothing new of course, but all the signs are that the fragile truce established at last year's Conference is in danger of cracking wide open by the end of this week. Of course, a key figure in all of this is likely to be Willie Moores, General Secretary of the powerful Transport and Allied Workers Union, who on Wednesday morning is expected to move a resolution critical of the government's economic and social policies, and calling for immediate and massive cuts in defence spending coupled with a phased withdrawal from NATO, no less. Now, I understand that the National Executive Committee will ask Conference to remit this particular resolution back – which often simply means to shelve it. It's by no means certain whether this will in fact happen, of course. And if it *doesn't*, it could set a rather large wedge between the Labour Government and may of its most committed supporters, which is unlikely to please a Labour Prime Minister contemplating – if indeed he is, and the evidence is less than overwhelming on this point – if he is, as I say, contemplating a snap election some time in the autumn.

Chairman calls Conference to order.

ROBERT: You'll get the chance, I know, to continue that speculation, Jim. Meanwhile Conference is about to begin. One thing I imagine you'd agree with me on, Jim, and it's this: whatever else is likely to go on in Blackpool this week, in caucuses and fringe meetings, in bars and hotels rooms around the town, it is here, on the floor of Conference, that the final decisions will be taken …

JIM: Yes, indeed, Robert. The Labour Party has always prided itself on being a democratic party …

Last's hotel suite. Scotch being poured into a glass on a table. Sounds of talk in another part of the large room.

LAST'S VOICE: Say when.

BRAND'S VOICE: Fine.

Last hands Brand the glass. It's a room in Last's suite at the Imperial. Doors lead off it, to other rooms and corridors. Several people sit or stand, chatting and drinking, down the room. A colour tv on a shelf is on, sound right down, in a sort of half-recessed area. A laid supper table.

Brand stands with Last at a drinks table, removed from the others. Last has poured himself another.

LAST: Cheers.

BRAND: Cheers.

LAST: Glad you could come.

BRAND: *(grinning, flicking head towards room)* Glad to be asked.

LAST: I'll introduce you in a minute. You'll know one or two of them.

Brand has caught sight of Winnie Scoular, who raises her glass. Brand returns the gesture.

LAST: You know Winnie, of course.

BRAND: We share a house. In Clapham. Tom Mapson, Jim McNab.

LAST: Lynnett Road?

BRAND: Drive. How did you know?

LAST: *I* used to live there. Thirty years ago. I didn't know it was still going.

BRAND: *(grinning)* Maybe I should see the Council about a plaque.

Last laughs, pours more scotch into Brand's glass. Phil Renshaw, his PPS, joins them.

RENSHAW: *(Scots, from Edinburgh; 40; alert)* I'm counting. *(indicates the drink)*

LAST: *(easy)* So am I. Two. Phil Renshaw, Bill Brand.

RENSHAW: We've met at Journal Group. Hiya, Bill.

BRAND: Hi.

LAST: Malcolm, give Larkin a ring and see what time we can expect the PM. He promised eight and it's his damned idea anyway ...

RENSHAW: Will do.

He leaves for the phone.

LAST: Good PPS. I'll be sorry to see him go.

BRAND: He is going then?

LAST: Megan's done a deal with Watson for another Under Secretary – at Social Security. *(he sips at his glass, studying Brand)* November. *(Brand takes a drink, detached, diffident, listening hard)* You're clearly not going to *ask*, so ... It's yours if you want it. *(Brand looks at him, impassive, alert)* Think about it. I shall need to know by the end of the week.

BRAND: *(simply)* Thanks.

LAST: Thank me when you've done it for a month. There's one small problem. It's in my gift, technically I can offer it without reference. But in practice it'll have to be approved by the PM. Which is why you're here tonight, so that he can put an eye over you before your name hits his desk. *(pause)* Now, if you're seriously considering accepting, you'd be as well to maintain a fairly low profile this evening.

BRAND: *(smiling suddenly)* Damn. And I left my invisible pills back at the hotel.

LAST: *(dry)* It's all right, I always carry a spare pack.

BRAND: *(scanning room, slow irony building)* Even so, I can assume, can I, that the main event of the evening is *not* the long-awaited meeting between Watson and Brand, however epochal that encounter may come to seem to future historians.

LAST: I think you can assume that, yes.

BRAND: I don't see the Minister of Defence.

LAST: *(shutters up halfway)* No. He's on holiday. In Spain.

Renshaw returns.

RENSHAW: I've tracked him down. He's in reception. Wants a word with you.

LAST: Right.

Smiles at Brand, leaves with Renshaw for the phone at the far end of the room.

Brand stands a moment, then wanders over towards the main knot of guests. Winnie Scoular detaches from her chat with Moores and intercepts him.

SCOULAR: Hey, what a surprise.

BRAND: Me? Darling of the leadership. I suppose *you're* wearing your NEC hat ...

SCOULAR: Saw you on the box again.

BRAND: Yeah? What was that?

SCOULAR: The Textile Workers demo. It *was* you, wasn't it?

BRAND: *(slight hesitancy)* Yeah, I was there.

SCOULAR: *(smiling)* It's all right, it was in long shot. I really had to peer ...

BRAND: What are you on about?

SCOULAR: *I* know why you're here. Has he offered?

BRAND: Yeah.

SCOULAR: So. He wants the royal assent from Watson.

BRAND: And a more common assent from me.

SCOULAR: You picked a great week to be vetted.

BRAND: Listen, how are you?

SCOULAR: I'm fine.

BRAND: Yeah?

She nods. Smiles. He smiles back.

SCOULAR: Come and meet the others.

They cross to the knot of guests, Frear talking with Wiltshire, Moores waiting for Scoular to rejoin him. In the background, Last talks quietly to Watson on the phone, Renshaw by his side.

SCOULAR: Tom, let me introduce a good friend of mine – Tom Wiltshire, Bill Brand.

WILTSHIRE: *(standing; short, slim, round-faced, a slow country voice)* Nice to you know you, Bill.

BRAND: *(handshake)* Hello.

SCOULAR: *(to Brand, uncertain)* Do you know Malcolm Frear ...?

FREAR: *(nodding, curt)* Yes, our paths *have* crossed ... How are you?

BRAND: *(cool)* OK.

WILTSHIRE: You're putting the textile resolution aren't you?

BRAND: Wednesday.

WILTSHIRE: You heard the NEC were asking for it to be remitted.

BRAND: Yeah, I heard.

WILTSHIRE: You've got a lot of support for it on the Executive. *(smiles at Scoular)* You could do worse than leave it with us ...

BRAND: *(eyes alive)* We'll have to see. I don't think the other two'd wear it. Couple of *real* roughnecks ... They eat MPs for dinner, with a pint of bitter and a pickle on a plate.

Wiltshire smiles, enjoying the mild flavour of joke in the air. Brand catches Frear's cold eyes.

SCOULAR: Come and say hello to Willie. Excuse us.

Willie Moores sits flicking through a book he's taken from a small table, sees them approach. At the phone, Last is arguing now, controlled, serious, miming to Renshaw for pen and paper to write something down.

MOORES: *(late 50s, largeish, deceptively warm, once a Hull docker)* Gideon Bible. Seen a few of them in my time. *(standing, hand out)* How are you? Willie Moores, Transport and Allied.

BRAND: *(shaking big mitt)* Bill Brand, hello.

MOORES: Leighley, yes? *(Brand nods)* I've had a few reports. All good. Frank Hilton?

BRAND: Yes, he's a good comrade.

RENSHAW: *(arriving: to Scoular)* Can you spare a minute? David wants a word.

Scoular leaves. Moores drains his glass.

MOORES: Let's have a drink.

He leads Brand back across the room to the drinks table on the edge of the recessed dining area. Begins pouring.

MOORES: Good demo this morning?

BRAND: *(cool masking surprise)* Yes. Pretty effective.

MOORES: Lots of my lads there ... It's not getting better, is it.

BRAND: Better? It's not even getting worse more slowly ...

Moores turns, studies his face, smiles wanly.

MOORES: Right.

BRAND: Would you mind if I talked Conference for a minute?

MOORES: *(checking watch)* Make it two.

BRAND: I wondered if you'd decided yet how to cast your vote on the textile composite. *(pause)* Twenty-four. Tomorrow.

MOORES: We caucus each morning, 8.30. Can't say I remember it exactly.

Brand takes out a copy of the composite, hands it to him, Moores smiles at his efficiency, begins reading, lips puckering.

MOORES: *(eventually)* Mmm.

BRAND: *(not pushing, yet insistent)* What do you think?

MOORES: Mmm. Yes, I remember it now. Makes a good read.

BRAND: Better than the Gideon Bible?

MOORES: Almost as long. Is the Textile Workers Union backing you? *(Brand smiles)* I thought not. *(pause)* You think you know better than them?

BRAND: I'm not alone. You saw the demonstration.

MOORES: *(his microscope out)* Demonstration? Oh yes. What's the NEC got to say?

BRAND: They want it withdrawn ... remitted.

MOORES: Ahunh. I'll see what my delegates think. We've er ... we've a resolution of our own to think about. *(an owlish grin)*

BRAND: *(deadpan)* I'll do a deal with you. You vote for mine, I'll vote for yours. I can't say fairer.

Last begins organising the others down the room. Waiters have appeared with trolleys of food.

MOORES: *(dry)* That's some deal, brother. Where'd they train you, Chicago?

Last arrives, the others following.

LAST: Willie, I'm sorry, Arthur's going to be a little late, he sends his apologies and suggests we eat without him.

MOORES: All right by me ... Bill here's keeping me amused ...

LAST: Good. Well, let's take the table, shall we ... *(people move into the half recess)* ... leave that one for the PM, will you. Thanks. Winnie, sit by Bill there, that's it ... Phil, switch the tv off will you ...

The waiters are splaying dishes onto the table. Last's directions continue, as we follow Renshaw back into the room proper. He stands before the mute set, watches a moment. Wilkinson is being interviewed in a make-shift studio. Renshaw clicks off.

Later, the meal over. They sit at the long, oval table, with coffee and cheese. A waiter takes wine round. Last sits at one end, facing the PM's still empty chair. Brand sits on his immediate right, then Scoular and Wiltshire; Renshaw, Moores and Frear to his left. Frear and Wiltshire talk quietly across the table. The others focus on Moores.

Moores has removed his jacket and loosened his union tie. He's showing Scoular his big fist, bristling with 10p pieces half buried in the slits between the fingers.

MOORES: Nobut a kid, but that were my introduction to politics. Two bob pieces in their fists and every punch took a slice … *(he pushes his hair back, shows a thin silver scar on his temple)* … And the coppers stood and watched 'em. For every fascist they arrested, they took ten of us. Halcyon days. *(he grins suddenly, pocketing the coins)* We learnt fast though … Trouble was, we couldn't afford the technology, we had to make do with pennies … No edge, you see. *(he runs his finger over a new penny, chuckling)*

SCOULAR: Don't be so romantic, Willie.

MOORES: *(in the spirit)* What are you talking about, I'm giving you the facts. Am I right, David?

LAST: *(him too)* Oh absolutely. Though in my part of the world …

MOORES: *(winking at Brand)* Hampstead.

LAST: *(ignoring him)* … Hampstead … we got a better class of fascist.

MOORES: Naturally.

LAST: There they used ten bob notes …

The apartment bell rings. Renshaw goes to stand, but Last holds him back, rising swiftly.

LAST: OK Phil. *(to table, yet only obliquely)* Hors d'oeuvres over, now for the meat …

He leaves. Moores gets up, begins mooching for cigarettes, away from the table.

BRAND: *(to Scoular, quietly)* I've a feeling I shouldn't be here.

SCOULAR: Last knows what he's doing.

BRAND: *(unconvinced)* Yeah?

SCOULAR: You think you're here just for Watson to put his eye over? You're here to see some … dealing. *(pause)* Last needs to see … how you … respond.

Movement in the doorway. Watson in, flanked by detective and secretary. Last follows.

WATSON: *(to secretary)* Geoffrey, I think it's better you take the car and collect Lucy at the Pavilion. Go now.

The secretary retreats.

WATSON: *(to Last, indicating detective)* You know Stan. He's eaten. *(he winks at the detective, who melts into the darker edges of the room, away from the recessed dining area)* Here we are then. *(approaching table)* Sorry, sorry, I got held up. *(indicating empty chair)* This me, David? *(sitting)* Good. *(to Moores, returning to the table)* Apologies, Willie. How are you?

MOORES: *(lighting a cigar he's found)* Fine, Arthur. You?

WATSON: Never better. Tom, Malcolm, Winifred *(each beckons a response. He's stopped at Brand)*

LAST: Bill Brand.

WATSON: *(clicking)* Oh yes. *(deeply dry)* Nice of you to turn out with my reception committee this morning. *(pause. Brand smiles neutrally, unsure of the ground)* Whose idea were the eggs?

BRAND: *(buying Watson's dry twinkle)* I honestly don't know. I argued against 'em. Some of the lads wanted them hardboiled ...

FREAR: A bloody disgrace.

Brand studies Frear's face. Frear drinks coffee, ignoring him.

WATSON: Another suit for the cleaners. *(cryptically, most of his meaning underground)* Enjoy your fling while it lasts ...

LAST: *(in his place now)* Will you eat, Arthur?

WATSON: Nothing heavy, David. I tell you what I wouldn't mind ...

Last begins a covered silver platter on its way up the table, through Brand, Scoular and Wiltshire. Watson takes off the lid. We see the contents: some nuts, an apple, a little cheese, celery and a yoghurt.

WATSON: *(at last, admiring but dry)* No pickled onions?

LAST: *(to Renshaw)* Phil?

RENSHAW: *(crossing to waiter, standing discreetly by)* Could you possibly bring a bowl of pickled onions? Otherwise we're fine now thanks ...

He ushers the waiter from the room.

WATSON: *(munching celery dipped in salt)* ... and a bottle of ale, mm?

Renshaw nods, half out of the room.

WATSON: *(friendly, open)* Well then, Willie, what are we going to do about this resolution of yours then?

MOORES: *(relighting cigar pufflingly)* I hope we're going to pass it, Arthur.

WATSON: *(still light)* Think that's likely, Tom?

WILTSHIRE: *(guarding his position)* That's up to Conference, Prime Minister.

WATSON: Oh yes. Conference. *(to Wiltshire)* But the NEC oppose, don't they?

SCOULAR: Not at all ...

WATSON: *(grinning)* I didn't expect *you* to, Winnie ...

WILTSHIRE: The NEC will ask for it to be remitted ... so that it can be examined more closely and costed ...

WATSON: What about the Engineers?

WILTSHIRE: Hard to say. They meet tomorrow ...

MOORES: *(mild, to no one in particular)* Oh I think they like it ...

Pause. Watson fiddles with a cut of cheese. The waiter returns with ale and onions. Renshaw relieves him of both, places them by Watson, who smiles appreciatively.

WATSON: *(forking onion)* We've had two full scale defence reviews since we came back, Willie. We clawed best part of a thousand millions out of the armed services. It's not a bottomless pool ... there's no way we can take more just now ...

MOORES: My resolution says there is.

WATSON: By withdrawing from NATO? *(pause)* That's not a possibility, Willie.

MOORES: *(unemphatic; this is, in tone and feel, light years away from confrontation)* Well I'll tell you something else that isn't a possibility, Arthur: my one and a quarter million members being thrown out of work or working for peanuts during your elasticated 'period of severe restraint'. You've got to find some money from somewhere and you've got to find it soon.

WATSON: *(mild, deliberate)* The money isn't *there*. We need another year ... Talk to the Chancellor ...

MOORES: My members will be talking to the Chancellor next month, at the Annual Conference. Fairly emphatically, I should imagine.

WATSON: Malcolm, tell Willie what, for example, a four-week dock strike would do to our trade account ...

Frear has begun to take out some notes he's prepared.

FREAR: A four-week strike in the docks ...

MOORES: I think you'd be better off reading that out at the next Cabinet meeting. *(Frear stops, nettled. Watson indicates he should hold his tongue)*

WATSON: *(as though passing on to the weather; opening his ale)* David, what's it likely to mean in terms of unemployment ...?

LAST: *(some slight reluctance to be drawn)* I think it would depend what form it took and what action you took to combat it ...

WATSON: You could set us back five years, Willie. More.

MOORES: I'm sorry, Arthur. You just can't go on squeezing the people who put you there in the first place ...

WATSON: We're squeezing every section, top to bottom, you know that ...

MOORES: Oh come on now Arthur ...

Watson's eyes have gone milky, distant, cold, though the smile remains. Brand refills his glass, hands the wine bottle to Winnie.

LAST: *(finest timing)* I suspect Willie would be a deal happier if he could be certain we were still going to hold the reins beyond the autumn ...

Attention regathers palpably, as yet another pebble hits the sand.

WATSON: *(the faintest surprise)* Autumn? What's autumn got to do with it? You mean these election rumours ... ? Ha.

MOORES: I think David has his finger on it. The Tories have all but promised an immediate wage freeze the moment they come back, I can't see my members running the risk of letting that happen without first getting in with a substantial wage claim ... No chance. *(Watson pours out the rest of his ale. Moores watches him, looks at Last, back at Watson)* Might make a difference, if you were to settle that this week ...

WATSON: You've been reading too many Tory papers, Willie. *(studying bottle label)* Theakston's ... that's Newcastle, isn't it?

BRAND: North Yorkshire.

WATSON: *(looking at him, unsmiling)* Is it? I must remember that. I tell you what, Willie, Lucy'll be back about now, why don't you pop up for a nightcap and say hello ... She's bought a William Morris traycloth or something she wants to give you for Elsie ...

MOORES: Fine. Let's do that.

WATSON: *(rising)* Well, nice to see you all ... Sorry I couldn't have joined you earlier ... Tom, Malcolm, pop up later for a chat, eh? ... Give us an hour or so ...

Moores puts on his jacket, lifts another cigar from the box on the sideboard, joins Watson. The detective materialises, still half-invisible. Watson smiles at him.

WATSON: No rest for the wicked, Stanley.

He waves a hand over his shoulder as he leaves, affable, benign, sharp as a ferret.

People stand as he leaves, stretching legs, relaxing.

WILTSHIRE: *(his use at an end)* I've a bit of work to do in my room, David. Thanks for the supper.

LAST: Nice to see you, Tom. Sorry we didn't have a chance to talk ...

FREAR: *(him too, and making little effort to hide it)* I'll go off as well, I think, David ... I had a coat somewhere ...

He leaves for the vestibule. Wiltshire approaches Brand on his way out.

WILTSHIRE: About that textile resolution ... We really do want to look at it ... If you insist on *putting* it as it stands, we'll have to oppose ... Which would be a pity ... Sleep on it, eh?

Brand finds himself taking the friendly proffered hand. Wiltshire smiles goodnight to Winnie, leaves, Last in their wake. The phone rings. Renshaw answers.

Brand sits in Watson's chair, looks down the table at Winnie, picks up the bottle.

BRAND: *(Watson's voice)* Theakston's. That's Newcastle, isn't it?

SCOULAR: If you're not careful he'll take you on himself ... just to stop you correcting him in public ...

BRAND: That'll be the day.

Last back in, less relaxed than earlier. He looks for Renshaw, sees he's on the phone, turns to Brand and Scoular.

LAST: Drink, anyone?

They shake their heads. Last pours a large drink, his back to Renshaw.

LAST: *(bitter)* Jesus ... Christ.

Takes a gulp, another. Straightens. Holds himself on rein.

BRAND: *(not aggressively)* Am I finished for the evening?

LAST: Stay. Have a drink.

BRAND: Small scotch.

Last pours, hands it to him. Sits down at the bottom of the table. Renshaw returns.

RENSHAW: That was Martin. He's got the revised unemployment figures for the last month. They're six and a half thousand worse than we said ... He wants to know whether he should release them now or hold them over till ...

LAST: *(vicious)* Now.

RENSHAW: *(tentative)* Are you sure?

LAST: Now.

RENSHAW: *(slowly)* OK. *(pause)* I'll ring him back.

Last gets up, pours himself another scotch.

RENSHAW: *(remembering)* Oh Winnie, there's a message at reception for you.

SCOULAR: *(standing)* Fine.

She crosses to the phone.

RENSHAW: I'll turn in, if that's OK, David.

LAST: *(at drinks table)* Ring Martin, OK?

RENSHAW: OK.

LAST: Goodnight.

RENSHAW: Take it easy. 'Night Bill.

BRAND: Take care.

Renshaw leaves. Last returns to his seat, faces Brand across the length of the table.

LAST: Grisly?

BRAND: Oh yes.

LAST: He liked you.

BRAND: He's a ghoul.

LAST: *(tireder than he knows)* It doesn't have to be this ... disgusting.

Long silence. He looks up finally from his glass, to meet Brand's eyes.

BRAND: *(gently)* Doesn't it?

Winnie returns to the table.

SCOULAR: *(grim)* That was Tom Mapson's sister ... He's had a heart attack ...

BRAND: Oh Jesus ...

SCOULAR: He's in the Middlesex. Listen, I think I'd better drive down and see him ...

BRAND: I'll come with you ...

SCOULAR: No, don't do that, Bill ... You've your resolution first thing ... I'll ring you when I have news.

BRAND: You've got my number, 281 ...

SCOULAR: I have it, I have it ... Oh God, poor Tom ...

LAST: *(by her side)* Give him regards, Win ... And drive carefully. All right?

She pecks his cheek, leaves. Last goes with her to the door. Brand pours himself another scotch. Brand listens to stray indistinct murmurs from the vestibule. Last returns from the door eventually, taking fractionally longer than expected.

BRAND: I think I'll get back.

LAST: Bill. *(Brand turns to face him)* I've asked Winnie, I'll ask you. Don't mention Tom Mapson ... to anyone ... at least tonight. OK?

BRAND: I don't understand. I mean ...

LAST: *(carefully)* I think it would be ... better if Watson didn't hear, at least until tomorrow ...

BRAND: Watson?

LAST: Bill, Watson floated this election rumour himself, way back in the summer. It's an old tactic, he's used it before, but it still works ... He's up there with Willie Moores right now, letting himself be persuaded that he shouldn't call an election this autumn he has no intention of calling anyway ... In return, he'll get Moores – and the others, this won't be his only meeting – to 'moderate' their demands this winter ... The unions know only too well what life under the Tories will be like.

BRAND: Go on.

LAST: Possibly the one thing that could tilt Watson towards an autumn election is the knowledge that his majority could be down to three by the time Parliament reconvenes and possibly to two by January ... What's Tom's majority, two thousand?

BRAND: *(frozen)* Fourteen hundred.

LAST: *(grave)* He's got to do the deal first. Give his pledge there'll be no election ...

BRAND: Is that what's most important then?

LAST: Yes. Listen, if we lose office now, this party will break up ... It's not the time, Bill. This is a mass party, that's its strength ... In ten years, five maybe, we can split on our terms ... the left's terms ... because we'll be the leadership then ... and we'll take most of the party with us, unions and constituencies. But it isn't now.

Brand stands, returns his glass to the drinks table.

BRAND: Listen. About this job ...

LAST: Leave it. We'll talk before you leave.

BRAND: *(slowly)* What's your advice about the resolution I'm putting tomorrow?

LAST: Do what you have to.

Brand nods. Lingers. Leaves.

PART THREE

Last's hotel suite. The large room now cleaned, cleared. Last works at the desk, the tv set in his eyeline.

On tv:

ROBERT: Now in the Textile Debate the radical and critical composite resolution, which is to be moved by the delegate from Leighley, Mr Bill Brand MP. He is a relative newcomer whose record to date both in the House and out has found him few friends in the Labour leadership. Though whether this causes Mr Brand any particular concern is a matter of merest speculation ...

Renshaw comes from another room carrying papers, files.

RENSHAW: Anything from Willie Moores yet?

Last silences him with his hand. Renshaw turns the sound up further. Brand is taking the rostrum, to a perhaps surprisingly warm and sustained reception from the morning delegates. Last puts down his biro.

On tv – closing in gradually so that the tv picture fills the screen, with the acoustic changing to conference hall, and reaction shots of Scoular, Wiltshire etc on the platform and Moores in the audience.

BRAND: Bill Brand, Leighley CLP. Comrades, I want to deal with the composite before you in a moment. I want to say one thing first though. When this debate's over, somebody up there on the high table is going to stand up and ask me to withdraw it. Of course that's not the word they'll use ... They'll ask for it to be referred to a committee, which will report its findings in time for next year's conference. Well, I have this to say to that, comrades: the problems of the textile industry are too catastrophic to be kept hanging around for yet another year. Because in a year's time there'll be no textile industry for the NEC to report back on. So I give my answer to the high table in advance of the question. And that answer is No ... This composite will be put ... and *Conference* will decide, not the Executive Committee, whether it should become party policy ...

Applause from the floor. Brand fiddles some notes, in a hurry to proceed. Pull out to hotel tv set, then further out to take in Last and Renshaw, watching in silence.

LAST: *(quietly)* Who does he remind me of?

RENSHAW: *(laconic)* Give me a clue.

Phone rings. Renshaw turns sound down (though not right down, Brand continuing). Answers phone, carries it over to Last, hand over mouthpiece.

RENSHAW: P.M.

LAST: *(to phone)* Hello, Arthur. Yes, I'm watching. *(listens)* ... James Cagney, that's very good. *(listens again)* Well, it's a composite, Arthur, there are others involved ... *(he gestures to Renshaw to turn the sound up, listens. Brand is lashing the government's record on textiles)* Yes, I hear it ... *(surprised)* What? Fine, fine, glad you think so. *(listens again, rustles the morning papers in front of him on the desk. We see a small front page item on Mapson's condition in the Mail and the Express; stop press in The Guardian – all ringed in biro)* Yes, I saw it in the papers. I don't think it's as bad as they make out, Tom's a leathery old so-and-so ... Mmm. Ahunh. Well, we've been there before, Arthur ... Fine. Will do.

Puts phone down, indicates with his hand for the volume to be lowered.

LAST: He's said yes to Brand.

RENSHAW: Yes?

LAST: Wants the muzzle on him. Fast.

Brand's hotel room. *Brand lies on his bed, his hand over his eyes. Knock at door. Brand calls it's open. Jowett in, grave-eyed. Stares at Brand. Brand stares back. Silence. Jowett's face cracks slowly into its version of a smile. Brand grins back. Jowett takes his hat off, throws it at Brand. Brand catches it, puts it on his own head.*

JOWETT: You did it, you bastard.

They embrace, gurgling and yipping like schoolkids.

JOWETT: Sod 'em, sod 'em, you did, you got it through.

BRAND: Right, right.

JOWETT: How did you do it, man?

BRAND: Tongue of silver, heart of gold.

JOWETT: Three and a half million.

BRAND: Right, right.

They sit down, silent again, wheezing a little.

JOWETT: *(finally)* Jesus.

Watson's hotel suite. *Watson's head, rear view. In his eye-line, a tv set. Willie Moores at the rostrum. Close in on set, glide through to hall and hall atmosphere. Reaction shots of Brand in hall and Scoular, Last etc on platform.*

MOORES: *(he's been speaking for several minutes)* ... as I've said, comrade delegates, there can be no cant talked about creating a caring and compassionate society when a Labour government is slashing thousands of millions of pounds off essential social services – health, education, welfare, pensions – when a Labour government is striking, with its ever-expanding 'period of severe restraint', on wages that is, not prices – at the very heart of working class living standards, and when a Labour government is apparently content to see a million workers out of a job as a deliberate instrument of economic – or rather Treasury – policy. In our view, comrade delegates, the rhetoric of a just and caring society will not be justified until fundamental shifts in policy have been effected ... and I don't mean in our lifetime, I mean *now*, comrades. I want this Conference to tell our government to get on with its job, which is to advance the health and wellbeing of the working people of this land, the people who create the national cake in the first place. *(appropriate rhetoric, appropriate response)* And so, comrade delegates, in view of assurances received, from the platform and elsewhere, we're prepared to withdraw the resolution in its present particular form, we do it in the confident belief and expectation that this government can and will rally the whole country behind it on a programme of full social justice and radical redistribution of wealth away from the rich and idle and towards the wealth-creating masses we're all of us here to represent. I so move.

Applause. We move back into the hotel room, as far as the tv set. Then close shot of Watson. He pokes his tongue inside a front cavity, very carefully.

Outside Broadcast van, the bank of monitors. Watson stands at the microphone, huge ovation cascading over the hall.

DIRECTOR'S VOICE: *(over)* Hold it there, Tony. Fine. You all right, Mike? OK.

ROBERT'S VOICE: *(over)* Say what you like about the Prime Minister – and most people do – he's not short of supporters here in this hall today ...

Brand's hotel room. *Brand and Jowett eat snacks off a tray, watching the monochrome tv set. Watson is beginning his speech. Brand passes Jowett the salt for his chicken sandwich.*

JOWETT: Well, now's his chance to let us all in on the secret ...

BRAND: What?

JOWETT: Autumn election.

BRAND: *(lips pursed)* Oh yes.

Cut to tv set, mix through to same shot of Watson in conference hall, with reaction shots of audience.

WATSON: ... a fine conference. A comradely conference. Where we've talked hard and thought hard. And where we've faced the world and its problems without flinching. A conference worthy of this great Party of ours. But let me, before I proceed, set one little ... contentious matter straight ... Just for the record, you understand ... and the Mail, the Express, the Sun and all the rest of the moaning minnies. Rumour has it that your Prime Minister is considering an election in the autumn. Let me tell the country – and the world at large – unequivocally and in words of one syllable ... There will be no election this autumn. *(huge applause, bordering on pandemonium)* This government was elected by the people of this land – the people, mind, not the press and the other media – to do a job. And we're going to see it through. All right. *(stamping and cheering)* We were elected on the policies we proclaimed with total clarity in our Manifesto. And we were elected because the people of Britain recognised the nature and depth of the challenge we face as a nation. They realise the going from now on will be tougher than we have known in this generation. They recognise that this national challenge cannot be met by confrontation and divisive conflict, but only by comradeship and co-operation and care and concern. Our mandate is still with us: to ensure that as the going gets tougher and tougher up the hill – as it will – that, in the words of the old Socialist story about the stage-coach going uphill – the order must go out to the nation: 'Everybody who is able-bodied, regardless of rank or class, gets out and shoves. But if there are any among us who are unable to play their part through illness, age, infancy or disability, they, and they alone, are free to ride ...'

Knock at door. Brand answers it. Last in.

LAST: Still on, is he?

BRAND: Mmm. You remember Alf Jowett, my agent?

Jowett has stood, removed his napkin.

LAST: Yes. How are you?

JOWETT: Fine, thanks. I'll go and pack.

He leaves, making few bones of it.

LAST: Mind if I ...?

BRAND: Let me.

Brand clicks the set off. Last sits down in Jowett's chair.

LAST: So?

BRAND: Tell me one thing. Why did Willie Moores support my resolution?

LAST: *(greyly)* I don't know. Perhaps he simply wanted to record one ... principled
act in an otherwise thoroughly nasty week's dealing ...

BRAND: *(a statement)* You don't believe that, do you.

LAST: No. I'm just too tired to figure it out. He's after leverage somewhere ... I
just don't see it at the moment. I rule out spite as a motive. Just. You haven't
answered.

BRAND: *(carefully)* I don't think so.

Last absorbs it a moment; sniffs; stands.

LAST: OK.

BRAND: Go well.

LAST: And you.

They shake hands, a late, odd, almost missed contact.

LAST: Winnie rang. Tom's still in danger. If he sees the weekend out, he's a fifty-
fifty chance of pulling round.

Brand nods, impassive. Last leaves.

*Brand switches tv back on. The Red Flag being sung badly. Delegates holding
hands etc.*

He watches for a long time.

- *end* -

Episode 7

Tranquility of the Realm

was broadcast on Monday 19th July 1976

The cast was as follows:

Bill Brand   Jack Shepherd

Jane Brand   Karen Silver

Michael Brand   Philip Cox

Miriam Brand   Lynn Farleigh

Clare Cranston   Ann Pennington

Sandiford   William Hoyland

Starr   Douglas Campbell

Venables   Peter Howell

Alex Ferguson   Cherie Lunghi

Mrs Martin   Rosalie Crutchley

Waverley   Richard Leech

Latey   Michael Macowan

Labour MP   Richardson Morgan

Wale   Michael Gover

Bealey   Alex Scott

Henson   Malcolm Terris

Hinchcliff   Basil Henson

Mace   David Henry

Conservative MP   Neville Barber

Wilkinson   Gary Roberts

Pakistani   Albert Moses

Police sergeant   Bernard G. High

Designers: David Ferris, Harry Clark

Executive Producer: Stella Richman

Producer: Stuart Burge

Director: Roland Joffé

PART ONE

Miriam's house. Evening. Dark. Streetlights darkly illumine the garage, whose up and over door is open.

In a corner, Brand, in jeans and sweater, is mending the chain on Jane's bike. Jane squats by him, watching intently. He shows her the sprained link, how the new one is fitted. She strains to see, nodding, absorbed.

Over this, Commons chamber acoustic, desultory background chatter.

SPEAKER'S VOICE: Order. Order. *(chat dies)* Almighty God, by whom alone kings reign and princes decree justice, and from whom alone cometh all counsel, wisdom and understanding, we Thine unworthy servants here gathered together in Thy name do most humbly beseech Thee to send down Thy heavenly wisdom from above, to direct and guide us in all our consultations.

Brand poised delicately on the brink of fitting the new link.

BRAND: Pin goes through, see?

JANE: Ahunh.

BRAND: And ... click. There it is. Wind it on.

He sits back, wiping his oily hands on a rag, as Jane refits the chain on the cog wheels.

SPEAKER'S VOICE: ... And grant that we, having Thy fear always before our eyes, and laying aside all private interests, prejudices and partial affections, the result of all our counsels may be to the glory of Thy blessed name, the maintenance of true Religion and Justice, the safety, honour and happiness of the Queen, the public wealth, peace and tranquillity of the Realm, and the uniting and knitting together of the hearts of all persons and estates within the same, in true Christian Love and Charity, one towards another, through Jesus Christ our Lord and Saviour.

BRAND: OK?

JANE: Yes. Thanks.

BRAND: *(watch)* Better get my skates on ...

JANE: Mummy saw you on the television last week. I was at Brownies.

BRAND: How's school?

JANE: All right. There's a man coming to teach us to play the guitar ...

BRAND: *(standing)* Terrific.

JANE: But it's only for children with big hands.

BRAND: Let's have a look. *(he puts his palm up and out. Jane presses hers against his, shy, smiling a little anxiously. He studies the match)* You'll be all right. You've got a hand like a foot.

JANE: *(laughing)* Daddy!

Michael appears from the side door of the house, which opens directly into the garage. He wears a white and blue plastic apron. He has flour on his face.

MICHAEL: Mum says she's made some tea and it's seven o'clock.

BRAND: Just finished.

JANE: *(slight aggression)* What've you been doing?

MICHAEL: *(friendly)* Baking.

Jane goes into the house. Brand rights the bike, checks the brakes, places it against the wall at the back.

MICHAEL: You can have jam tarts if you like.

BRAND: *(his back to him)* Love some.

MICHAEL: I wish you lived here. *(Brand says nothing, wipes the handlebars with a rag)* Dad.

BRAND: *(turning)* What?

MICHAEL: You know that gerbil? At school?

BRAND: *(reaching for it)* Yes ...

MICHAEL: It's had children.

Miriam calls from the house. 'Michael. Bath'.

MICHAEL: *(calling)* Right.

BRAND: *(approaching, hugging him to his side)* How many jam tarts am I allowed?

MICHAEL: Many as you like. Save some though won't you.

They walk into the house together.

Living room. Miriam has placed a tray on a low table, is saucering cups, pouring tea from chrome pot, spreading toast and jam tarts onto a plate. Brand calls from the hallway.

BRAND'S VOICE: See you before I go, OK?

He enters the room, takes his jacket from a chair, puts it on, closes his black attaché case, laid open on a table.

MIRIAM: I made some tea.

BRAND: *(crossing to sit by the low table)* Thanks.

MIRIAM: *(point to tarts)* Those are what Michael made.

BRAND: *(picking one up)* He's good, isn't he?

MIRIAM: He brought sausage rolls home last week from school ...

They sit back in their chairs, tea cups balanced. Brand checks watch.

MIRIAM: You look thin.

BRAND: *(ironic)* No, it's the light.

He bites into the tart.

MIRIAM: *(quietly)* Can we talk some time?

Brand looks at her. She's leaning forward, to spread jam on her toast.

Michael in, undressed, ready for bath.

MICHAEL: *(to Brand)* Something else to tell you, Ollie.

BRAND: What's that, Stanley?

MICHAEL: *(very pleased)* I finished the reading scheme.

BRAND: Good. Good on you, comrade.

MICHAEL: What do you think of that?

BRAND: Over the moon. Come here.

He takes Michael to him, kisses him fatly on the lips.

MIRIAM: All right, now go and finish your bathing scheme.

MICHAEL: *(turning to go: to Brand)* Do I get anything?

BRAND: I'll talk to Mum.

MICHAEL: *(winking several times, conspiratorial, whisper)* Fishing rod. Cheers, Ollie. Good tarts, eh?

He leaves, giving Miriam a sillytooth smile as he leaves. She make a mock-threatening gesture at him.

Brand leans forward, to replace his cup and saucer on the tray.

BRAND: Anything … special?

Miriam gets up, begins to draw curtains.

MIRIAM: I just thought it might be … useful to see what shape we were in for … after the divorce …

BRAND: *(finally)* Yeah. I'd like that.

She picks up a darning basket and a pile of children's socks and other garments, places them by her chair. Brand watches her covertly.

BRAND: *(finally)* Thanks, Mim.

She sits; looks at him; smiles.

MIRIAM: You'd better get off. Are you driving?

BRAND: Mmm.

MIRIAM: Take care.

Brand stands, picks up his case. Crosses to where she sits. Looks at her. Wants to touch her, as friend, as colleague. Can't risk the ambiguity of the gesture.

BRAND: You too.

He leaves the room. Miriam takes out darning needle and wool. Begins threading. Upstairs, sounds of Brand joshing the children, in the bathroom. All played off Miriam's process. Finally, we hear him on the stair again.

BRAND: *(over, from front door, calling)* Bye.

MIRIAM: *(in close shot; hesitating a fraction only)* Bye.

Fade slowly.

Fade up blackboard: *'Further Containment of Terrorism Bill, Standing Committee 'B', First Sitting'*

Pull back to show section of corridor outside Committee Room B, first floor, House of Commons. It's a broadish corridor, carpeted, oaken, defined at its edges by padded benches. This section is at one end, with a suggestion of other corridors leading off the T-junction at the end.

Knots of MPs, staff and others stand or sit around the open Committee Room door. Some pass in to the room itself, where a fair number, as we can hear, have already taken their seat. A tea trolley does good business, a small queue of members waiting their turn.

We pick out the details, the separate but interlocking processes; end the sequence on Brand himself, seated, somewhat apart from others, his black case open by his side, a bulky file open on his knee. He works on the file, quiet, absorbed.

A woman in her late 20s, long fair hair, attractive, well-dressed in loose, flouncy clothes, rounds the corner, asks directions. A member points in Brand's direction. She approaches.

CLARE: Mr Brand? *(he looks up, a bit startled)* Clare Cranston.

BRAND: *(standing)* Oh yes. Hi. Nice to meet you. *(takes her hand)* Erm … look, have a seat, give me that … *(she hands him his case, he puts it on the floor, she sits)* Erm … coffee?

CLARE: No, I'm fine thanks.

BRAND: *(sitting again)* Jeff Rawlinson said you might let me have a few hours a week …

CLARE: It's possible.

BRAND: Say … ten?

CLARE: *(thinking)* Yeah, that should be all right.

BRAND: Where do you work, at home?

CLARE: Yes, I've a seven year old daughter. I like to be around when she gets back from school.

BRAND: What, you've a typewriter there and ...?

CLARE: That's right.

BRAND: Good. It's mainly correspondence. How long did you work for Jeff?

CLARE: A year. A bit more.

She avoids his eyes on the question, looking down the corridor. He studies her milky face carefully.

BRAND: Is Wednesday morning OK for dictation?

CLARE: Fine.

BRAND: I'll send the rest. In longhand. Or you can pick it up, if you prefer ...

CLARE: We'll see how it goes, shall we?

BRAND: *(fiddling in his file)* Maybe you'd better have a look at my writing ... It's not without a certain quirkiness, I'm told.

She takes a sheaf of handwritten notes from him, begins reading them.

Sandiford, the smooth young Whip, arrives. The corridor is thickening with arriving members. Some laughter, ribaldry. Sandiford closes in on Brand.

SANDIFORD: Got a minute, Bill?

Brand closes his file slowly, places it on his seat, moves to join Sandiford, who eyes the girl on the bench.

SANDIFORD: *(to tea-man)* Two coffees, Alf. *(seeks Brand's assent. Brand nods)* I'm whipping on 'B' ... *(gesturing to door)* First committee, isn't it?

BRAND: That's right.

SANDIFORD: Thanks, Alfred. *(hands Brand his)* There we are. *(sipping)* Don't worry too much about procedure, it's not a great deal different from the Chamber ... We stand when addressing the Chair, the usual forms of address, no smoking, reading newspapers, eating or drinking ... *(Brand remains toughly quiet)* I must say it's a blessed relief to be on a committee that isn't going to be a parliamentary version of the Third Battle of the Somme ... I can't remember the last time we had Tory support on a second reading ...

BRAND: *(terse)* It was a year ago. When you introduced the 'period of severe restraint'.

SANDIFORD: Yes, of course. Ah well, let us count our blessings. *(order paper in hand)* You know about tabling amendments?

BRAND: Yes.

SANDIFORD: *(laughing a little)* Not that it's encouraged, mind. We expect support here just as much as in the House. *(Brand says nothing, drinking his coffee)* I read your speech on the Second Reading. The Chief Whip took it as a speech in support of the Bill. *(pause)* Which is why he agreed to your request for a seat in committee.

Brand places cup and saucer on the trolley.

SANDIFORD: Well ... I'll be around, anyway. Should you need ... advice.

BRAND: *(levelly)* Thanks, Jeremy.

Sandiford joins a group of members by the door. Brand takes in Clare Cranston, still studying his manuscript, pen in hand, making the odd deft marginal query with her green Pentel.

VOICE: The member for Leighley, I'll be bound.

Brand turns. Starr, Chairman of the Journal Group, is buying himself a coffee.

STARR: How goes it, Bill?

BRAND: Fine, Reg. You?

STARR: *(tightlipped)* Not complaining.

BRAND: I noticed.

STARR: Meaning?

BRAND: Doesn't matter.

Slight pause. Some unease between them.

STARR: I hear you turned the PPS job down with Last. *(Brand nods once)* Not interested in the scenic route, eh? He's pretty disappointed. Set his heart on having you.

BRAND: *(carefully)* He'll survive.

STARR: Oh yes.

Another slight pause.

BRAND: You on this committee?

STARR: No, I'm on 'D'. Finance Bill.

BRAND: *(pointing to his door)* What's the line on this one?

STARR: No line. Save a low profile. A question of priorities. You should come to more Journal meetings, Bill.

BRAND: Will you vote for it on Third Reading?

STARR: Probably not. Not that it'll make any difference, with the Tories supporting it ...

BRAND: Yet you did vote in favour at the Second Reading ...

STARR: *(draining coffee)* Not true. I wasn't there for the Second Reading.

BRAND: I meant the Group ...

STARR: *(sniffing)* Did they? Didn't you?

BRAND: Yes.

STARR: Why was that then?

BRAND: *(slowly)* Isn't it obvious? *(Starr gives nothing away)* Do you think they'd have given me a seat on this committee if I'd spoken against?

STARR: *(lips pursed, nodding)* Nice ... Nice. *(pause. studying Brand's face)* You're getting good at it, aren't you.

Venables, the Home Secretary, arrives, flanked by Minister of State etc. His Minister of State is Henson, tall, thin, stooped, about 40; Under Secretary is meek, young, keen, bright, impassive; his PPS is Lambert, late 40s, a faded ex-Post Office Union man, untalented, correct. Venables greets people cordially, without show. A good entrance nonetheless.

He passes Starr and Brand to enter the room.

VENABLES: Morning, Reg.

STARR: Morning, John.

Venables smiles at Brand, disappears into the Committee Room.

STARR: Our next leader? *(Brand says nothing)* I'll leave it to you then. I'll keep an ear out for explosions ...

He waves an airy goodbye, stumps off round the corner, against the tide of committee lawyers, counsellors, chairperson etc. arriving for this first sitting. Brand returns to the padded bench where Clare Cranston sits.

CLARE: *(sheaf of letters in hand)* They seem OK. There's no address for this one – Wilkinson, Textile Action ...

BRAND: Just leave it blank. I'll need to find it ...

CLARE: Shall I do them then?

BRAND: Fine. Sign them tomorrow?

CLARE: I'll sign them if you like. Jeff Rawlinson never minded ...

BRAND: No, I'll sign them, OK? *(she nods)* Don't I know you from somewhere?

CLARE: I don't think so.

BRAND: I'm not being corny. Really.

CLARE: I was an actress for a while. That's probably it.

BRAND: *(quietly)* What happened:

Silence. She's collecting her things.

CLARE: *(finally)* Nothing.

She looks at him eventually. He smiles slowly.

BRAND: *(hand out)* Good to meet you, Clare.

CLARE: *(taking it)* Good to meet you.

Brand sees Alex turning into the corridor. Blinks. Clare follows his eyes. Alex talks to a liveried official, who points up the corridor. Clare withdraws her hand, smiles, leaves, passing Alex on the way. The corridor is emptying, as members enter the committee room.

Alex wears trousers, shirt, tank-top and jacket, and a funny, old knitted beret. The two women look at each other curiously as they cross. Brand frowns at the approaching Alex.

ALEX: Hi. I got an early train. Thought I'd call in before I go.

BRAND: *(dawning)* Christ, it's today. I'm sorry, I'd clean forgotten ...

ALEX: *(calm)* S'all right. *(staring at the Committee board)* I'd forgotten your committee ... What time does it start?

BRAND: Ten thirty. *(watch)* Two minutes.

ALEX: Well. There we are.

BRAND: Hang on, hang on. Listen. I hope the interview goes well.

ALEX: Thanks.

BRAND: Do you want the job?

ALEX: I'm not sure. In principle I wouldn't mind it ... I'll know better when I've met the people I'd be working with ...

BRAND: *(smiling)* Go easy on them, eh?

ALEX: *(smiling back)* Of course. *(she looks at the blackboard)* That's a filthy bill.

BRAND: I know.

ALEX: *(level, but quite intense)* You don't belong here, Bill.

BRAND: Listen, I've got to go in ...

ALEX: Yes.

BRAND: Stay down. We'll talk.

ALEX: I'm on a day return ...

BRAND: You can drive back with me Friday ...

'Order, Order' from inside the committee room, as Mrs Martin, the Committee Chairperson, begins the sitting.

ALEX: I don't know, I'll ring you this evening ...

BRAND: Think about it.

She leaves. He turns from the empty corridor into the small, quite crowded committee room.

The room is squarish, panelled, with portraits on walls, windows overlooking the river and the members' terrace. As in the Chamber, massed ranks of Government and Opposition members face each other across a central well. At the top of the well, the Chairperson sits behind her desk, flanked by two clerks, Parliamentary Counsel and several Home Office experts. At the bottom, 'below the bar' as it were, a scattering of press and other observers.

The Home Secretary and his team sit on the Government's front bench nearest the Chair. The Opposition shadow ministers match them.

Brand threads his way in, through the gate and up to the back row of the Government's benches, as the roll is taken. He answers while still in movement, squeezes gratefully down onto his seat, surveys the room and its occupants.

Venables rises.

VENABLES: Madame Chairman, following consultations with Right Honourable members opposite, I should like to move that during proceedings on the Further Containment of Terrorism Bill the Committee do meet on Tuesdays and Thursdays at half past ten o'clock.

MRS MARTIN: Please show ... *(general agreement)* Resolved.

A Tory – Waverley, who shares a desk-room with Brand – rises on the Tory back benches.

WAVERLEY: On a point of order, Mrs Martin. This is my first appearance in this room and it's my distinct impression that it's freezing. Is one to understand that this is yet one more Government attempt to save the nation's fuel? If it is, might I suggest members be issued with blankets, as we move into the winter ...

Some laughter from Opposition benches. Derisory calls from Labour.

MRS MARTIN: I thank the Hon and Gallant member for Coventry West, but the temperature in this room had not escaped my notice. The fact is, there's been a partial central heating failure which I am assured will be rectified by the second sitting ...

WAVERLEY: *(on feet again)* May one ask whether that assurance came from the Government or from House staff? If it was the Government, I think we should still lay in a stock of blankets, in view of their unequalled record of broken promises and assurances over the last two years ...

Tories 'hear hear'. Jeering shouts from Labour benches. A Labour back-bencher rises.

MRS MARTIN: Mr Latey.

LATEY: *(old, gnarled parliamentarian)* Might I ask the Chair for guidance, Madam? I had understood that we were gathered to discuss the Further Containment of Terrorism Bill, not the Provision of Blankets Bill ... Perhaps I'm in the wrong Committee ...

Labour laughter. Tory frontbenchers turn to frown. Waverley is already on his feet again. The Chair refuses to name him.

MRS MARTIN: *(dry as ever)* I think we've said enough about blankets ...

Some cross-chat developing, as the Chair continues ... A Labour member in the row down from Brand's turns round to Brand and others.

MEMBER: Welcome to Upper Four Remove ...

Brand's face is stone. Venables rises.

MRS MARTIN: Mr Venables.

VENABLES: *(from time to time during his speech we see Brand's stone face over his shoulder)* Before we begin to dicuss Clause One and amendments, may I draw attention to the Explanatory and Financial Memorandum that prefaces the Bill. The Bill before you is an attempt to build upon the undoubted success of the temporary and renewable Act we placed on Statute two years ago, as an immediate response to the terror that was being waged in our cities. When we introduced that first Act, we were anxious that, in pursuing law and order and the protection of citizens in Britain, we should not make inroads into the area of democratic rights and individual freedoms. On the whole, our fears were unjustified. The vast majority of our citizens continue to lead their lives, untouched by the workings of the new law. Which is as it should be ... Law is always an assistance to good living, not the inhibition of it ... While, at the same time, the police and other security agencies have undoubtedly had their hand strengthened by the new powers of arrest, detention and, where applicable, deportation the new law has afforded them. As I said in the Chamber on the Second Reading, the time has now come – many may think it long overdue, in view of the awful events of the last weeks and months – to integrate still further elements of those *temporary* laws into a permanent legal structure ... *(hear hear from both sides of the room)* I'd like to say here ... that it's particularly gratifying to have produced a Bill that has won the whole-hearted approval of all sections of the House ... It's a ... closing of the ranks in time of danger to the people ... that I have personally sought across a broader spectrum of governmental policy than simply that of security ...

Two men rise requesting the Home Secretary to give way. Venables gives way to his opposite number, Wale, Shadow Home Secretary and leader of the Tories in the Committee.

WALE: I thank the Minister for giving way. May I remind the Right Hon member for Pemberley, however, that Conservatives had a long and unbroken record of patriotism in such matters, and that the Bill before us is at least as much a result of persistent opposition pressure as of the Minister's personal initiative ...

Pick up Brand picking his way down the gangway, through the gate, past the press and out into the corridor. It's not a demonstration – members are free to do it throughout, so long as divisions are not being called. Yet we read it as stronger than stretching his legs. Sandiford alone notices him.

Brand hits the corridor. Lights a small cheroot. Paces a little. Stares at the blackboard with the Committee details.

Sandiford joins him.

SANDIFORD: All right? *(Brand turns to look at him, nod once)* I shouldn't wander far. We're looking for a division on Clause One by noon or so ...

From inside the room, the Chairperson is listing her selection of amendments and consequential amendments to be taken with them.

SANDIFORD: By the way, you forgot to bow ... *(Brand sucks on his cigar whitely)* You know ... just like the Chamber ... coming and going.

He leaves. Close shot of Brand.

PART TWO

Brand's bedroom in the Clapham house. Brand and Alex lie in bed, separate, not touching, lit only by the street lamp shining through the uncurtained window. They've just made love poorly, a coloration for the scene that follows. Brand's right hand rests on a heap of work files by the bed. Their speech is spaced, half disjointed.

ALEX: *(eventually)* I should've taken the train ... yesterday.

BRAND: No.

ALEX: That was terrible.

BRAND: Yes. I'm sorry.

ALEX: Wasn't you. It was us.

BRAND: Alright.

ALEX: You take the blame as a way of avoiding the problem.

BRAND: Which problem? What's a problem? We didn't make it. It happens. *(she says nothing. He reads the criticism)* OK, it's a problem.

They lie in silence.

BRAND: Will you take it or what?

ALEX: I don't know.

BRAND: How long have they given you?

ALEX: A week.

BRAND: But you like the team? And it's a good job?

ALEX: Ahunh.

BRAND: So?

ALEX: I'm not sure how much I want the job qua job, how much it's because you're here.

BRAND: *(eventually)* Oh.

ALEX: I've spent the last five years trying to rid myself of dependence on men. It's a hard habit to kill.

BRAND: Al ...

ALEX: I don't want to talk about it actually. I'll sort it out.

Silence again. He lifts his wristwatch from the floor, seeks light to see it in.

ALEX: *(softly)* Do *you* want to talk?

BRAND: *(flat again)* I wouldn't know where to start.

ALEX: Doesn't matter where. Start.

BRAND: I have these two voices, in here. *(hand on head)* I say two, it's never less than two, sometimes it's in the upper thirties.

ALEX: What do the two say?

BRAND: They say might, right; power, principle; pragmatism, precept; slow, quick; one day, now.

ALEX: Parliament, people; consensus, struggle?

BRAND: I've stopped feeling real. *(scraping his hair back along his skull)*

ALEX: *(finally)* What are you going to do about that?

BRAND: *(deliberately)* I don't know. *(pause)* I'm ... blocked ... there's no way I can move.

ALEX: Go on.

BRAND: *(lighting a cheroot)* The logic of being in Parliament is to struggle for power. It has to be. Yet I don't. Won't. Because I can't. Partly because I suspect that struggle, very deeply ... a glance at the shrunken giants of the Left currently behaving like elegant miniatures in the Cabinet room makes the point, I think. Partly because I think the Parliamentary struggle is illusory – a chimera, or a mystification – circular, perfectly self-contained. *(searching)* A pea, three wooden cups. Find it. The conjuror's job is to keep us guessing. And while we guess, he wins. Take his wrists in your hands, while someone else lifts the cups ... Eureka. The pea is discovered. Where it is. P is power. Yes?

ALEX: Say more.

BRAND: It's messy. Won't focus.

ALEX: I'm sorry I haven't ... helped.

BRAND: I wouldn't ask, would I. *(pause. Thinking)* So, I'm left doing these hundreds of ... little things, some ... marginally valuable, some silly, some ... ugly but 'necessary', some ... hugely idiotic. I help widows get their pensions, homeless get houses, I write to ministers about inner ring roads, I open bazaars ... I preside at speech days ... I bow to chairs.

ALEX: You do other things.

BRAND: Listen. A Labour government, kept in power by the likes of me, is currently fulfilling – yet again – its historic role as the supreme agent of international capitalism in Britain. And all the classic features of that process re-emerge: chronic large-scale unemployment, massive sustained cutbacks in public spending – you know, education, nursery schools, social welfare services, hospitals – coupled with the steady, sheltered recovery of profits in the private sector. And what do I do – what do *we* do, we men of the Left? Mmm? David Last ... lies low ... raises hell in private but makes no waves in public ... dreaming of the final push that gives him party, government and power ... Reg Starr and the Journal Group 'take soundings', 'establish priorities', trapped in the same metallic logic of social democracy, unable to do what is incontestably *right* because their definition of the Left *ends* with a Labour government ... which they must then keep in power at all costs ... And what do *I* do? God, it's pathetic. I treat parliament ... *this* ... as an arena for the exercise of moral repugnance. Like any ... Liberal. *(the word is ugly in his mouth)* That's not what politics *is*, for Christ's sake.

The phone rings by the bed, shrill in the quiet room. Brand leaves it, checking his watch. Picks it up eventually.

BRAND: Yes. Who? Oh yes ... That's all right. *(listening)* Ahunh. *(listens for a while. Interrupting finally)* Look, Jeremy, what's the *status* of this call? *(listens briefly)* I've spoken to *nobody* ... *(listening again)* Don't do me favours, all right? You want to talk about the amendment, see me tomorrow before Committee ... Fine. Yes. Goodnight.

He clouts the phone down, stubs his cheroot. He's sitting now, his back against the wall. Alex studies him, still prone. Brand turns to her.

BRAND: Committee Whip.

ALEX: What's he want?

BRAND: Wants to discuss my amendment to Clause Two of the Further Containment of Terrorism Bill.

ALEX: Isn't it ... to his taste?

BRAND: He thinks I'm hatching something.

ALEX: Are you?

BRAND: Yes. A wooden egg.

He lies down again, pulling the duvet over his shoulders.

BRAND: Hey. Sorry about the miseries. Your turn tomorrow night. *(she smiles, strokes his nose in the darkness)* Do you want to try again?

ALEX: If I have to try, I'd sooner not.

BRAND: *(after pause)* OK.

Committee Room 'B'. Clock has 10.25. Complement pretty much as before, though Venables, the Home Secretary, and Wale, his Tory shadow, are absent, and the front benches are being led by the Minister of State and the Tory No.2. The press and visitors' seats are considerably fuller than for the first sitting. Members and others still arriving. Greetings etc.

Sandiford quietly checks Labour turnout, swivelling from the front bench to do so. Brand's seat is vacant. Sandiford notes it, gets up, moves out of the room by the lower door, against a tide of members making their way in.

From the doorway, Sandiford's point of view, we see Brand seated on the other wall, dictating letters to Clare Cranston. Brand looks up, mid-sentence, sees Sandiford, returns to the sentence.

BRAND: *(dictating address, a file in his hand)* ... Nottingham ... I'll find you the post code ...

CLARE: It doesn't matter, I'll find it.

BRAND: 'Dear Ken, I'll be delighted to speak at the forthcoming Workers Control Conference in Birmingham. I'd intended coming anyway, but I'll now consider it a definite commitment. Para. I don't know whether you'll be doing a separate seminar on textiles this year, but you should in any case make contact with the Textiles Action Committee, whose headquarters are in Leighley. The man to write to is Bill Wilkinson at ... *(fiddling letters)* ... 177 Manchester Road, Leighley. He organised the Bryant's sit-in, you may remember, and would be of enormous value at a conference such as yours. Para. Please send me details of programme and venue when you have them. Fraternally ... Oh – p.s., am in touch with the National Organisers of the Right to Jobs campaign. What do you think?

CLARE: *(closing notebook)* Fine. May I take the file?

He hands it to her, stands.

BRAND: Thanks for coming so early. *(she smiles, gathering her things)* Erm ... how shall I pay you?

CLARE: How does 'regularly' sound?

Brand takes a cheque from his wallet, already made out. Hands it to her with a tiny, ironic flourish of the wrist.

CLARE: *(laughing)* Touché.

BRAND: A hit, a palpable hit. See you Tuesday.

She leaves. He watches her briefly, closes his case, moves towards the committee room door.

SANDIFORD: *(continuing a dialogue they've had half an hour earlier)* I don't see what you're after with this amendment.

BRAND: Don't you?

SANDIFORD: There's a good chance it won't even be called. My own view is, it's not in the spirit of the Bill ...

BRAND: We'll see, shall we?

SANDIFORD: You have no hope of getting it through anyway. The Tories will vote with us. You know that. *(the Chairwoman calls 'Order, Order' from inside the committee room)* The Home Secretary wants you to withdraw it.

BRAND: I can imagine. Excuse me.

He walks into the committee room. Sandiford follows him, bowing to the Chair, crosses the well to speak quietly with Henson, Minister of State, who nods, lips pushed forward importantly. Venables sits quietly studying a large file of papers. The roll is being called. Labour members look curiously at Brand as he takes his seat on the end of the back row and furthest from the Chair.

MRS MARTIN: Clause Two. Special powers and functions.

BEALEY: *(shadow number two, standing)* I beg to move Amendment no. 63, in page 4, line 15, leave out subsection 1 and insert: 1: 'The law-enforcement agencies as described in Clause One shall be empowered to detain without trial such persons as fall within the terms of the Bill for a period not exceeding *two* weeks.'

He sits down.

MRS MARTIN: With this we are to take the following amendments: No. 73, in page 6, line 25, leave out paragraph B and insert: B, 'the immediate creation of a National Fingerprint File'. No. 84, in page 4, line 15, leave out subsection 1 and insert: 1 'the law-enforcement agencies as described in Clause One be empowered to detain without trial such persons as fall within the terms of the Bill for a period not exceeding three days'.

Close shot of Brand, impassive, as Labour members turn to look at him.

Henson is on his feet.

HENSON: *(suave, alert)* On a point of order, Madam Chairman.

MRS MARTIN: Mr Henson.

HENSON: The selection of amendments is properly the business of the Chair, of course, but I would argue that amendment no. 84, to be moved by my Honourable Friend the Member for Leighley, is so obviously against the spirit of the Bill before us, and so patently, therefore, contrary to the will of Parliament, who sent the Bill to this Committee, that a prima facie case for not calling it is clearly made.

Hear hear from Tory benches. Bealey stands as Henson sits.

BEALEY: On the same point of order, Madam Chairman, it is surely clear to all honourable members present that powers of detention limited to three days are tantamount to there being no powers of detention whatsoever. I would strongly urge, Madam Chairman, that in the light of this you would reconsider your decision to allow amendment no. 84 to be called.

MRS MARTIN: *(dry, tough)* I'm grateful to the right honourable gentlemen for raising the points they raise, though as points of order they lack a certain … lineage, I think. As both right honourable gentlemen agree, it is for the Chair to decide on the selection of amendments to be discussed. I am very happy, however, to explain my thinking in calling amendment no. 84. The principal amendment to Clause 2 paragraph 1 – amendment no. 63 – contains a crucial variation of the period during which persons might be detained without trial under the then Act, the Bill asking for ten days and the amendment calling for fourteen days. In logic, any variation of the period of detention, as contained in an amendment, should be allowed to be put. I have consequently selected amendment no. 84. *(pause)* Since there is no indication that amendment no. 84's leading sponsor wishes to withdraw the amendment, it will be taken as indicated.

The government front bench turns to look at Brand. Brand stands.

BRAND: Thank you, Mrs Martin, I have no desire to withdraw the amendment.

MRS MARTIN: Mr Bealey.

BEALEY: *(standing)* Very well, Madam Chairman.

HENSON: *(standing)* Would it be possible to ask for clarification as to procedure, Madam Chairman.

MRS MARTIN: Mr Henson.

Bealey sits, complicit.

HENSON: Could the Chair say whether division will be called on all amendments or simply on the substantive amendment as selected? The Chair will recognise that the government is anxious to place an Act on the Statute Book at the earliest possible moment, in view of the terrible events of the past few months. *(a flurry of vigorous assent from the committee)* It is, I believe, not only the will of Parliament, but of the country as a whole, to see to it, as expeditiously as possible, that these men of blood be brought to justice and that this wave of terror should be halted and peace restored to our towns and cities. *(sustained cries of hear hear)*

MRS MARTIN: *(even drier)* It is practice, as the Right Honourable Gentleman possibly knows, to take divisions on principal motions only …

HENSON: *(pleased but contained)* Thank you Madam Chairman.

MRS MARTIN: *(continuing, deliberately)* However, I should point out to the Committee that where amendments are grouped, as in the case we have been discussing, if the sponsors wish to have separate divisions, they should make it known to me when we reach the appropriate point. *(close shot of Henson, nibbling his lip, then muttering to Meek, the Under-Secretary, on his right)* Mr Bealey?

Shot of Alex being admitted to the visitors' 'gallery' by uniformed House attendants.

BEALEY: *(rising yet again)* I want to stress at the outset, Madam Chairman, that there is no fundamental difference of principle between Opposition and Government on the measures here before us. Conservatives, in office or out, have always striven to follow bipartisan policies on such matters as the defence of the realm. What we seek, in this Committee, with our amendments, is an Act that will enable the forces of law and order to do the job we ask of them – to find these ... murderers, to secure them, and to bring them to justice. *(Tory hear hears)* In later sittings we will be considering the proposed arrangements for deportation and the like ... but our amendment to Clause Two is, in our view, an essential bridge to those later clauses. The temporary and renewable Prevention of Terrorism Act of 1974 operated on a period of detention following arrest not exceeding seven days. In seeking, in a new Bill here before us, to extend that period to ten days, the Government ipso facto concedes that their original surmise was inadequate. We have canvassed, I might add, far and wide throughout the land, we've spoken to magistrates and police officers, we've put the question to them: what is a realistic length of time you need to build your case against those suspected of terrorist connections. And the answer has come back loud and clear: at the very least, a fortnight. Now, I'm confident that the Government will agree that the people best placed to advise us in these matters are the people who have to do the job at the dirty end: the police themselves. I have here ... *(he holds them up)* letters from leading officers throughout the land, all asking for that longer period our amendment suggests ... I won't bother to read them out ... they've received a fair bit of newspaper and television coverage in the last weeks, and Honourable Gentlemen will doubtless be aware of them ... In effect, they are saying: 'Give us the powers, give us the time, and we'll do the job. But if you tie our hands, out of some misguided concern for the 'democratic rights' of these suspected killers, then the situation will grow worse, until the whole fabric of our democratic society is ripped into shreds and terror and anarchy stalk the land'. It would be a particularly stubborn Minister, in a particularly purblind Cabinet, who failed to heed such calls. And I beseech the Minister, in the strongest possible terms, to reconsider the terms of the Clause and to accept our amendment, because the consequences of his not doing so may well be horrible beyond description, for which he might well be held, in some measure at least, personally responsible.

Calls of 'hear hear', loud, heavy, as he sits down. A Tory back-bencher stands.

MRS MARTIN: Mr Hinchcliffe.

HINCHCLIFFE: Madam Chairman, I should like to support the amendment and the statement of my Right Honourable Friend the member for Ryton. As member for Wallsover, I have the honour to serve a constituency in which a good many Irish live and work. Good people, decent people, hardworking and god-fearing. Overwhelmingly it is their view that the 'patriots' who perpetrate these horrific outrages – these 'men of blood' as they have been named – must be hunted down and brought to justice with the full rigour of the law. But that law must be strengthened, in favour of the agencies of detection and apprehension. Let us have no more cant about 'democratic rights', it is *democracy* we seek to preserve, against these alien anarchistic and subversive elements in our midst. The Government's extension of the period of detention without trial to ten days is like everything else they've enacted over the last two years – too little and too late. I personally would have favoured an amendment giving the police specific powers of immediate re-arrest, should the situation in their view warrant it ...

LABOUR BACKBENCHER: *(interrupting)* Like South Africa, you mean?

HINCHCLIFFE: You may smear by association as much as you care to, sir, the *facts* are that our law enforcement agencies have asked for *this* amendment, and it would be a desperately foolish man who did not pay them heed.

He sits down to Tory hear hears, some Labour raspberries. Several people stand, on both sides.

MRS MARTIN: Mr Mace.

MACE: Thank you, Madam Chairman. As the only Liberal on the Committee, may I say that we do not support amendment no. 63.

Tories mutter 'shame'.

MACE: I see nothing to be ashamed of in seeking to preserve that delicate and vital balance between the essential democratic rights of our fellow citizens and the need to provide an effective legal framework within which those rights might be enjoyed. That is what political maturity means – though I would not expect too many of the honourable gentlemen on this side of the aisle to be over-familiar with the concept. *(Labour loud hear hears. Tory sneering, mocking laughter)* Liberals will oppose the amendment because it would represent, at this point in time, an unwarrantable, and indefensible inhibition of democratic rights and freedoms. We have no doubt that some such Act as this should be placed on the statute book. But its strength must be based in morality, for it is a moral idea – the idea of individual freedom within the law – that we seek to uphold.

He sits down, to Labour hear hears. Several Tories stand, Venables raises a lazy arm.

MRS MARTIN: Mr Venables.

VENABLES: *(rising)* Madam Chairman, there are many reasons why the Government will seek to have amendment no. 63 defeated, some of which have already been touched on in that excellent speech we've just heard from the Honourable Member for Leaming. *(the Liberal acknowledges with a nod and a smile)* We too have taken soundings, but of a rather more ... official kind than those of the Opposition. Members will remember the Conference of Chief Constables, and the Army Seminar, that I as Home Secretary called and presided over in the late summer. These and countless other meetings and consultations and correspondences – reaching far out into the country as a whole – have led us to the drafting of this particular Bill, and in particular this Clause. In our judgement, a period of detention without trial not exceeding ten days is the correct balance to be held between freedom and security. *(pause)* I am empowered to give this assurance, though. *(weighing words importantly)* Should, in the course of a reasonable period of time, the new law prove defective, in relation to this clause, I will not hesitate to seek to pass a new amending act to put the matter right. *(Tory backbenchers call 'too late' etc. Bealey looks well pleased, however, whispers something to his subordinate)* On amendment number ... *(he checks order paper to get it right)* ...

TORY BACKBENCHER: *(standing)* Would the Minister give way?

VENABLES: *(not budging)* I'd rather not if you don't mind, I think you've had a generous bite of the carrot ... On amendment 73 I shall dwell only briefly ... *(looking round)* ... since nobody has actually spoken to it ... and I see no sign of the honourable member sponsoring it ... the Government is opposed, at this point in time, to the setting up of a National Fingerprint File, or for that matter, if I may anticipate other amendments tabled but not yet called, the creation of special military anti-terrorist units on the model of West Germany and other sovereign states. To us, this smacks of impetuosity bordering on panic. The measures to be taken must be calm, they must be rational, they must be fair and seen to be so, and they must inconvenience the law-abiding citizens of this land as little as possible. *(brief, frosty pause)* As to amendment no. 84, of course we oppose. *(pause)* Speaking personally, I cannot believe that anyone who voted for the Bill on Second Reading can seriously be proposing it.

He looks at Brand coldly before sitting down. Other members follow the look. Brand waits a moment, then stands.

MRS MARTIN: Mr Brand.

BRAND: I beg to move Amendment no. 84. And I give notice that I would like that Amendment to move in due course to a division, Mrs Martin.

Strong cries of 'shame' and 'traitor' from Tory benches. Brand listens, impassive. Chairwoman calls order several times, her voice sharpening to quell the din. Finally:

MRS MARTIN: Noted, Mr Brand.

BRAND: *(through a mounting barrage of interruption and expostulation, and increasing requests to speak, which he steadfastly ignores)* The Home Secretary rebukes me with the charge of inconsistency, in voting *for* the Bill at Second Reading and urging this amendment here. I would ask the Minister to bear two things in mind. First, the polite fiction that a member is responsible for his vote is a piece of cant that even a minister should be able to recognise, unless the iron has bitten very deep indeed. Like all the other Labour members on this Committee, I was enjoined to vote *for* the Bill at Second Reading by a process known as a three-line whip. Now it know it's not ... customary to talk about these things in gatherings like this, but it *is* important that we try to separate *reality* from the fictions that surround it. *(Henson asks to interrupt. Brand presses on)* In spite of which organised requisitioning of all available fodder *(disquiet in Labour ranks)* fifteen members voted against. Four of them are co-sponsors of Amendment 84. And here is the second thing I would ask the Minister to note. *(looking round the Labour benches)* How many of those opposing members find themselves on this Committee here today? Not a single one. *(pause)* I cannot say I am surprised.

Several members clamour to interrupt. Cries of 'shame' and 'withdraw' from the Opposition benches. Brand remains standing. Labour benches very uncomfortable.

MRS MARTIN: Order. Order. Order, order. *(order returns slowly)* I would remind the member for Leighley that he is moving an amendment and must confine himself to it.

BRAND: Thank you, Mrs Martin. I simply felt that the Minister had imputed something that required some answer of me. But I'll continue. We heard on Tuesday, from the Home Secretary, the way in which the temporary and renewable Terrorism Act has worked. We heard the statistics for last year – eight hundred-odd arrests and detentions, over seventy deportations, something like twenty persons brought to trial, eleven found guilty of offences under the Act. Yet the terror continues, spreads, worsens. Why? Because police powers are inadequate? *(cries of 'yes, yes')* The police have greater powers now, under that Act, than at any time outside of war since the eighteenth century. *(cries of 'rot' etc)* The police have powers to arrest a man as he leaves the factory or the building site, without charge, without basic rights of habeas corpus, which that Act specifically *waives* – to lock him up for seven days and interrogate him, often without informing workmates or employers of his whereabouts, and then to present him before a tribunal for deportation, on 'evidence' that has been in no way challenged in or by a court. In my own constituency such things have happened and will continue to happen. *(cries of nonsense, rubbish, sit down etc)* And in yours. *(further inflammation)*

MRS MARTIN: The member for Leighley will confine himself to the Amendment ...

BRAND: The problem of Ireland will not be solved by passing punitive anti-democratic laws in Britain. It will be solved, by the Irish, only when a British Government, on behalf of the British people, relinquishes the imperialist role it has exercised these last three centuries and accepts that the Irish must be allowed to settle their own affairs in their own way, however painful that way may seem to be. *(catcalls, brays, shouts, quite deafening. Brand is unmoved. He looks only at the Chair)* The present Bill, with this clause, if enacted ... *(the Chairwoman subsides, at the mention of Bill and Clause, halfway to another admonition)* will cause proliferation of a process already well under way. Already, police are using existing powers to spread the net even wider. Men and women who have lived here all their lives, who have never had any connection with Republican parties, are being taken in, some of them to be eventually deported, to a country they left twenty or thirty years ago. And who are these people, what characterises them? They are Irish. *(deliberately)* And they are industrial militants, trade unionists, shop stewards, convenors, organisers, or they are political militants, members of parties, or officials, or even local councillors. *(cries of outrage, shame, slur, out, out. Chairwoman 'order, order'. The press seats are alight. Over din:)* I will not support a Bill that in any way infringes on the rights of the working class of this country – or any other – to organise itself so as to struggle more effectively. *(hubbub of communist, traitor, disgraceful, shame, withdraw, out. Brand stands on. Bealey tries to interrupt. Brand declines icily.)*

HENSON: On a point of order, Madam Chairman.

MRS MARTIN: Mr Henson. *(to room)* Order, order. *(calms down, but still dangerous)*

HENSON: *(struggling for elegance)* With respect, Madam Chairman, there seems pretty common agreement among members of the Committee that we are in the presence of a dilatory motion in abuse of the Rules of the House.

The Chairwoman has listened with half an ear, leaning sideways to consult with the Committee Counsel.

MRS MARTIN: Thank you, Mr Henson. The Chair is familiar with the powers of the Chair in these matters. *(deliberately)* I am mindful of the fact that the Honourable Member for Leighley is a relatively new member, possibly less familiar than many here with the … rules and procedures of the House. But I must ask him once again to speak more concretely and more precisely to his motion.

Loud hear hears.

BRAND: I am obliged, Mrs Martin. I shall finish in a few sentences more.

Cries of 'finish now' and half-uttered expletives.

BRAND: If I might be permitted a tiny reference back – *(the Chairwoman frowns)* simply on a point of information, Mrs Martin – *(she concedes warily)* I have collected evidence supporting these last allegations on fourteen cases of arrest and detention under the Act in my own constituency. A dossier was sent by me to the Home Secretary two months ago. Despite frequent reminders, I still await a reply. *(Venables rises to interrupt. Brand marches on)* Let me say in conclusion. The politics of terror, of bombing, is bankrupt politics. I do not oppose this Bill – or this Clause – because I support the politics of terror. But when honourable gentlemen on both sides of the aisle talk of those 'men of blood', let them consider *all* the men of blood, not just those who kill with bombs and guns. Let them reflect a moment on others in our society who might equally bear the soubriquet. Currency speculators, for example, *(uproar beginning)* who murder by telephone, who bring the pound down until a Labour government 'sees sense' and gives cast-iron guarantees that it will carry out *their* policies … which inevitably include extended wage-standstills, vicious cuts in social services, and a huge increase in the 'reservoir' of the unemployed. Old people will *die* this winter – thousands of them – of hypothermia or something else as a direct result of such telephone calls. *(frenzy on Tory side)* Let us bring the 'men of blood' to justice by all means, but let us be sure who we mean. Let us pass laws that prevent the 'men of blood' who run the multi-nationals from juggling plant from country to country in search of maximum profit, regardless of the havoc it causes to working people's lives. Let us have laws against the employers and capitalists who have engineered the largest investment strike in our history, over the last two years, as a means of clubbing a socialist government into accepting capitalist policies. *(huge uproar. Brand raises his voice above it, yet remains calm and controlled as stone)* These people kill facelessly, with pen and ink and telephone and telex machines. But they are 'men of blood' nonetheless. *(shouting over din)* I beg to move Amendment no. 84 and I call for it to be put!

Most members are now on their feet, howling anger, abuse. The Chairwoman is on her feet, banging the table and calling for order. Brand has sat down. Sees Alex over the rail. Stares impassively at her, giving no recognition. She nods, once, twice. The uproar grows, in spite of the Chairwoman's calls for order. The press are greatly amused.

Brand stands suddenly, treads a careful way towards the well and the gate, about to leave the room. A youngish, stocky Tory MP flaps his order paper in Brand's face, as a cover for striking him on the cheekbone with his ringed fist. Brand has half-anticipated the attack, rides it fairly well, chops the man with a short right to the mouth. The man falls backwards, mouth bleeding quite a lot, begins to struggle to his feet. MPs on both sides struggle to keep them apart. Over the chaos, the Chairwoman can be heard adjourning the session.

Brand shakes himself free, walks carefully from the room. Press, Alex with them, follow him, rather more quickly, but not a cliché stampede, chatting with some animation as they go.

Tory MPs continue the uproar. Some Labour backbenchers jeer at their frothing, begin to argue. Henson and Bealey stand in front of the Chairwoman's desk, talking closely with her.

PART THREE

Clapham house. Brand's bedroom. That night, towards 11.30. Brand sits on the floor, speaking on the phone. He's in blue bathrobe.

BRAND: Yeah, I know that, Alf ... *(listening patiently)* Yes, I'll take your word for it it was on News at Ten ... the man hit me, I hit him back ... I don't even know his name ... *(listening)* I don't know, to be honest. I might have to go before the Speaker ... Did you read what I said? ... Well, read it, get The Guardian tomorrow ... And then tell Frank a constituency party vote of total confidence wouldn't go amiss. *(he turns. Alex has come into the room, in white bathrobe, rubbing her wet hair. He covers the mouthpiece)* Jowett. *(she nods, crosses to mirror, begins to comb her hair, watching him in reflection)* Anyway, never mind that, Alf, tell me more about these attacks on the Pakistanis ... *(listens attentively)* ... Christ, houses! What, burnt! Who's behind it, the Front? *(listens again)* What're the police doing? ... Ahunh. Ahunh. Look, I'll be up and see for myself tomorrow, I want the details, OK? ... Don't *worry,* Alf. You'll get ulcers ... Cheers.

Puts phone down. Alex takes off her robe, slips naked into the bed.

ALEX: Hairdryer still bust, I take it?

BRAND: Yeah. I'll get it fixed.

Pause.

ALEX: What time are we likely to be leaving tomorrow?

BRAND: *(sitting on bed, in profile to her)* Four, maybe. Around four.

ALEX: I've fixed up a meeting for the Women's Press. That'll be OK.

Another silence. He's drained suddenly.

ALEX: What's going to happen? *(he shakes his head numbly)* Will they kick you out? Suspend you?

BRAND: I don't know.

ALEX: *(the only hint of congratulation permitted)* You took ... flak, as they say.

BRAND: I went there to say it. I said it.

Silence

ALEX: What was that about Pakistanis? On the phone?

BRAND: There've been half a dozen beatings-up down Hillmoor. And two houses have been set on fire ... petrol bombs.

ALEX: Christ. Is anybody hurt?

BRAND: None seriously, Jowett says.

ALEX: Who is it?

BRAND: What do you think?

ALEX: Bastards. What are the police doing?

BRAND: *(without coloration)* The police are conducting enquiries.

She sucks her lips, disturbed.

BRAND: *(slowly, simply)* It'll get worse.

He removes his robe, slides into the bed beside her. She watches him for a moment, then carefully turns out the light by a switch above her.

They lie in darkness, breathing quietly. A cat yowls somewhere. A jumbo gropes its way towards Heathrow. He turns to face her. She faces him. They lie on their sides, eyeing each other. He pushes forward, to kiss her on the lips. She meets him. They kiss, short swirling pecks, growing fleshier, deeper, tongues working.

The phone rings. They continue to make love. It rings maybe twelve, fourteen times, then stops. Alex moves across him, kisses his nipples, positions herself along his body. He makes to enter her from below.

The phone rings again. He has tensed. She rolls slowly from him. He reaches for the phone.

BRAND: Hello. Oh, hello. *(he looks quickly at Alex, as though in warning)* What? No, no, it's been blown up out of all proportion … *(he listens, sharpens, tenses)* When? … No … start at the beginning, eh? When was the first one? Ahunh. A man? *(listens)* Go on. Ahunh. Ahunh. Have you told anyone? *(listens again)* All right, but ring the police anyway … They'll probably send somebody round to keep watch. Then er … *(he's reaching into his open attaché case, urgent, precise, finds an address book, fiddles pages)* then ring a man called Bill Wilkinson at Leighley 58132 … that's it. Tell him who you are and what's happening, he might be able to help in some way … keep the door locked, keep the kids away from the windows … I'll come up now … Three, three and a half hours … No, I'd rather, Mim … Yes. Yes. Take care you. Bye.

He puts phone down. Alex puts on light.

ALEX: Miriam?

BRAND: *(socks on, underpants)* Yes. I'm sorry, we've got to go up north.

ALEX: What is it, Bill?

BRAND: Probably nothing. Some joker's making threatening phone calls … started this evening …

ALEX: Who are they threatening?

BRAND: Me. The kids …

ALEX: With what?

BRAND: *(tight-lipped, zipping trousers)* You name it.

Night. *Brand, alone, turns from main road into steepish crescent leading to the estate. On the bend at the top, his headlamps sweep across two men standing, hands in donkey jacket pockets, on the edge of the pavement. He drives past them, stops, slowly reverses. They approach the car. Brand rolls down his window. Wilkinson and Patel (the Asian from episode 3) loom up out of the dark.*

WILKINSON: Your wife phoned. There's a copper there. Won't let us near.

BRAND: Hop in.

They clamber into the back of the car. Brand continues to round the bend.

BRAND: *(through driving mirror)* Thanks.

WILKINSON: They've paid a visit.

Brand's eyes shift into cracks, through the mirror. Fear splashes his face. He turns into the square, his headlights flood the front of the house. The white wooden laths that screen the front of the house are badly charred, over an area of maybe six or seven feet. Glass has showered onto the unraised paving area and through into the front patio.

PATEL: *(voice over, from back of car)* That's the fascists. No question.

Brand switches the engine off, moves quickly towards the house, Wilkinson and the Asian follow.

Brand is met at the door, by a police sergeant. Miriam stands behind him.

BRAND: I'm Brand. These are friends.

MIRIAM: It's all right, sergeant. It's my husband.

BRAND: Are you all right?

MIRIAM: *(calm)* We're fine. The children are sleeping on the sofa.

He puts his arms around her, hugs her for one moment, then leads her into the living room. The kids sleep, one at each end, pale under the blanket.

MIRIAM: I'll make some tea ...

SERGEANT: It's all right, ma'am. You stay here. I'll make the tea.

He leaves for the kitchen.

BRAND: These are the friends I asked you to ring. *(Miriam smiles palely)* Bill Wilkinson, Mr Patel.

MIRIAM: *(sitting down by fire)* How do you do. I'm sorry you're missing your sleep.

WILKINSON: That's all right.

BRAND: What happened?

MIRIAM: I rang the police. They said they'd come at once. About ten minutes later I heard a car coming into the square. I pulled the curtain, to see if it was them. The car pulled up, there were two men in it, one threw something at the house – a petrol bomb, the sergeant says – it hit the fence and exploded into flames. The car drove off ... the police found it abandoned by Hillmoor Park. They think it was stolen. George Peters and the Bates helped me dowse the fire.

Brand looks at the two men.

BRAND: Can we talk tomorrow sometime ...? *(checking watch)* Today.

WILKINSON: Sure. Give us a ring. I'm still out of work. *(they rise)*

BRAND: Stay for a cup of tea.

WILKINSON: No, we'll get off, now you're back.

Brand crosses to the door, holds it open as they say goodbye to Miriam.

BRAND: Thanks.

WILKINSON: No need. Take care.

They leave. Brand turns back into the room. Stares at Miriam, at the children, face hardening, bittering.

MIRIAM: *(standing)* Who'd want to do it, Bill?

BRAND: Yeah.

She walks to the door.

MIRIAM: I'll help the sergeant with the tea.

She leaves, closing living room door behind her. Brand crosses to the sofa, studies the sleeping kids, kneels quietly, to see them more closely, leans forward to kiss each in turn on the lips. Jane wrinkles her face – shy even in sleep – wipes it with the back of her hand.

Brand crouches, holding the children under his spread arms. Phone rings. Brand crosses to the table, picks up receiver, very tense. Miriam and the policeman (carrying tray) come in from the kitchen.

BRAND: Yes? *(listens, relaxes visibly)* Hello, Alf ... No, it's under control, I think ... How'd you find out? Ahunh. No, just burnt the fence a little. She's fine. They're fine. No. I'll be there in the morning ... Early surgery ... Yes. Thanks for ringing. Sorry you were bothered. Yes. Goodnight.

He stares at the receiver. Miriam watches him as she pours tea by the fire. He puts the phone down, draws the front curtain aside, stares out at the charred fence.

- end -

Episode 8

Rabbles

was broadcast on Monday 26th July 1976

The cast was as follows:

Bill Brand   Jack Shepherd

Alex Ferguson   Cherie Lunghi

Irene   Eileen Kennally

Alf Jowett   Allan Surtees

Hughie Marsden   James Garbutt

Albert Stead   John Barrett

Young Socialist   Ian Liston

Policeman   Ken Kitson

Postman   Mike Henson

David Last   Alan Badel

Call boy   Duncan Faber

Eddie Brand   Dave Hill

Barman   Barrie Fletcher

Designers: David Ferris, Harry Clark

Executive Producer: Stella Richman

Producer: Stuart Burge

Director: Stuart Burge

PART ONE

Leighley Labour Party Central Committee Rooms. Alex stands in the doorway, sheltering from thin November drizzle. Mid-evening. Down the street a police car draws up, two men inside. She watches the lights go off on the car. The men sit on.

She stands a moment longer, tugs the collar of her short, belted plum coat around her ears, the wool hat pert on her head. To her left, a row of lit windows running the length of the main hall. Sounds of a biggish meeting build: some rancour, expostulation, a hint of Brand trying to reason. To her right, the lit window of Jowett's office, the inner sills piled high with old literature and other debris. The thin pick of a typewriter, slowish, sporadic, from within, and light music from Radio Manchester.

Alex puts down her small grip, checks the watch on her left wrist. The drizzle thickens. She stares up into it, her face pale in the lamplight, clicks her teeth together, a bare hint of annoyance there. Turns through the door into the ill-lit hallway beyond.

She stands a moment, re-orientating. The din from the meeting plainer, though the double doors are closed. Some jeering, the occasional expletive. She approaches Jowett's office, opposite, its door ajar. Pushes it quietly open, locates Irene, (44, blonded, immaculately dowdy) at the typewriter addressing envelopes. Vera Lynn puts the finishing touches to 'The White Cliffs of Dover' on the radio.

ALEX: *(finally)* Excuse me.

Irene doesn't hear her, goes on typing.

ALEX: *(louder)* Excuse me.

Irene turns quickly, eyes wide, startled, embarrassed at once at her startlement.

IRENE: Yes, what can I do for you?

ALEX: Do you know when they're likely to be through? *(she motions with her head towards the main hall)*

IRENE: *(what a bizarre question)* Eeh, I've no idea. *(pause)* I could say ten but it'd be a guess. *(pause)* They'll not be later, not with the pubs shutting at half past. What was it you wanted? *(she eyes Alex's bag carefully)*

ALEX: I'm meeting somebody. Do you mind if I wait in here?

IRENE: You're Mildred Braithwaite's girl aren't you? *(reaching for it)* Erm ... Cath, Cathleen.

ALEX: No. No, I'm not.

IRENE: Aren't you? Goodness me, you're the spitting image.

A flat-capped policeman, wet from the walk from the car, enters.

POLICEMAN: Any idea what time they're likely to finish in there?

IRENE: I've told you, I don't know. Pop your head round and ask. For goodness sake, I just work here.

Violent outburst of invective from across the passage. We hear, quite distinctly above the hubbub, Brand's 'That isn't what I said, comrades, that isn't what I said, that isn't what I said ... that isn't ...' Somebody clouts the table repeatedly with an ashtray. Some straggling order ensues.

POLICEMAN: *(rebuke in his mild mimicry of her tone)* OK.

He withdraws gently, pulling door to behind him, cutting noise a good deal. Irene lights a cigarette, offers one to Alex, who refuses with a smile.

IRENE: Have a seat. If you can find one. *(Alex is making towards Jowett's battered swivel)* Not that one. He'd throw a fit.

Alex removes some box-folders from a roundback kitchen chair, sits by the dinted gas fire to dry the soles of her boots and the wet bottoms of her trouser suit.

Irene types another address, errs, sees it, rips it from the carriage.

IRENE: Sh ...ugar!

She continues to mutter to herself, as she threads another envelope in the machine. Alex glances at the contents of Jowett's desk top. A dozen or so newspapers are spread out on it, red biro ringing the articles, stories and pictures that chart the aftermath of Brand's activities – stance and punch-up – on the Prevention of Terrorism committee. She stands to scan them more fully. We take a flavour of the treatment: hit, eventually, as her hands shift upper layers, a Mirror's 'Manchester Massacres' and Express's 'Manchester's Night of Terror'. Both carry the same huge pic of a class hotel bar blown out by a bomb, a policeman clearing debris on the pavement, a body half covered by a blanket in the gutter. Shouting again from the meeting hall, aggressive, sustained, drowns the music from Irene's transistor radio.

IRENE: *(half-turning in her chair)* Oh, they want blood tonight. Definitely.

ALEX: Any idea whose?

IRENE: *(frowning slightly)* You're not ... press ... by any chance, are you?

ALEX: *(evenly)* No I'm not. I'm just waiting for someone in there.

She returns to the paper. Brand's pic stares up at her from a 'Sun'. Irene passes her with a bunch of envelopes, which she stacks in a tray on Jowett's desk.

IRENE: His. *(returning to her desk)* He's been trouble since we got him. The wild man of Leighley they call him. I've nothing against him personally, mind. He's always very charming and considerate with me. He just doesn't seem able to stay out of bother. You must have read about him. *(she gestures at the papers. Another outburst from the hall)* And as you can hear, he's never likely to make the Guinness Book of Records for Pouring Oil on Troubled Waters, is he? Listen to it. I can remember when General Management Committee monthly meetings meant twelve old fellers, two women, a pat on the head for each of 'em from the MP, a vote of thanks from the floor and home by nine at the latest. *(she checks the wall clock: 9.50)* There was never any of this with Mr Horton.

She clicks a few keys, searching for her place on the list of addresses.

IRENE: Mr Horton was a man you could respect. *(pause)* Look up to. *(pause)* It's respect wins votes in these parts. *(more shouting, if anything louder and angrier)* Listen to it.

She clicks the radio off, disgusted now, her world threatened. The noise subsides, under Hilton's makeshift gavel.

ALEX: *(carefully)* I understood he was pretty popular in the constituency ...

Irene swivels again in her chair, as a surge of noise from the meeting beats against the door.

IRENE: Oh he is. The Tories love him. By the time we've weathered this lot they could put up a dead horse against him and still win comfortably.

Jowett cracks through the door, tight, hard. Rather pale.

JOWETT: Right, that's that lot. *(he sees Alex, flicks through to Irene)* All finished?

IRENE: *(tough)* Aye. As much as I'm doing. I'll do the rest tomorrow. I've a home to go to. *(she stands, covers the machine in battered leather)*

JOWETT: Take a few with you.

IRENE: Some hopes. Ha. *(Jowett glances at Alex, who picks up her grip carefully)* She's waiting for someone. In there.

Jowett says nothing, moves to his desk. Alex threads a careful way towards the door area. Irene puts on her heavy wool coat and scarf, and rather silly rainhat.

JOWETT: *(fiddling in a card index)* How's your mother?

IRENE: All right.

JOWETT: Good. See you tomorrow.

Sounds of hall door flapping, animated chat, as people leave.

IRENE: Right. *(to Alex)* Good night.

Alex smiles goodnight. Wavers. Irene leaves.

JOWETT: I should wait out there, love, if I were you. You'll miss him else.

Alex looks at him a moment. Jowett looks up at her eventually. Nothing suggests he knows her.

JOWETT: I take it it's a feller. Yeah?

Brand in fast, eyes wide with anger. Sees Alex at once. The anger holds, burning the ground she occupies between him and its principal object. She holds the ground, very cool, unyielding. Jowett watches, long enough to read what he needs, walks towards the door area.

JOWETT: *(soft, unobtrusive)* Excuse me.

He walks between them, leaves, with managed ease, missing rather than avoiding Brand's steamy eyes. Brand advances into the room, closes his attaché case on a table by the window.

ALEX: *(eventually)* Sorry. I didn't mean to be here. *(pause)* I came in out of the rain.

BRAND: *(his back to her)* S'OK.

ALEX: *(waiting for more; it doesn't come)* Are we going or what?

BRAND: Yeah. *(turning, car keys in hand)* I've got to see one or two people. *(she takes the keys, holds them in her hand, palm up, open, weighing them)* I'll be five minutes.

She nods, terse yet yielding, closes her hand.

ALEX: OK. *(pause)* Take it *easy*, eh?

He nods, smileless. She leaves. Brand takes down his parka from a peg, puts it on. Sits down eventually in the chair Alex had by the fire, fighting the anger. Loosens his red wool tie, but stays alert, coiled, no sense of sprawl there.

The policeman pushes his head round the door, wet again.

POLICEMAN: Ah, you're there, sir. All finished have we? *(Brand nods)* Now, if you could just give me some idea of your whereabouts tomorrow, I'll pass it on to the station.

BRAND: I'll be home most of the day.

POLICEMAN: *(polite)* Which home would that be, sir?

BRAND: Foundry Street. I'll ring in if I'm moving about.

POLICEMAN: Grand. We'll just see you back, sir.

BRAND: Fine. I'll be a few minutes.

Hilton and Marsden pile up behind the policeman.

POLICEMAN: Right you are, sir.

He smiles pleasantly at the arrivals, leaves. Marsden and Hilton, coated for off, crowd the tiny office. Brand stares at the gas fire. Hilton sits just inside the doorway, Marsden takes Irene's chair. Hilton fiddles with his diary; Marsden eyes Brand with stiff-faced circumspection through steepled fingers, as the building quietens about them.

Jowett says goodnight to stragglers, the front doors flap. He enters, winks grimly at Marsden, crosses to his chair, draws it away from Brand, sits to face him. Brand stares on at the fire.

JOWETT: *(finally, quietly)* You wanted a word, I think.

Brand looks at him, hard, level, cold.

BRAND: Yes, I did. *(he takes the others in deliberately, returns to Jowett)* I want to know what that ... *(he blows, the anger biting his chest)* ... *fucking* pantomime was *about*.

Jowett lights a cigarette carefully, hands the spent match into a basket beneath the desk.

BRAND: I was thrown to the wolves, I want to know why. I want to know why not one of you had *anything* to say in my defence. I want to know why copies of my speech in the Committee weren't circularised to every member of the GMC as I requested. And I'm asking *you (he includes them all)* because you know the answers. *(pause)* So what's it all about? Mmm?

HILTON: Look, Bill ...

MARSDEN: Hang on a bit, Frank. All right? *(to Brand)* You stepped out of line ...

BRAND: Look, don't give me ...

MARSDEN: Do you want to hear this or not? *(Brand holds, on an edge of something ugly)* You're a marvel at raising questions, you're bloody hopeless at listening to the answers. *(on his fingers)* One: you took a deliberate, calculated, anti-Party line on terrorism ... Let me *finish*, for Christ's sake. Two: you got involved in a punch-up in the House. Three: throughout the last week, with people dead and maimed down the road, you manage to alienate all sections of the party and most of the voters in this constituency by persisting with this futile – and to my mind callous – defence of what you said in London. Four: you sat there tonight like some ... little intellectual tin god ... asserting your right to be right when everybody else in that room knew you'd blundered. *(pause)* I've read your speech. It stinks.

Long silence.

BRAND: So you set me up.

HILTON: *(firm, not harsh)* Nobody set you up, Bill. This is a democratic Party. Delegates to the General Management Committee are entitled to ask their Member to give an account of his actions. *(pause)* They *are* the Party, Bill. You'd do well not to forget it.

Brand looks at Jowett, who scribbles something in a ledger, apparently unconcerned; at Marsden, who stubs his cigarette in a saucer. He cares for Hilton: can't blast him as he would like.

BRAND: *(to Jowett principally)* Anyone else?

Jowett keeps himself busy, looking at no one, cool, detached.

BRAND: *(taking a copy of the Committee minutes from his pocket)* All right. Let me say something. When the prorogation is over and we all troop back to the House, that Bill will come back to the Chamber for its third reading. *(pause)* I shall vote against it. I shall vote against it, comrades, not as a little intellectual tin god, but as a socialist committed to the defence of democratic freedoms. Because, comrades, when these are ... threatened, it's the working class, and especially its more militant leaders, who feel the pinch first. As I tried to show in my speech. *(to Marsden specifically)* Which you have read. *(to all again)* Bombing, shooting, urban terror – these are bankrupt politics, crude, ugly, indiscriminate, pointless. *(tapping the paper in his hand)* This I also said. But the answer, comrades, does not lie in turning the country into a paramilitary state, with laws that can trap a militant worker called O'Reilly more easily than a terrorist called O'Flynn. *(to Marsden specifically)* Now if you don't agree with all this, Hughie, that's fine, that's your privilege. But don't pull the bloody roof down on me because I do.

He sniffs heavily, the anger dragging at his chest again.

HILTON: *(asserting himself over Marsden's imminent retort)* Lad, nobody's questioning your integrity. It's the way you set *about* things. On an issue like this, I mean my God we've a right to be consulted. All right, it you're voting with the Group, that's one thing. On your own, and often, that's just maverick, that's just death. What are we supposed to do, eh? This Party isn't made up of people with university educations and teaching certificates. A vote against a bill that tries to do something about senseless, terrible murders is a vote for the people who commit them ... *(hand out, to quell Brand)* I know, I know. But that's not the point. It's what our people *think* you said – what the TV and the radio and the papers made you appear to be saying – that's at issue. This movement's ... *(he looks for his meaning: finds it simply)* ... our people don't believe in violence, Bill. It goes very deep with them. You've touched a nerve and you mustn't be surprised when people shout.

Another lengthy silence. Brand slumps a fraction, or perhaps merely retreats into his own process, unable to cope with Hilton's firm but gentle correction. Marsden checks his watch, stands.

MARSDEN: I'm away. *(to Jowett)* I think we'd better talk this out, though, before he goes back down.

Jowett nods, non-committal. Marsden's on his way when Jowett remembers.

JOWETT: *(moving to join him)* Oh, I've got those leaflets in the boot, Hughie, you may as well have them now ...

MARSDEN: Fine.

They leave together. Brand sits up, looks down at his boots. Hilton begins buttoning his coat.

BRAND: *(smallish voice)* I can't do this job with one eye over my shoulder to see what the *people* are gonna say, Frank.

HILTON: I know that, Bill. But you can't do it despising them either.

Brand looks at him for a moment, searching for meanings.

HILTON: You've gotta stay in touch. You can't run *all* the time. Sometimes you've gotta walk. So that people can see where you're going. *(Brand looks down at his boots again, head on hands)* Do you know what Gorki said when he arrived at some godforsaken spot in outer Russia somewhere to lecture the peasants on socialism? He said 'Is this the rabble on which we are to build a revolution?' Well, the answer's yes, Mr Gorki, yes, Mr Brand. Because without them there *is* no revolution. We're all you've got, comrade.

Brand looks at him again, sucks his upper lip, says nothing. Hilton stands.

HILTON: I'll get one in at the club before they close. Will you join me?

BRAND: No, I won't, thanks.

HILTON: Think about it.

Brand will not yield; yet his resistance is mannerly, respectful.

HILTON: Give my regards to Mrs Brand and the kiddies, won't you.

BRAND: Yeah, sure. Thanks, Frank.

HILTON: Good night now. *(pause, at door)* Comrade.

Brand smiles wanly, throws his head back as Hilton leaves, rubs his eyes with the heels of his hands. Sounds of chat in hallway, as the returning Jowett says goodnight.

A young man pops his head round the door: long hair, thin face.

MAN: Don't let the bastards grind you down, comrade. The Young Socialists are with you. Cheers. *(Brand nods. The man withdraws)*

Brand stands, picks up his attaché case, holds it loosely, waits. Jowett in, crosses to desk, begins piling papers and files into raddled briefcase, picks up phone, dials, waits, still selecting items for briefcase. Brand has swivelled to watch him.

JOWETT: *(phone)* Hello, Ethel. I'll be back about eleven, all right? *(listens)* Yeah, that'll do, I had a sandwich earlier. No, you get off to bed then. Right.

He puts the phone down, clicks his case shut, looks at Brand.

JOWETT: Anything you wanna say to me?

BRAND: *(rather frozen, dead)* It'll wait.

JOWETT: *(neutrally, without animus)* You asked why copies of your speech weren't distributed. *(pause)* There weren't enough. I'd 've needed fifty thousand of 'em to make good the damage it's done, and twenty WEA tutors working full time for a year. The problem isn't what the General Management Committee think, it's what that lot out there are thinking. You're out in space, comrade. And you'd better come down.

BRAND: *(slow, quiet, thinking it through, almost innocent)* What makes you think you know them ... better than me?

JOWETT: *(as slow, as quiet)* Because if I didn't, I'd be out of a job, friend. How long since you called in at the Labour Club?

BRAND: I don't know. A month, six weeks.

JOWETT: Try it tonight. See if you get the smiles and pats and handshakes you're used to.

BRAND: *(turning)* I've gotta go.

JOWETT: Where'll you be?

BRAND: *(turning back)* I'm going away for a few days. *(he takes a card out, with an address written on it, hands it to Jowett, who studies it)*

JOWETT: What's here?

BRAND: Nothing.

JOWETT: What about the family?

BRAND: They're in Scotland. Kids' half term. The police know.

JOWETT: *(card up)* Do they know about this?

BRAND: No. I'll ring in tomorrow and tell them.

JOWETT: Be sure you do, eh. There's nutters loose.

BRAND: Yeah. *(he turns again, reaches the door)*

JOWETT: Hey. *(Brand turns in doorway)* In case you think we treated you badly, I spent the whole of last week with Frank and Hughie getting rid of a motion to withdraw your nomination.

Brand blinks, the only visible indication of the deep surprise he's experiencing.

JOWETT: Go well, comrade.

Brand leaves. Jowett sniffs, fiddles for his car keys, finds them, studies the card again, frowning, the keys jangling in his free hand.

Brand's car, *Brand driving, no one in passenger seat. Gradually we become aware of Alex, curled, dozing, on the back seat. The radio is on low (Luxembourg); it's just after midnight. Brand checks his watch, turns the radio up slightly, as the news ident comes up.*

NEWSREADER: Two minutes past midnight, Fran Flynn here with tomorrow's news headlines, brought to you from the resources of the Daily Mirror, Britain's biggest selling paper. *(beepbeepbeepbeep)* Britain's Prime Minister cancels all engagements for the next four days, due to what his doctors call 'a mild virus infection and an associated chill'. *(beepbeepbeepbeep)* British Chancellor Maurice Kearsley in New York crisis talks with officials of International Monetary Fund and US Treasury, as pound slides. *(beepbeepbeepbeep)* Fifty thousand women crowd Trafalgar Square in pro-abortion lobby. *(beepbeepbeepbeep)* England thrashed four goals to one in vital cup tie. The news behind the headlines in just a moment. But first ... *(the Daily Mirror plug begins. Brand turns it down, as Alex sits up behind him)*

ALEX: What did it say?

BRAND: The usual. Watson's down with flu or something. The pound's down and out. England took a pasting in Prague.

ALEX: Did it mention the march?

BRAND: Fifty thousand, it said.

ALEX: Crap. Eighty at least.

BRAND: How was it?

ALEX: Good.

BRAND: Ahunh.

Alex looks at the place she's had her head. Picks up a stack of unopened letters and packages.

ALEX: Damn. I've crushed this lot …

Brand turns to look at them.

BRAND: Doesn't matter. Go on down, get some sleep, you must be whacked.

ALEX: *(propping herself on back of front passenger seat)* I'm fine.

He drives on. Clicks radio off. She pushes a strand of hair behind his ear, then one on the other side.

ALEX: You've got odd ears.

BRAND: Peculiar, or non-matching?

ALEX: *(thinking)* Both.

BRAND: *(serious)* I'll put in for a new pair.

Alex returns to the letters.

ALEX: Do you want me to read some of these for you?

BRAND: *(no)* Uhunh.

ALEX: *(nose wrinkling)* Can you smell something?

BRAND: *(sniffing)* Like what?

Alex sniffs again.

ALEX: I don't know. *(pause)* Like dog-shit.

Night. Living room, agricultural labourer's cottage. *Low, beamed, plastered, hardly treated. Brand crouches over the fire he's just built, ensuring the wood will hold. Over the fireplace, a flow-mastered poster note: 'Vladimir Ilyitch and Nadezhda, Enjoy your exile, love, Pru and the Galloping Caries'. Alex is in the small connected kitchen, plain, primitive, unpacking food etc. The cottage is calor-gas lit. Their tone, when they talk, is flat, familiar, habituated, unexcited.*

ALEX: *(calling through)* How's it going?

BRAND: It's going.

ALEX: My watch has stopped.

BRAND: Half twelve.

ALEX: Do you want tea?

BRAND: Ta.

He gets up, still in his parka, studies the room, the old makeshift furniture, the Sony portable tv, the upright ancient piano, the seat beneath the window, their bags by it. Crosses to the long table, where he's thrown his attaché case and mail, checks the aged phone works. Begins to open a letter.

Alex places tea bags in the mugs, pours water on them, removes bags, milks the tea.

ALEX: *(carefully, casual)* I think I should take the job in London. *(no answer. She sugars the teas, carries them into the room, approaches the table)* I said I think I should take ... *(she sees his face. Follows his stare to the open package on the table)* What is it?

BRAND: It's a ... turd.

He picks up the crumpled newspaper that holds it with tips of fingers, straightens it out. It's a copy of the Leighley Recorder, with a pic of Brand and a lead story. His face is disfigured by the excrement. Alex stares at it, fairly stunned, a little horrified.

BRAND: *(after long pause)* Folk art?

Alex puts his mug down by his hand, crosses to the fire with hers, sipping, working things out. The air between them is flat, hopeless.

PART TWO

Morning. The grounds of the cottage. Tough, knolly grass, some ragged pear trees, a light covering of early hoar. Alex chops brushwood and dead branches for the fire. She wears her woollen hat, short wellington boots, a rough, worn denim jacket over a thickish sweater. She swings the axe purposefully, and well; adds pieces to the pile she's making against a stone wall.

Kitchen and living room. Brand watches her through the tiny kitchen window, as he prepares breakfast. He takes a warm plate from the oven, puts bacon, grilled tomatoes and fried eggs onto it, returns it to the oven. Lifts the coffee percolator lid, checking. Wipes his hands on a pot towel, carries bread, butter into the living room, lays them on the half-laid table, sees her again through the window. Goes out to join her down the garden.

The grounds. Alex chops on, as Brand arrives. He studies the pile.

BRAND: Waiting for coffee.

Alex stops fractionally, a fractional acknowledgement, hits the log again, splitting it.

BRAND: *(eyeing pile)* It's just till Wednesday, you know. Just a few fires. We're not rebuilding a fleet.

She straightens up, stares at him levelly. Neither smiles. She stands the axe up carefully against the wall, begins to stack the split pieces with the rest.

Brand looks around for a moment, wanting her to speak. She's wrapped in process. He climbs onto the wall. Walks a few paces, until he's immediately above her.

BRAND: *(to the fields around them; American – Groucho, even)* Good morning, countrymen. Correction, countrypersons, we're all persons now. A man walks into the surgery, he says Doc, I feel terrible. Doc examines him, he says you've got two weeks to live. The man says, Doc I can't pay. The doc says I'll give you another six months. *(he squats on his haunches, to bring his head closer to hers as she stoops over the wood)* Old Polish story. Two peasants walking down the road. First peasant says, Chaim, see de frog, I bet you five kopeks I can swallow him. The peasant picks up the frog and takes it, one gulp. The money changes hands. They walk a hundred yards, the second one says, Ladislaw, see de frog, I bet you five kopeks I can swallow him. Ok says the first man. Picks up the frog, gone. The first one hands him back the five kopeks. Another hundred yards and the second one says to the first one: Chaim … *(long pause. Alex looks up at him, straightening, the wood in her arms)* Why did we eat the frogs? *(they stare at each other for a while, neither moving. Brand looks away to say the next bit)* Al, we didn't screw because I couldn't. I couldn't because I didn't want to. I didn't want to because I knew I wouldn't be able to. *(he looks down at her again)* Why are we here?

ALEX: *(finally)* I wanted to talk.

She walks down the grass to the house. He remains squatting on the wall, his hands together between his thighs, watching her.

BRAND: *(calling suddenly)* So talk.

She stops, half turns.

ALEX: Who to?

She goes on. Brand, absorbing it, watching her.

Slow fade.

Living room – *about two in the morning. Alex sleeps on her stomach in front of the dozing fire. Her head rests on a fat hardback, open. A biro still loosely nestles in her right hand, on the floor, a pad with notes on it a foot or so away, by an ashtray from Portugal bearing the words: 'Avante! Proletarios de todos os paises: Uni-vos.'*

Brand in from stairs, in old sweatshirt and underpants. He carries an oil lamp. Locates her at once. Approaches. Stoops. Sets the lamp down. Reaches for a cushion. Tries, very gently, to replace the book. She wakes very suddenly, half turns, sees him, a flick of fear on her face, on the way to recognition. She shivers.

BRAND: Hang on. *(he reaches his parka from a chair, puts it over her. She's awake. He kneels by her)*

ALEX: What time is it?

BRAND: After two.

ALEX: Is it?

Brand nods. She rubs her eyes a little. Brand examines the book, marking the place with fingers. Alex sits up a little, gathering herself.

BRAND: What are you working on?

We get the sense, from Alex, it's the first interested question he's asked about her since they left Leighley. She deliberates whether to mark it; resists the pettiness, though only just.

ALEX: I'm working up some talks about sex for fourteen year olds.

BRAND: What, in schools?

ALEX: Ahunh.

BRAND: Terrific. *(he opens at the held page, shifts the lamp so that he can see it. Reading as he speaks)* That in London or up here?

ALEX: London.

BRAND: Ahunh. *(still reading)* When do you go?

ALEX: *(lighting cheroot, handing it to him, lighting another)* End of the month. Maybe sooner. I have to fix somewhere to stay.

Pause. Brand reaches forward, to knock some life into the fire, turns, in half-lotus, book still open on his lap, to face her. She leans against an old armchair, the parka round her shoulders.

BRAND: *(interrogative statement)* My place no good then. *(she shakes her head, a tight, minimal movement. He looks down at the book, not seeing it, searching for words, images)* All I can think of, wheeling and wheeling round an empty head, is ships in the night. *(pause)* It's so sodding ... pedestrian.

She crushes her cheroot in the Portuguese ashtray, not looking at him.

BRAND: You stay, I go. You go, I come back. *(pause)* Sounds like bloody Itma.

ALEX: Sounds like what?

BRAND: Doesn't matter.

ALEX: You ... come back?

He looks down at the book again.

BRAND: 'Epididimis'

ALEX: On, sitting on, the testicles.

BRAND: I don't think it's possible any more. Down there, up here. You heard it Friday night.

ALEX: They can't get rid of you ...

BRAND: *(casual)* I could resign the seat.

She stares at him, eyes widening slightly.

ALEX: And do what?

BRAND: I dunno. *(pause)* A year ago I thought this was the place to push. I think I was wrong. If I'm gonna be a social worker, I might as well do social work. I just … can't find the politics. They aren't there. Maybe they never were.

ALEX: So what do you do? Go back to I.S?

BRAND: No. They're not there either.

She gets up, crosses to the window seat, looks out at the moonwhite garden. He watches her, book still in hands.

BRAND: *(softly)* What are you telling me, Al?

She doesn't answer, doesn't turn.

BRAND: *(as soft)* Al?

ALEX: How are your children?

BRAND: *(deep breath, patient)* They're fine.

ALEX: Are they?

BRAND: *(standing slowly, but not approaching, watching her back carefully)* We came fifty miles to talk. So talk.

She turns at last, looks at him evenly.

ALEX: *(direct)* I think I've moved on.

He weighs it, not moving.

ALEX: I think *you've* moved on.

BRAND: Stick with you.

ALEX: *(genuinely; not playing a game or for time)* I don't know how else to put it.

BRAND: *(slowly)* How about Goodbye?

ALEX: Is that what you'd like to hear?

BRAND: *(tersening slightly)* I just want to hear what you have to say.

ALEX: *(rather loud)* Christ, I haven't got anything to say!

BRAND: *(relentless)* You just want out.

ALEX: Yes! *(almost at once)* No! *(beat or two)* Yes.

BRAND: *(slowly)* The Ayes have it … I think.

ALEX: *(small voice)* No.

Brand sniffs, heartbeat slowing again.

BRAND: Do you want some cocoa? *(she looks down at her feet)* I'll make some cocoa. *(he's moving as she speaks)*

ALEX: I slept with someone else last week.

He stops.

ALEX: *(looking at him directly through the gloom)* No, that's not true. I've been sleeping with people since the summer.

BRAND: *(remote)* Oh?

ALEX: *(grave)* And that's not the point either. *(pause)* You make me feel married. I'm not a partner. Or a comrade. I'm a surrogate wife. *(pause)* I don't want the dependence, Bill. In me, I mean. *(simple, unemphatic)* I've started wanting a child, rather a lot. I don't think it makes any sort of sense, I just have the feeling.

BRAND: *(metallic, distinct, distant)* A child? *My* child?

ALEX: *A* child. *(pause)* It's not important. It's just symptomatic.

BRAND: And sleeping?

ALEX: In a way. I don't want to feel ... spoken for ... when I fancy another feller. I want to be free to make my own choices.

BRAND: And who are they? Anyone I know ...

ALEX: Christ, you're not listening ...

BRAND: *(lifting slightly)* I'm asking a question ...

ALEX: I'm trying to tell you something ...

BRAND: Then answer the bloody question ...

ALEX: It doesn't *matter!* Jesus Christ. It doesn't matter *who,* it doesn't matter *that,* it matters only that it makes a *difference.*

He sits down in an armchair. They face each other across the dim room, eerie in thin moonlight.

ALEX: *(almost shouting)* You make me feel guilty. And that's bloody childish. I don't want to feel guilty. I just want to feel ... honest. That's all anyone can ask of anyone else: honesty.

BRAND: *(slow)* Well, baby, you've got it in spades.

She looks up at him.

ALEX: Thanks a lot. *(pause. She can barely see him in the big chair, only feet away)* Why do you ... stagger on with this anyway?

BRAND: I don't know. Maybe it's something to do with loving you.

ALEX: Horseshit.

BRAND: Horseshit.

ALEX: You stagger on because you've always staggered on. You need guilt and dependence and deceit and mendacities like some people need heroin. You couldn't ... quit ... if you were chained to a puma. You couldn't cut free from anything, it's not in your training. You're like a ... snowball. You pick up everything in your path and take it with you. *(pause)* Well. *(long pause)* I'm getting off. *(pause)* While I still care for you. *(pause)* I'll catch a train back tomorrow.

He gets up, reaches for the lamp, face obscured in shadow. Picks up lamp and book – still opened at her page – carries them both to the table, puts them down.

BRAND: OK.

She stands, crosses to the table, joins him in the lamplight.

ALEX: Do you want the cocoa now?

BRAND: *(reading from the page)* 'Epididimis. Within this small lump of tissue, which does indeed sit on the testicle, the sperm mature, they become motile, and they wait, for this is the main storehouse. Both fertility and motility of sperm can last for several weeks, but if they are not ejaculated during this lifetime ... the sperm eventually degenerate ...' No. I want something else.

ALEX: *(her hand on his, very lightly; carefully)* As friends?

BRAND: *(finally)* Yes.

ALEX: *(softly)* Pass, friend.

He draws her to him, kisses her softly on the mouth. The kiss holds, strengthens. Fade slowly.

Cottage living room. Morning. *Phone ringing. Sound of car drawing up outside. Brand in, Sunday Times, Observer, Sunday Mirror in his hand. Crosses to answer phone. He's fairly tense; sombre.*

BRAND: *(to phone)* Yeah. *(unenthusiastic)* Hello, Alf. No, I've been out, I had to take someone to the station ... *(listening)* Who? *(listening)* What does he want? ... Well, didn't you ask? ... All right, so what did you tell him? ... Oh great, so he knows where I am ... Look, I don't give two stuffs for David bloody Last, I don't want to see him and I can't imagine why he wants to see me. *(listening)* Well, it's done now. Thanks very much ... I dunno, Wednesday I think, I'm not sure. *(pause. deliberately)* I'm considering the position. *(listens to Jowett's ferreting. Very casual)* I thought I might resign the seat. *(listens for a long time)* Yeah, well that's tough, Alf, but some things in life just are, aren't they ... *(listening again)* You too, sunshine.

He replaces the receiver, Jowett's voice still rattling at the other end.

He walks around the room a moment. Sees the book, still open on the table – Alex has forgotten it. The phone rings again. He picks it up, listens without speaking, then clicks the rest down until he cuts the line and lays the receiver down on the table. He looks down at the book, closes it. We see 'The Body. Anthony Smith'.

Slow fade.

Living room, early afternoon. 'Weekend World' on the tv. We start tight on the screen – Peter Jay explaining the economic plight of the nation and the financial crisis around the corner. Charts, tables, indices of non-growth, non-investment.

This is fairly lengthy, though we leave the screen early, to track and scan the room, arriving at the table, where a mug of cold tea stands on 'The Body', and the Sundays have been stretched out for reading. We take in several front page items, including the PM's doctors ordering him to bed and senior ministers (Venables, Kearsley, Last) undertaking his speaking engagements up and down the country. At the bottom of the front page of The Observer, Nora Beloff speculates on the possibility of a spring general election. Finally, the phone, receiver restored. It rings.

The shot moves round to bring Brand into view through the window. He sits on the wall, one leg up. Turns to look in the direction of the phone. No move. The phone stops ringing. Brand remains motionless. It begins to ring again. He turns his head back towards the Derbyshire hills, totally withdrawn.

Slow fade.

Cottage grounds. *Early morning. A postman, weasely, about 45, cycles to the cottage, props bike against wall, knocks on door, a telegram in his hand. He knocks again, louder, studying the name on the yellow envelope.*

Brand opens the door, hair wet from washing, half-shaved, cream down the left side of his face.

POSTMAN: *(thickish Liverpool accent)* Lovely morning.

BRAND: Yeah.

POSTMAN: Mr Brand, is it?

BRAND: That's right.

POSTMAN: Telegram.

BRAND: Thanks.

POSTMAN: Sign there, if you would. *(Brand signs against the door)* On holiday, are you?

BRAND: Yeah.

POSTMAN: Where you from, Manchester?

BRAND: *(handing him the pad)* Mmm. Leighley.

POSTMAN: *(not releasing telegram)* How do you like it round here then?

BRAND: *(hand on drying shaving cream)* It's very nice.

POSTMAN: I wouldn't live anywhere else. I worked in Derby for a bit, but I couldn't settle. What's money, eh? *(Brand says nothing)* So I came back.

Brand holds his hand out for the telegram. The postman hands it over, with some reluctance.

POSTMAN: *(dwelling)* Money's not everything, is it?

BRAND: Absolutely. *(the man smiles, hope there yet)* You know, they talk just like you in Liverpool.

POSTMAN: *(no smile now)* Oh aye?

Brand waits till the postman begins his withdrawal, then closes the door and turns into the kitchen, where his shaving gear is laid out before the mirror. He places the telegram on a ledge beneath the mirror, re-creams his left face, begins to scrape, his attention wandering insistently down to the telegram, which he sees bears a Manchester frank. He finishes shaving by an act of will, proving something important perhaps. Picks it up; carries it into the main room, where a good fire burns. Stands in front of it. Begins to open the envelope, some tension there now. Reads. We watch his face. He frowns a little, maybe with disappointment. Reads it again. Lays it down by the phone. Walks away towards the kitchen, cleans his gear, washing the tiny bowl clean. Returns – drawn – to the table again. Picks up the phone. Dials the operator. Checks a number in his address book.

BRAND: Yeah. I'd like to place a person-to-person call to Mr David Last …

We drift down to the telegram. It reads 'NOW IS THE TIME ETC STOP AM AT MIDLAND MANCHESTER STOP LAST'

PART THREE

A name card on a Granada TV studio dressing room door: 'Rt. Hon. David Last'. A fist knocks, twice. Call of 'Come in'.

Brand enters the cramped, narrow room: bunk, basin, primitive wardrobe. Last sits at the dressing table, a heap of papers in front of him, checking some figures. His reflection glints oddly from the bright, bulb-fringed mirror. He wears an old faded dark check jacket, patched at sleeves, brown shirt, red wool tie, dark trousers, heavily wrinkled behind the knees, and thick grey wool socks. His shoes are in the washbasin.

It's a moment before he looks up, the habit of concentration not easily broken.

LAST: *(standing at once)* Bill. Come in. You made it then.

BRAND: Yeah. Renshaw told me you were here. *(he looks around the room enquiringly)* This the best they can do?

LAST: *(looking around with him: a genuine innocence)* Is it not good?

BRAND: I bet Len Fairclough's is better. *(Last frowns his question 'Who?' but doesn't press it.)* What's the show?

LAST: Have a seat.

Brand sits in a chair along the long dressing table, his back to the wardrobe.

LAST: *(continuing)* It's some Granada Spectacular …

BRAND: 'Whither Britain'?

LAST: 'A Year from Now' I think it's called. *(beat)* It's on late tonight.

Last resumes his seat, notices his feet. Silence.

LAST: I was here anyway, filling in for the PM. *(Brand nods he knew)* I thought I might have seen you at the Free Trade Hall Meeting Saturday.

BRAND: I was somewhere else.

It hangs. No give, some wariness developing.

LAST: Mmm. *(long pause)* Still. You're here now.

BRAND: *(smiling)* You have a certain ... gnomic way with telegrams.

LAST: You didn't appear to be answering the phone.

BRAND: I had some thinking to do.

LAST: *(casual but keen)* Did you do it?

BRAND: Some of it.

Pause.

LAST: I hear you're in trouble with your local party.

BRAND: Yeah.

LAST: Word has it you've alienated the left.

BRAND: It would seem so.

LAST: Over the Terrorism Bill. *(Brand nods tersely)* Are you surprised?

BRAND: *(finally)* No, I don't suppose so. I'm angry. They could have told me I was about to have my legs torn off; they chose not to. *(pause)* We call each other comrade.

LAST: Did *you* tell them what you were going to do on that Committee?

BRAND: No. I felt I had to play it close, if I were going to make an impact ...

LAST: *(interrogative statement)* And expected your ... comrades ... to go along with you, whatever you decided.

BRAND: Not at all. I expected them to raise their ... objections ... in a principled way, not try to 'teach me a lesson' with a display of toy democracy.

LAST: Toy?

BRAND: Pulling strings doesn't suddenly become a democratic process because it's the left pulling them.

Pause again. Last looks at his several mounds of papers.

LAST: *(still casual)* Your agent mentioned you were talking of resigning the seat.

BRAND: *(slowly)* It ... crossed my mind.

LAST: All the way across?

BRAND: Not quite.

Last looks at him levelly for a moment.

LAST: I saw a copy of your speech. Read pretty well. *(pause)* It had one ... fairly
substantial flaw in it. Not of logic, not of morality. *(pause)* It just did rather read
like the views of a man recently arrived from Venus. *(Brand stays collected) Any*
law can be abused, used against its meaning. But that's no argument against *law* ...

BRAND: *(suddenly)* David, you know and I know that the present Home Secretary
is almost pathologically anti-trade union, a true man of the right, a 'middle
ground' man. He was one of the first in the Party to support statutory incomes
policy, he has spoken continuously over the last ten years and more about 'the
growing menace of trade union power', he has repeatedly rejected appeals of
trade unionists serving savage gaol sentences under laws of *conspiracy* devised
in other times for totally other purposes, most of them ugly. Now unless and
until we have a socialist as Home Secretary – and he'll be the first in history –
I will continue to do what I can to protect working class militants from the
likes of Venables.

LAST: *(weighing it: finally)* And the bombers?

Brand slows down.

BRAND: We're reaping the harvest of three hundred years of British imperialism.
Maybe we need a socialist Foreign Secretary too.

*Knock at door. Last pads over, opens it. Some low chat, clinking. Brand scans the
papers on Last's table, sees several Secret and Highly Confidential brown envelopes.*

*Last returns with a bottle of scotch and a glass on a tray. Smiles at Brand: places
it on the table between them. Crosses to sink for another glass, sees his shoes,
slips them on, returns with the glass.*

LAST: *(pouring)* We seem to need ... quite a few things. *(handing Brand his glass,
filling his own)* Cheers. *(he sits down, taking a large but controlled slug)*

*Brand holds his glass up at arm's length along the dressing table: drinks a little,
suddenly circumspect.*

LAST: If the dialectic teaches us anything, it's that everything we think, do, every
moment, every act contains its contradiction. There's nothing *wholly* anything.
Everything's a movement towards, a movement away from all at the same
time. *(long pause. Quoting, not at random but with some ease)* ' One step
forward, two steps back'? 'We shall not enter the kingdom of socialism with
white gloves on a polished floor'? And the unascribed locus classicus: 'You
cannot make an omelette without breaking some eggs'?

BRAND: I'm not against cracking a few eggs. I just want to know what happened
to the bloody omelette. *(grinning suddenly)* A quote for all seasons, eh?

LAST: *(putting more scotch away)* Futile to resist a natural ... eclecticism.

They laugh quietly together, some slow warmth growing now.

BRAND: *(draining his glass; takes telegram from pocket, spreads it out on table)* I still don't get the telegram, but thanks for the chat.

LAST: Wait.

He gets up, crosses to the basin, begins to douse his face in cold water, towels it, searching for facial tone in the mirror.

LAST: *(purposeful now: businesslike)* Phil Renshaw leaves for the DHSS Thursday, when we re-convene. As yet I haven't replaced him. I'm still prepared to put you up, in spite of everything.

BRAND: *(jolted a little, not expecting this)* Wouldn't that be ... rather foolish?

LAST: *(straightening his hair)* Possibly.

BRAND: Watson wouldn't buy it.

LAST: *(checking watch, straightening tie)* Probably not.

BRAND: *(watching him)* Why ... me?

LAST: *(facing him, ready)* I'll give you the short answer. You're bright, you're tough, you're principled. And fairly soon I think I'm going to need you.

BRAND: Need me?

Last checks his watch again, screws the cap on the scotch bottle.

LAST: *(undramatic, very detached)* This is confidential, all right? *(he drags agreement from Brand before continuing)* By the middle of this week we could be without a leader. On Tuesday, Arthur Watson's due to go into the London Clinic for an operation on his prostate. His doctors have already told him it's unlikely he'll be able to continue, whatever the outcome of the operation. Which suggests it's fairly grave. *(pause. There's a knock at the door)* Who is it?

VOICE: *(calling)* The director wonders if you'd care to make your way to make-up, sir.

LAST: Fine. Just coming.

He turns to the table, begins stacking his papers into the attaché case, locks it carefully, pockets the key.

LAST: *(talking through it)* If he goes ... when he goes ... I'll be seeking nomination in the ballot for the new leader. And for a while ... *(he smiles, dazzling but brief, at Brand)* ... we can openly share the same enemies.

BRAND: *(still trying to cope)* Jesus Christ. Can you win?

LAST: *(dry again)* It depends. On who stands for the right. On who stands down on the left. On who the centre will stand for. *(long pause)* The dealing has already begun. *(pause)* Will you take a hand?

BRAND: *(standing)* Jokers wild then, are they?

LAST: *(tough)* I'm asking you.

BRAND: How long have I got?

LAST: Twenty four hours. I'll need your answer by tomorrow evening at the latest.

BRAND: OK. You'll have it.

LAST: Good.

They exchange a long, searching look, each oddly puzzled by the other's interest.

LAST: I haven't time for the long answer to why you ... Except ... *(long pause, thinking)* ... there are thousands like you, tens of thousands maybe, just beyond us, just beyond the rim, full of energy and commitment and principle. And this party needs you. *(pause again)* And if I can't take you, them, *with* me, where the hell do I think I'm going anyway?

Brand smiles.

BRAND: I'll call you.

Last nods. Brand leaves. Last looks around the room, sees his telegram on the dressing table where Brand has laid it. Brand has written, in good italic, underneath the message: 'Now is the time for all good parties to come to the aid of the man.'

Night. Car. *Brand driving through Manchester.*

Night. Lit sign: Clayton Conservative Club. Brand stands in small darkish entrance, seeking orientation. Sees card players in a room to his right, goes in. The room is small, empty save for four men, three old and comfortable, and Eddie. The room has a small, rather shut-off back bar, a portrait of the Queen over it, and a small portable tv, sound right down, on it.

BARMAN: Can I help you?

BRAND: *(gesturing)* No, I just want a word with my brother.

The barman retires. Brand watches Eddie as he deliberates which card to place in the crib. They begin their play. Reach the count. Some laughter, groans, as the hands unfold. The pegs are put on. Hands reach under the table for beers, the game won and lost. Eddie laughs, taking the 10p from an opponent, draws deeply on his pint, sees Brand over the top of his glass, is surprised.

EDDIE: *(getting up)* No, I'll quit while I'm ahead. 10p's 10p. *(he takes the groans and 'miserable devil's with considerable aplomb, carries his pint to the bar, to join Brand.)* Hya, kid. What you doing here?

BRAND: *(ironic)* I was going to ask you the same question.

EDDIE: Best snooker table in East Manchester.

BRAND: It'd have to be ...

EDDIE: *(not at ease, though smiling)* What'll you have then? Good to see you.

BRAND: I'll get 'em.

EDDIE: You take a pew. You have to be a member. Two pints, Percy, when you've a minute.

Percy leaves his Sporting Chronicle, draws two pints.

PERCY: Ha bloody ha. 44p.

EDDIE: *(counting it out exactly)* Keep the change.

He carries the beers to a table in the corner, where Brand has already sat down.

EDDIE: *(sitting down opposite him, on a stool)* Are you on holiday or someat?

BRAND: Yeah, sort of. We start a new session Thursday.

EDDIE: Nice. I'm on holiday sort of too. Round here it's called unemployment. Million and a half of us ... I heard it on the news ... About the others, I mean, I knew about me.

BRAND: Owt I can do?

EDDIE: Not unless you're handing out jobs.

The feeling is tacky, under the surface ease of exchange, something aggressive at work in Eddie. Silence. They drink their beer. Brand lights a cheroot, hands the pack to Eddie.

EDDIE: No, I won't thanks. Trying to knock it.

BRAND: How's the family coping?

EDDIE: All right. Jane's waiting on at Dargai Street, brings in a bob or two. I mind t'kids. Give us a job any time. Phew. She took a night off tonight, just to let us out of the house.

BRAND: *(reaching into back trouser pocket for his money)* Listen ... here's a tenner ... *(Eddie pushes his hand away)* Take it ...

EDDIE: No no.

BRAND: Don't be daft, go on.

EDDIE: No, I don't want it...

BRAND: Take it.

EDDIE: No. Put it away. I don't want it.

Brand repockets the money. The tension is there but unacknowledged. Eddie drinks again. Brand watches him.

BRAND: I saw ma earlier.

EDDIE: I must call round. I haven't seen her for a week or two.

BRAND: She seemed OK.

EDDIE: D'you meet her bloke?

BRAND: What?

EDDIE: Aye, she's got a bloke. Some feller from Mather & Platts.

They laugh a little, not quite easy, the tension not properly dispersing.

EDDIE: How're you doing then?

BRAND: So so.

EDDIE: Been in the papers again haven't you. Saw it in the Express. *(Brand nods, crushing his cheroot in the glass ashtray)* Ma told us about you and Miriam. Tough.

BRAND: Yeah.

EDDIE: When's the divorce?

BRAND: Next month I think. Before Christmas.

EDDIE: Is there someone else?

BRAND: No. *(pause)* Just didn't work out, you know. *(Eddie nods, without understanding)*

EDDIE: *(suddenly)* How long's this lot going on for, Bill?

Brand looks at him, knows precisely what this means.

BRAND: I dunno, Eddie.

EDDIE: Well what are you doing about it?

BRAND: What I can. Which isn't much.

EDDIE: Well somebody'd better do someat and bloody quick. There's fellers round here bin outa work two years. They won't be voting Labour next time, I can tell you. And neither will I.

BRAND: *(carefully)* Will the Tories be better?

EDDIE: I don't know. They can't be much bloody worse, can they? I've voted Labour since I got the vote and every time it's the same bloody story, socialist paradise before, freeze and squeeze after, and the unions sit back and let it happen. At least when the Conservatives are in we can have a bloody go.

BRAND: *(helpless, finding himself saying it)* Look, they're tough times, Ed ...

EDDIE: Too bloody right they are! You must think we're bloody puddled. Rolls Royce make two thousand cars a week – I saw it on t'news the other night – who's buying *them* buggers then? Somebody's *minting* it. There's tough and tough, int there! I mean if that sodding Kearsley or whatever his name is, that Chancellor feller ...

BRAND: Kearsley.

EDDIE: Aye. Well if he's supposed to be a friend of the working man, he'll never need an enemy, by God he won't. Down there guzzling at the Lord Mayor's Dinner, white tie, tails, I saw him on the box, he wants to come up here, see how *we're* getting on ...

BRAND: *(suddenly, spitting a little, quite harsh)* So why don't you do something about it?

EDDIE: What you talking about? What can I bloody well do?

BRAND: You can bloody well struggle, like the rest of us. Join the Right to Work campaign. Don't just sit there and moan.

EDDIE: *(contempt more open now)* What're you talking about? Struggle! Lot of good that'll do. When it comes down to it, we're just bloody rabble.

BRAND: Well, as long as you feel that way, you'll always be in it up to your neck. *(pause)* Listen. *(very deliberate)* We'll do nothing unless we're made. And the only power *we* have is what *you* give us.

EDDIE: It's words, Bill. It's just words.

BRAND: *(insistent, earnest)* Eddie, it isn't just words.

EDDIE: *(peremptory)* Well, leave it anyway. I don't want to fall out with you.

They sit there tightly for a moment, not looking at each other.

EDDIE: Fancy another? *(Brand shakes his head)* I'd better get off then. She'll bollock us else.

BRAND: I'll drop you off.

EDDIE: *(thinking)* Yeah. OK. *(standing)* I'll just have a pee.

He walks out into the entrance. Brand gets up, fastening his coat, carries the dead glasses to the bar, where Percy is covering the pumps. The three oldish men carry their glasses, crib board and cards over to the bar, leave with goodnights. Brand focuses on the tv: there's a big studio discussion in progress. Suddenly Last comes up in close-up, talking with intensity, fervour, irony, despite the lack of sound. Brand watches, fascinated.

EDDIE: *(over)* Fit?

BRAND: *(turning)* Fit.

They leave. Close on Last, sweeping his lank hair from his eyes, his frame packed with energy.

- *end* -

Episode 9

Anybody's

was broadcast on Monday 2nd August 1976

The cast was as follows:

Bill Brand   Jack Shepherd

David Last   Alan Badel

Frear   Geoffrey Palmer

Marjorie   Stephanie Cole

Maddocks   Peter Copley

Winnie Scoular   Rosemary Martin

McNab   James Giles

Tom Mapson   Richard Butler

Reg Starr   Douglas Campbell

Corbishley   John Nightingale

Preen   Richard Beale

Blackwell   Hugh Martin

Edna James   Doreen Mantle

Armfield   Martin Fiske

Brent   John Woodnutt

Bullock   Anthony Woodruff

Kearsley   Godfrey Quigley

Wilks   John McKelvey

Venables   Peter Howell

Sandiford   William Hoyland

Designers: David Ferris, Harry Clark

Executive Producer: Stella Richman

Producer: Stuart Burge

Director: Roland Joffé

PART ONE

Brand sits in the back of a taxi, approaching the Palace of Westminster, reading an Evening Standard.

House of Commons. Ministerial ante-room. Brand stands by a small elegant table, studying a selection of the day's national and provincial newspapers laid out across it. His bags stand by an elegant chair. The large double doors behind him open, Last and Frear appear. Frear walks away down a corridor.

LAST: Bill.

BRAND: David.

LAST: Come in. You're early, your note said eleven.

BRAND: *(following him into his office, carrying his bags)* I caught an early train. Came straight here.

Last's ministerial office, leaded uncurtained windows, solid furniture, deep carpet. Doors connect it with other rooms. The desk is strewn with books, notepads, jottings, Hansards and other current work.

Last takes his seat at the desk. Brand sits in a comfortable chair to face him.

LAST: *(eventually)* Yes or no?

BRAND: When do I start?

Last blinks a little, smiles, chuckles.

LAST: I expected no.

BRAND: It started out no. I re-read your Tom Mann on the train. A man who hates capitalism as much as you do can't be all bad.

Last picks up the phone, waits.

LAST: Marjorie, I'll need another half hour or so. No, just take names, I'll call back. But I'm still in to Jim Wilks. Thanks. Oh, and … coffee. Thanks. *(he replaces the phone)* How about now?

BRAND: Fine.

Pause.

LAST: Why? *(Brand sniffs, not committing)* Just the book?

BRAND: *(slowly)* No. *(pause)* You're all we have.

Long silence.

LAST: Yes?

BRAND: *(deliberately, demanding agreement)* And it's now, isn't it?

LAST: Yes.

Another pause.

BRAND: So it's you.

LAST: Yes.

Marjorie in on a knock, carrying tray with coffee pot, cups. She places the poured cups by the two men, leaves the tray on the end of the desk between them.

MARJORIE: Mr Dalton's secretary rang. He thinks the Liaison Committee might meet late afternoon, depending on what the Palace does ... *(Last nods, reaching for a sandwich)* Mr Wilks is back in the House, Mr Dalton spoke with him ten minutes ago ...

LAST: Give him fifteen minutes, if he doesn't call, call him. OK?

Marjorie goes back into her room. Last fiddles among his papers, finds a piece of paper, hands it across the desk to Brand.

LAST: That's a probable timetable of events. *(he picks up his own copy)* I'll take you through it. Noon: Watson's resignation posted. 2 pm: Cabinet meets. Parliament re-opens. Wilks asks the Speaker to suspend the sitting pending a statement. 3 pm: Queen sends for Wilks and asks him to continue pro tem as Acting Prime Minister, question mark question mark. *(he looks across at Brand, smiles briefly)* 4 pm: Cabinet reconvenes, passes crisis measures including heavy Bank of England intervention on behalf of desperately plunging pound and suspension of dealing on Stock Exchange until Monday at earliest. 5 pm: Parliamentary Liaison Committee meets to draw up timetable for the leadership contest. *(long pause. He looks at Brand again)* We agree that balloting should begin the following morning at 11 am and shall be exhaustive. Tellers to be elected etc. Nominations by 10 am. *(he pauses)*

BRAND: *(surprised, as it sinks in)* Friday? Is that possible?

LAST: *(crisp, quiet, a hint of gun-metal)* If it's thought ... desirable. Certainly. 5.30. Meeting of Parliamentary Labour party to ratify PLC's recommendations. Early evening to early morning: factions. *(pause)* The Journal Group picks its candidate. Friday. 11.30 am. Results of first ballot. 11.30 to 1.30. Canvassing for second ballot ... *(slowly)* ... etc. etc. etc. *(looks at Brand)* It's all possible. If it happens like that, I have a chance. There are no precedents. ... Without precedents, anything can happen.

BRAND: You've been busy.

LAST: As have others.

BRAND: Shall I give you my reading?

LAST: Please do.

BRAND: *(studying the sheet a moment)* Kearsley's unstoppable.

LAST: Kearsley's in America.

BRAND: He'll be back by tomorrow.

LAST: Tomorrow might be too late.

BRAND: *(firming up)* All right. Runners. Certain: Kearsley, Venables. Possibles, you, Copple, Brent, erm … Morahan, I suppose … even Wilks. Morahan's too old, OK, leave him out, and Wilks has no base, him too. It's you if the left will have you against the rest. All two hundred and plenty of 'em. The winner will be the man who can hold the centre. That's not Venables. That's not you.

The phone rings. Last picks it up.

LAST: Is *he* calling *me*? … Fine. Put him through, would you Marjorie … *(to Brand)* Wilks. *(to phone)* Jim, it's David. How's Arthur? Ahunh. Ahunh. *(listening)* Dear dear. I'll try and see him tomorrow. Ahunh. It's still noon, is it, the er … Ahunh. … No, I think that's right, Jim. Absolutely. *(listens)* Just one or two thoughts, Jim. I've spoken with Rawlings and one or two others, and it does seem constitutionally there is just the faintest chance she'll be advised to appoint you pro tem and then at least explore the possibility of sending for the Leader of the Opposition. *(listening briefly)* Yes, well I say the faintest chance, we *are* the biggest party but we no longer command a majority over all other parties in the House, if the Tories decide not to pair with Arthur … Anyway, I offer it for what it's worth. Only it does point up, very sharply, I think, the need for expedition. I hope we can both argue this at the Liaison Committee tomorrow afternoon. *(checking his probable timetable sheet)* Around five, I hope. Quite seriously, I don't think the weekend is necessarily going to be ours to play around with. *(pause, as he listens. He looks at Brand)* One more thing, Jim. I've thought hard about this, I want you to hear me out. It don't believe there *is* a natural successor to Arthur, largely because Arthur spent much of the time making sure there wouldn't *be* one. Now, this is a crisis, for the country, for the government, and for the party. I believe it will be better for all three if violent upheavals can be avoided. I think the proper thing would be for you to be regarded as leader, preferably unopposed. I'll go further: if others will do likewise, I'll withdraw my nomination. *(long pause. He listens, staring at Brand's wide, gleamy eyes. Finally)* Precisely. Jim, I'm glad we talked. You have my numbers. *(checking watch)* Oh, hours. Please do.

He puts phone down, takes a sip of coffee, pours some more.

LAST: What then if we split the centre?

BRAND: By withdrawing?

LAST: My withdrawal is contingent upon theirs. Neither would dream of withdrawing. By which time – with luck – Wilks will have convinced himself and his supporters that it's in the national interest that he should stand anyway. *(pause)* But he'll split the centre and maybe let me in.

BRAND: Don't Wilks's votes return to Kearsley when he's eliminated?

LAST: *(quiet, almost detached)* Do they? How can we possibly know? None of us has ever played this game before. We don't even know the rules. We could wait for ever and never get a better opening … *(he looks questioningly at Brand)*

BRAND: One thing.

LAST: Yes?

BRAND: Isn't it … the only way for Venables too? If the revisionists get their hands on this party, that'll be the end of this party, right?

LAST: Probably.

BRAND: Isn't Kearsley preferable then?

LAST: Yes. But I'm preferable to both. Yes? *(Brand nods, tersening under Last's unrelenting acuity)* But if I'm to win, it's Venables I have to beat. Only if the party finds itself with *that* choice on Friday afternoon do I have a chance. See it?

BRAND: Yes. I see it. I don't like it.

LAST: Do you think I do? *(pause)* I think it has to be done. We'd have two years in which to earn the 80s for socialism. Kearsley would have two years to convince the electorate that the management of capitalist economies is better left to capitalists. *(plain; neutral; objective)* Not a very difficult task for Kearsley, I should have thought. All my political life I've worked to shift this party to the left. In two days we have a chance to move it further than it's moved in fifty years or more. Is that a chance we have the right to pass up? *(Brand doesn't answer)* I'm asking you.

BRAND: Well I can't answer. I'll have to think about it.

Some friction in the air, neither man yielding.

The phone buzzer goes on Last's desk. He picks up the phone, listens. Looks at watch.

LAST: … No, I'll see him, Marjorie. I'll let him in. *(puts phone down. Stands)* The Chief Whip. *(passing Brand on way to door; indicating tray of drinks on top of a cupboard)* Help yourself.

He opens the double doors, greets Cedric Maddocks with managed warmth, brings him into the room.

MADDOCKS: … just passing, I thought I'd drop in. *(he sees Brand)*

LAST: One for Cedric, Bill. Scotch. And a drop of water. Come and sit down, Cedric *(showing him to Brand's chair)* Brand's accepted my offer of PPS. So … you're among friends.

He smiles candidly at Maddocks as he resumes his seat behind the desk. Maddocks nods several times, absorbing the information. Brand hands him his drink.

MADDOCKS: Thank you.

BRAND: Will you have one?

LAST: Thank you, no.

Slight pause. Brand registers the refusal, then draws a chair round to face the desk; sits; sips his drink quietly.

MADDOCKS: Well. Here we are.

LAST: Yes. It's bad.

MADDOCKS: Could bring us down, David.

LAST: Ahunh.

MADDOCKS: Ted Bullock's asked me to take some ... unofficial soundings. There's a feeling we're going to have to move fairly and quickly and he won't be down until tomorrow. It'll save the PLP a little time if we have some idea who's likely to be standing. *(he waits for Last to speak. Last lights a cigarette, finds an ashtray)* I had a brief word with Kearsley in New York. *(checking fob watch)* He'll be en route now. He will definitely stand. *(pause; carefully)* He's very strongly opposed to the idea of an early ballot. Doesn't see the urgency. Doesn't see it at all.

LAST: He's a long way away.

MADDOCKS: Venables will stand. Come what may. He's in favour of Friday. For the ballot. *(a pause for Last again; again nothing)* Morahan's sleeping on it. That's to say, he's busy seeing what his support is. A year ago he was the man. But a year in politics, eh ...? *(he grins surprisingly. Last nods, a small smile)* Which leaves you, David.

LAST: *(hands forward on desk, clasped)* I favour an early ballot. Friday. By tomorrow afternoon the water could be up to our chins. We swim or go under.

MADDOCKS: So you'll stand.

LAST: Not necessarily.

MADDOCKS: How do you mean?

LAST: I think a leadership struggle now, with the country in the state it is, will tear the guts out of us. I think there's someone we could return unopposed this Friday.

MADDOCKS: *(brows up a fraction)* Who's that?

LAST: Jim Wilks.

Pause. Maddocks drains his glass, sets it on the desk.

MADDOCKS: Jim Wilks. Mmm. *(pause)* And you'd what, withdraw, give him the field?

LAST: He's honest, middle-of-the-road, well-respected, experienced and dull. He has a following. He's what we need. If Venables and Kearsley can't agree then they must be made to explain why not.

MADDOCKS: You don't seriously imagine they will agree, do you?

LAST: Why not, if I'm prepared to? They're both young men, their turn will come. We're talking about the life of a government and of a party, Cedric. In that perspective, personal ambition's a miserable thing, is it not?

Maddocks checks his watch again, begins buttoning his jacket.

MADDOCKS: Can I talk ... about this?

LAST: By all means.

Maddocks rises.

MADDOCKS: Good. Well, I'll toddle off.

LAST: *(rising)* I've already spoken to Wilks.

MADDOCKS: Ah. Good.

LAST: He's thinking it over.

MADDOCKS: I'll have a word with him. What's the word on Arthur?

LAST: Not good. Jim's just come from the Clinic, he'll tell you.

MADDOCKS: Ahunh. *(he sees Brand suddenly, holds a big flapper out to him. Brand takes it)* Congratulations young man. *(leaving, then turning back, chuckling a little)* Though whether your boss here will have a job by Monday is something else entirely, eh? *(he pokes his deaf-aid, turns to Last)* Or any of us, come to think of it.

He leaves. Brand finds himself closing the double doors after him; frowns a little. Marjorie in from her office, with several letters. Last signs them efficiently, scanning each in turn.

MARJORIE: Mr Frear rang. He left a number.

LAST: Thank you.

She picks up the letters, leaves. Brand stands by the drinks, glass in hand.

LAST: Frear's Venables' man. We're in touch.

BRAND: *(a statement)* You're enjoying it.

LAST: No. *(pause)* But I'll do what I have to. Ends ... always ... and only ... justify means. If the ends are ... large enough.

BRAND: Lenin?

LAST: Tom Mann. Born in Warwickshire, 1857.

BRAND: *(gesturing at doors)* Did he buy it?

Last laughs.

LAST: Buy it? He came to sell it. *(Brand sits down, some confusion showing)* Maddocks is a Wilks man from way back, came into the House together, docker and railway clerk, brothers-in-arms, hugging the centre like drunken drivers after the cats eyes. *(pause)* Wilks sent him round to check it out. *(pause)* If Wilks gets it he'll give Cedric a ministry. *(pause)* The question is: did he know I knew he knew.

The question hangs between them, grows odd, bizarre, in the silence. Brand laughs suddenly at its fatuity. Last joins him.

BRAND: It's pathetic.

LAST: Yes. Very.

Big Ben booms the half hour outside the window. Brand checks his watch.

LAST: *(simply)* I'm glad you said yes.

BRAND: *(slowly)* I think I'm glad you asked me.

PART TWO

Meeting/committee room. Two horseshoe tables, one inside the other, set out for a meeting. Members have already begun arriving; some thirty or so have taken their places, sitting on both sides of the two tables but orienting their chairs towards the Chair, set at the outer apex of the inner horseshoe. It remains vacant, awaiting Starr.

The atmosphere is lively, tense, expectant; greetings tend to be excited, a little overloud, overemphatic. A tv monitor, mounted on a cabinet in one corner, bears a date, day and time caption: Thursday, November 11th; 6.57.

Brand sits on the outside of the inner table, away from but clearly facing the Chair. He scans an Evening Standard, smiling occasionally at people who greet him as they arrive through the door behind him. We take in the strap head: 'WATSON GOES. WILKS TO PALACE'. Brand's fingers tap out a slow, irregular rhythm on the edge of the page.

Winnie Scoular and Jim McNab arrive, stop at Brand. Are greeted by several people in the doorway en route.

SCOULAR: *(slightly tense; quiet; non-committal)* Hello, Bill.

BRAND: *(seeing them)* Winnie. Jim.

MCNAB: *(quite tough, but not heavy)* You're taking it, then, eh?

BRAND: Yes.

MCNAB: Picked an odd time, didn't you. *(he gestures at the room)* I wish you luck, comrade.

He walks off to join a group of men up the room. Brand eyes Winnie, whose eyes are on but not engaged with the front page of the Standard.

BRAND: Something to say?

SCOULAR: Why *did* you take it? *(pause)* Why *you*, do you think? Again. And now.

BRAND: *(toughening slightly)* Tell me.

SCOULAR: Don't you know?

BRAND: I know what he told me. And it's hardly calculated to impress the right with the maturity of his political judgement.

SCOULAR: It's not the right your appointment's intended to impress, Bill. *(pause)* He needs *us*.

A uniformed House servant arrives with an envelope, hands it to Brand. Brand takes it, smiles his thanks, studies Winnie Scoular obliquely as he opens it and reads the note inside, then folds it back again into the envelope. Looks at her directly, indicating she should go on, his face impassive.

SCOULAR: Your role is ... emblematic. *(pause)* He's a very clever man.

She walks off up the room, takes a place in the outer ring of the inner table, on the opposite side to Brand and nearer the Chair. The room has filled considerably; more than fifty MPs, making considerably more noise.

Brand fingers the letter a moment, takes it out, rereads it, catches Reg Starr arriving in the corner of his eye, with two or three others. Starr strides heavily by him, en route for the Chair, deep in talk, a stack of folders and pamphlets in his arms.

MAPSON: *(voice over)* Now then, comrade. Any chance of a hand?

Brand swivels to see him. Stands at once. Mapson's in a wheel chair, very pale, drawn, tired but vital.

BRAND: Hello, Tom. How are you?

MAPSON: Fine, son, fine. Shift me one of them chairs so I can slip in beside you with this thing.

Brand begins the manoeuvre. A fair number of members move up to greet Mapson. Scoular waves a fond greeting from across the table.

MAPSON: *(finally in)* That's better. *(Starr waves from up the table, Mapson waves back)* Good turnout.

BRAND: I thought you weren't supposed to be up for another month.

MAPSON: Aye, well you know what thought did, don't you lad. Followed a muck cart and thought it was a wedding. *(grinning)* I'll see bloody Watson out, anyway.

BRAND: *(quietly)* And who *in*, Tom?

MAPSON: *(not answering for a moment, studying people in the room; seriously)* That's what I've come to find out, isn't it.

Starr bangs the table, those with seats take them, those without crowd the walls. The room's now packed, with about sixty four men and half a dozen women.

STARR: *(over the subsiding din)* The meeting has begun. As Chairman of the Journal Group I think I might be permitted a few words by way of introduction to this evening's deliberations ... First, the constitutional position. We're still the government of this country. By tomorrow evening the party will have chosen, by due process, our new leader. It will then, in my opinion, be the duty of the Queen – and I use the word duty advisedly, in my view she has no area of discretion whatsoever in the matter – it will be her duty to send for that person and appoint him Prime Minister. *(he stares slowly round the room)* And if she sends instead for someone else not of this party, God will indeed have his work cut out to save her. Comrades, these are grave times. Country, government, party face the most enormous problems. Whether we call it the 'agonised death-rattle of late capitalism' or something less hysterical, it's vital that the left at least keeps its head, its nerve and its heart in working order. Let me say this and then I'll sit down. The best outcome of this meeting would be the unanimous nomination of a single candidate wholly assured of the total voting strength of this Group. I don't of course in any way wish to pre-empt the search for that person; but at the end of the day, whoever it is should be able to count on the support of a united left in tomorrow's ballots. That's what the Group is for. Let us prove it works.

He sits down, scans the room for the first speaker.

CORBISHLEY: *(about 38, tall, angular, roughish voice, lank hair)* Could I ask what the latest information is on the field, Reg?

STARR: Would comrades mind standing while speaking? It's a crowded room and I think it would help at this particular historical conjuncture.

CORBISHLEY: Comrade Chairman, I think it's important we should consider other runners when deciding who to enter. Is Jim Wilks in or out, for instance? Do you know?

STARR: Venables and Kearsley are in. Wilks I don't know about. He's been busy in Cabinet most of the day, but as far as I know he hasn't yet made up his mind.

PREEN: *(45; balding; trade unionist; continuing Corbishley's line of attack)* I must say, comrade Chairman, I find the whole Wilks business difficult to comprehend. Can I ask for a kick-off whether Comrade Last's announcement that he would withdraw in favour of Wilks if others did was discussed at all with you, comrade Chairman, or with anyone in the Group?

Close shot of Brand, reading his letter again. It says: 'Bill. Hold all forts. Cavalry arriving. David.'

STARR: *(over this)* Nothing has been discussed with me, comrade …

BLACKWELL: *(50 or so; short; stocky; Scot; not rising)* Has he gone bananas or something? Since when has Jim Wilks been a friend of the left, for Christ's sake. He was a statutory incomes policy man, the last I heard of him …

STARR: Through the Chair, if you wouldn't mind, comrade …

CORBISHLEY: *(standing again)* I'll tell you what I resent, Reg. I resent the assumption David Last makes in all this; namely, that he already has the left vote in his pocket, to trade with as he sees fit. Because as far as I'm concerned, that's very far from being the case …

Some growled agreement, not large but significant.

EDNA JAMES: *(mid-30s, dull clothes, determined face; standing)* I couldn't agree more, Mr Chairman. I don't think I'm alone in finding the Minister of Employment's record in office somewhat ... uninspiring. Speaking personally, I think we should be examining other records and credentials ... Trevor Brent's, for example. *(some limited muttered agreement round the tables)* If it's a convincing left-wing record in office we're looking for, I submit that Trevor Brent's – particularly in his work with the trade union movement – has much to commend it.

Some hear hears around the room. Several people now want to speak. Calls of Reg, or Comrade Chairman.

STARR: All right, all right, hold your horses ... I thought I saw Wally Armfield here *(Armfield indicates. He stands on the far wall, in a ruck of others. He's around 40, swarthy)* Could you throw any light on whether Comrade Brent would be prepared to stand if nominated?

ARMFIELD: I understand that Trevor will be here directly. I'd prefer to leave it until he comes ...

STARR: *(relentless)* I spoke with him this morning and he indicated to me then that he would be unwilling to stand. Do you know if that is still the position?

ARMFIELD: *(reluctant)* The Minister has been in Cabinet most of the afternoon. We've barely spoken. *(pause)* As I understand it, that was certainly the position this morning ...

STARR: *(peremptory)* Thank you. *(returning to meeting. Hands shoot up again. He picks Winnie Scoular. She stands deliberately)*

SCOULAR: It's just possible, comrades, in all this frothy chat about personalities, that we'll forget to talk about *politics. (calls of 'not while you're around, Winnie' etc)* What are we actually talking about? We're asking who should represent the left in the coming leadership struggle. But there's a prior question. Does a left candidate stand a chance of *winning*, given the present composition of the Parliamentary Labour Party? We're rushing into *tactics* before we've assessed the nature of the battle. So. Can we win? Out of a vote of three hundred odd, how many can *we* count on? Eighty? Ninety? Venables will pull the same, maybe more, maybe less. Kearsley will take the rest. We could lose on the first ballot; but even if we won, what possible chance do we have of eating into Venables' supporters to beat Kearsley on the second? If Kearsley were a wholly bionic man who had to go on trickle-charge after every Cabinet meeting, they'd make him leader before one of us.

MAN'S VOICE: So what're you saying, Winnie love?

SCOULAR: Several things, Dickie *love*. I'm saying, one: do we put up a candidate at all? Two, if we do, it should be the second and deciding ballot we should be discussing here tonight, not the first; and three, if we cannot win, why should we automatically assume that the left candidate should already be a member of the government? *(some assent quietly growing, in sections of the meeting)* David Last is a comrade. Let that be quite clear from the outset. But three years in government have taken their toll. It makes it not a whit better that he is honourable, brave and uncorrupt, because on the left these are expectable virtues. What does matter is that in certain important respects he has done the right's dirty work for it ... and has been seen to do so, comrades, by the Constituency Labour Parties, themselves overwhelmingly left. *(pause)* If we can have no reasonable expectation of victory at this ... particular historical conjuncture ... *(she looks at Starr, who does not smile)* ... should we not see to it that we are at least represented by someone who most nearly matches our view of what a socialist leader should be like? Not to put too fine a point on it, I believe Comrade Last should not receive the nomination, but someone else. *(pause)* And ... *(with no particular drama)* just to start the ball rolling, I nominate comrade Starr.

She sits down quietly and at once, so that it takes those at the back some time to realise she has ended. Some low murmuring chat grows around the room. Brand stares at Scoular across and up the table. She's grave, contained – looks once at Brand, expressionlessly. Brand looks down at the table, turns to look at the doorway, turns back to look at Starr. Starr bangs the table once, to quieten the room.

STARR: If I might make my position clear, comrades ... I was approached last night by a dozen or so members of the Group, to see whether I would be willing to stand for nomination. I answered quite simply: I will stand if, and only if, one: it is the expressed desire of the Journal Group that I should stand; and two, if my standing did nothing to damage or divide our democratic faction. Shall we proceed, comrades. Tom?

Mapson gets a helping hand up, stands with difficulty, his knuckles under stress on the shiny table. Applause for him.

MAPSON: Thank you, Reg. *(pause)* I shan't be treating you to an extended peroration, comrades, so you can relax. Three minutes in this position's about my limit, just for the moment. *(some smiling chuckles, the tension slackening a mite)* And I'm not about to cross swords with Winnie Scoular. What I will say, though, is that while it's an interesting enough analysis she's offered, it's not necessarily a correct one. For example, what if Jim Wilks does decide to stand, out of pique, ambition, a genuine desire to serve the party, whatever – it doesn't matter. If the right and centre can be induced to split to our advantage ... that's a new ball game, as they say, isn't it. Is Kearsley so impregnable *then*? *(pause)* I honestly believe we should fight as if we mean to win. And that means – no disrespect to you, Reg – we must put up our most politically and electorally credible candidate. Who, unless things have changed drastically since I went sick in September, is David Last. *(Last's support, substantial but relatively muted till now, begins at last to materialise in vocalised assent. Mapson lets it grow a moment.)* But if I can go on a moment longer, comrades ... *(quiet again)* ... I believe his nomination should be conditional upon his furnishing us with some fairly detailed outline of the way he would handle matters as PM and Leader of the Party. *(he looks around the tables briefly)* Because if this is the sort of attention he's going to pay the organised left when in power, it's going to be a bloody sorry show for everyone concerned. Right, that's me.

*He levers himself down carefully, his face grey and sweaty. Hear hears and
applause from most parts of the room greet his speech.*

*Brand's hand has gone up immediately. Starr sees it, takes in other hands around
the room, returns to Brand.*

STARR: Comrade Brand, perhaps you could tell us something about his
whereabouts?

BRAND: *(rising)* Thank you, comrade Chairman. Comrade Last was meant to come
here directly Cabinet broke. I have a note to say he's been detained but will be
here shortly.

STARR: *(looking around for other speakers)* Thank you, comrade ...

BRAND: *(not yielding)* Might I be allowed a word or two more, comrade
Chairman?

STARR: By all means, comrade.

BRAND: Thank you. *(pause)* I speak as Bill Brand, a member of this Group, not as
... junior campaign manager ... or apologist ... for David Last. *(pause)* It seems
to me there are two distinct but interconnected areas of problematic. Comrade
Scoular touched on the first – can we win? Comrade Mapson on the second –
win to do what? The first clearly depends, as Tom says, on whether the right
and the centre can be induced to split, to our advantage. *(deliberately)* We're not
likely to be in full possession of the facts on this until tomorrow morning. But
as long as Jim Wilks is a possible entry, we have a chance of pulling it off.
(pause) Think what that means, comrades. *(he looks levelly round the room)* But
if we win only to become prisoners of the right, of the revisionists and
pragmatists and opportunists and careerists that have filled and still fill our
benches in the House, we'll have won for nothing. The only genuinely political
reason for offering someone our nomination tonight would be if that person,
man or woman, were prepared to commit – publicly – to the kind of economic
and social programme we as a Group were prepared to endorse.

*He becomes aware of movement and low chat, follows stares behind him to the
doorway, sees Last there, Copple and Brent flanking.*

STARR: *(to group in doorway)* Welcome, comrades. Would you care to move in a
little, I'm sure we can find a bit of room for you up here ...

LAST: Apologies for lateness, Reg. We'll squeeze in somewhere when the
comrade's finished speaking, if that's all right ...

STARR: As you wish. *(he looks to Brand to continue)*

BRAND: *(pausing a little, perhaps pondering possible adjustments before rejecting
them, aware of Last only feet behind him)* ... Speaking for myself, I'm very
clear what a Socialist Government's priorities must be in this present crisis.
Some facts. In the last year, under a Labour government, unemployment has
risen to close on one and three quarter millions: seven per cent of the total
workforce is now jobless. And the graph continues to rise. In that same period,

the average employee has experienced a six per cent reduction in real disposable income. Under a Labour government. In that same period, industrial output – wealth-producing output, comrades – has continued to plummet. In that same period, the current account balance of payments has continued to deteriorate: it now stands at two billion in deficit. *(pause)* Now, unless we can solve these problems, comrades – and I don't mean simply incant magical socialist slogans over them and wait for them to disappear – unless we can *solve* these problems, we will not be fit to govern. *(uneasy assent; some tension developing again)* I don't know comrade Last's thinking on all this, but I'll give you mine. As Trevor Brent and others have consistently pointed out, industry and the stock market will not undertake the investment this country needs. As a nation we need six billion pounds a year for capital investment in manufacturing, double what is currently being spent. So, whether through the National Enterprise Board or new institutions – to be created overnight if necessary – we must make these sums available at relatively low rates of interest. So that at a stroke we begin to reverse the trend in unemployment, with still more jobs to follow, as the new investment bites. In the short term, of course, we add to the already enormous government borrowing requirement … but we make sure *this* time that this reflationary money goes into production rather than consumption; that's to say, into factories instead of extra houses … *(some protest, which he rides)* … Yes, comrades, these are the iron contradictions, face them … Into extra machines, not extra cars; extra product, not extra services. And if this rapid growth in money supply proves inflationary, as it's bound to, a Socialist Government must be prepared to introduce *at once* a system of Special Deposits similar to the one used just after the war, whereby a sizeable proportion of all bank deposits are compulsorily frozen, with minimal interest rates. As we must be prepared to oblige life insurance and pension funds to invest a fraction of their money in industry – if necessary by direct intervention. *(pause)* Industry itself could not of course expect to receive these low-interest loans from the state for nothing. The new lending institutions would need to be empowered to explore the taking of equity or of direct ownership *and* the requirement of all borrowers that acceptable models of workers' control be immediately set up in their particular enterprises. *(he checks his watch)* There's the bones of it, comrades. *(pause. Deliberately)* It's my view that whoever gets our nomination should commit himself to putting flesh on them.

He sits down. Silence. People look round and down the table.

STARR: Thank you, comrade Brand. *(several hands shoot up)* I think if I may I'd like to use a Chairman's privilege and call on David Last to speak – David.

He makes a space for him on his left. Last dwells a moment, then walks forward up the room. Considerable applause.

STARR: *(as the room settles again)* I should say at the outset, David, that there is some feeling in the Group that you are no longer the … automatic choice as left candidate … And further, that a nomination of another Group member has already been lodged, though not as yet seconded.

LAST: Thank you.

MAN'S VOICE: You left out Trevor Brent, Reg. Will he stand if asked, or what?

STARR: Forgive me, Alf ... I must be getting old ...

He looks in Brent's direction. Necks creak to see him. Brent – mid-40s, pale, composed, steely, youthful – steps forward to a point immediately behind Brand's chair.

BRENT: I've given the matter much thought, Chairman. And I've spent hours discussing my position with David, Edna ... *(he acknowledges her)* ... and others. I can see no useful purpose being served at this juncture by allowing myself to be put forward. I believe David Last to be the only person capable of leading us to victory. And I trust his socialism implicitly.

He withdraws into the shadows, a strange, grey melting achieved effortlessly, oddly impressive. People begin to clap around the room, slightly surprising themselves. Last stands and listens, hardly watches. Brand watches Scoular, whose hands remain on the table. The applause mounts, shifting imperceptibly from Brent to Last. Its meanings are multiple; but audible among them are genuine respect and considerable relief at finding at last a focus for their approval in the room.

Last waits for Brand's eye, gets it. A short stare, difficult to read on each side. Last looks away, to the clapping Mapson, smiles a glad greeting for his return.

The applause falls away. Some excited expectancy takes its place. Last holds a moment longer, staring down now at the table he leans flat-handed on.

LAST: *(finally, looking up; moved)* Comrades. I have little to say. Except, perhaps ... it's good to be home ...

Applause again, hands first, then voices. Brand studies Last's extraordinarily emotional face.

Chess room, Westminster. *Night. The room is in darkness, save for one brightly lit table at which Brand and Last sit playing in silence. Brand's clock ticks: 1 hour 20 mins. Last's is silent: 43 mins. Last gets up eventually, stares briefly out of a window at the dark windy night; hears his clock punched; returns to study the move; looks at Brand, surprised and impressed, then back at the board. Brand stands, stretching a little. Outside, Big Ben strikes three. Brand checks his watch. Studies Last studying the board. Last has red; rook, queen, knight, two linked pawns on 5 and 6; Brand has two rooks, bishop, a knight, three linked pawns, the most advanced on 7.*

LAST: Mmm.

BRAND: Aren't you tired?

LAST: No. Are you?

BRAND: Not so I could sleep.

LAST: *(glancing up at him)* Perhaps you're offering a draw.

BRAND: *(smiling, looking at pieces)* No no. Not now.

Last's clock ticks on.

LAST: *(hand hovering, then retracting)* I've always found draws ... unreal, somehow.

He moves his rook up to cover his front pawn. The move is fast, precise. Last punches Brand's clock. Brand stays where he is to study the move, confident of his advantage.

BRAND: The unions didn't exactly offer you unqualified endorsement on the 'Tonight' thing, did they.

LAST: They stayed clear of everyone ... That's all I asked of them ... Moores and Wigan, I mean. *(pause)* I didn't want them playing safe in public by lining up behind Kearsley.

BRAND: *(studying Last's face)* Kearsley almost haemorrhaged when Venables announced he was in favour of Jim Wilks being returned unopposed. *(Last studies the board carefully)* You, on the other hand, never batted an eyelid.

Silence. Last looks up at him, smiles briefly, looks back at the board.

LAST: Kearsley's problem is, he only expects the expectable. Your clock.

Brand steps back to the table, forks rook and pawn with his knight, clicks Last's clock back into life.

LAST: *(finally)* All right, I'll give you the draw.

BRAND: *(smiling a little)* I'll accept your resignation.

Last grins suddenly, lowers his king to the board.

LAST: Who taught you this?

BRAND: I taught myself. Long nights with books filled with great games and commentary. Morphy, Anderson, Reti, Capablanca ...

LAST: Another.

BRAND: Shouldn't you sleep?

LAST: No. I need to be awake. Two each. *(he palms a white and red pawn, holds his fists out across the table)* Decider.

Brand points to a fist, Last shows the red pawn. Smiles. Brand sits down, they exchange pieces, begin to set the board and reset their clocks.

BRAND: What do you imagine *they're* doing now ... Venables, Kearsley?

LAST: *(dry)* No idea. Hate to think.

BRAND: Sleeping, both of them. Venables will have prayed to God rather hard. Kearsley will have knocked back several Mogadon cocktails.

The board is ready. They look at each other across it.

LAST: As it happens, for the moment, neither matters. *(pause)* I hope Jim Wilks sleeps soundly. Dreaming of power.

He pushes pawn to Q4. Clicks clock. Brand matches. Clicks clock. They look at each other again.

LAST: Dreaming of something.

PART THREE

House of Commons. Grand committee room, large enough to hold the whole of the PLP (300 plus). A large, very ordinary cardboard box is in transit to the platform. Sounds of crammed, excited meeting over. The box hits the desk; hands slide it to the centre.

BULLOCK: *(over)* Thank you Fred. Thank you John.

Bullock's hand receives a white envelope. His right hand teases it open, careful not to tear the contents. A single slip of white paper.

Brand, some tension in the eyes. He looks to his right towards Last, stroking his nose with thumb and forefinger. Over this, sounds of Bullock (Chairman, PLP) banging the desk for order. The room quietens at once.

Kearsley, in close-up. He's around 50, fleshy, blowing a little with tension: the face of a disappointed bully, capillaries bright with whisky.

Over this, the announcement:

BULLOCK: *(over)* Result of the first ballot. I read in alphabetical order. *(clearing throat)* Kearsley, Maurice. 83.

A suppressed gasp from the room. Kearsley's lips move, half-involuntarily, towards a smile they have no chance of achieving.

BULLOCK: *(over)* Last, David Russell. 81.

Last mutters something quite urgent to Brent, who nods twice: understood. Brand is entering the tallies in a notebook. Venables, very relaxed, civilised, is leaning back slightly to hear what the man behind him is whispering.

BULLOCK: *(over)* Venables, John Winston. 85.

Some clapping from Venables' supporters. Venables nods to the man behind him, looks at the pad the PPS on his left is holding up for him.

BULLOCK: *(over)* If colleagues could just contain themselves … Wilks, James. 61.

A gasp again, a few 'Jesuses' etc of surprise, then separate vollies of applause from the separate camps.

BULLOCK: Is it your wish that the tellers remain the same? *(loud ayes)* Thank you. I declare that Messrs Kearsley, Last and Venables shall go forward to a second ballot, to be cast ... *(checks his watch)* ... at 1.30 pm. Will the tellers stay behind please? Thank you.

Noise, surprised, excited, a little boisterous, ensues, as members begin to leave for the corridor and probably the bar. We pick out the contenders in the ruck. Maddocks shakes Wilks's hand, claps him on the shoulder. Venables, Frear and four others leave as though drilled. Last and Brand remain seated, talking quietly with Starr, who leans between them from the row behind. Kearsley is in a huddle with half a dozen men, faces taut, serious. Kearsley shouts 'bloody idiot' several times, only half-heard in the din. Wilks's party prepares to pass them. Kearsley turns to look at Wilks.

KEARSLEY: I hope you're bloody satisfied, James ...

WILKS: *(statesmanlike; irritatingly pompous)* I did what I had to, Maurice.

KEARSLEY: Don't be dim, man. You've been *used*. See it, for Christ's sake ...

Kearsley's men know he's way over. One takes him by the arm to calm him, Kearsley draws it away from him, reddening. Wilks, face white at the insult, struggles for dignity. Maddocks shakes his head at Kearsley, purses his lips. Wilks draws himself up, leads his parade from the room. Kearsley's men envelop Kearsley, calming him.

Last, Brand and Starr have watched the incident.

LAST: Dear dear. Maurice is having difficulty remembering he's a gentleman. Again.

BRAND: *(handing him the tally slip)* You've under two hours. Kearsley or Wilks?

LAST: *(standing)* Neither. Cedric Maddocks. Preferably in his office. I'll be upstairs.

He leaves quietly. Brand looks at Starr, who remains impassive. Looks up at the big wall clock over the desk: 11.40.

Maddocks's office. *Maddocks stands and stares at the picture of sheep on the wall above his desk, his pocket-watch in his hand. Big Ben strikes the half. He checks his watch, makes a minute adjustment to it: 12.30. Clacks the watch shut. Turns into the room. Nods to Sandiford, who exits. Maddocks sits down at his desk, face settling into stone for a moment, then reanimating into kingmaker-grave as Sandiford returns with Last and Brand.*

MADDOCKS: *(rising)* Sorry you were kept waiting, David, it's been a busy ... *(he sees Brand)* ... hour. *(looks enquiringly at Last)*

LAST: *(matter of fact)* I thought it better if Brand came along. He has fast legs.

MADDOCKS: Well, I had expected erm ...

LAST: What passes between us is wholly confidential ... We all know that ... May I?

He points to a chair. Maddocks nods; sits; waves Brand and then Sandiford to join them on the fringe.

MADDOCKS: Well, David, what can I do for you?

LAST: *(mildly)* I want to talk votes, Cedric.

MADDOCKS: With me?

LAST: *(simply)* With you.

Maddocks looks at Brand carefully, then back at Last.

MADDOCKS: I'm flattered ... talk on.

LAST: *(glancing at clock)* I tried to see Jim Wilks. He's seeing no one, I understand.

MADDOCKS: Isn't he. *(pause)* I suppose he's a little upset. Quite naturally, in the circumstances.

LAST: I understand Kearsley's offered his apologies for his ... behaviour downstairs. *(Maddocks purses his lips; noncommittal)* Word has it Jim's refused to accept them.

MADDOCKS: He's a proud man.

Pause.

LAST: *(very plainly, without hesitation)* Do you happen to know if Jim intends to ... advise his supporters on how they might cast their vote in the second ballot?

MADDOCKS: *(carefully)* We've discussed it briefly, yes.

Pause. Last waits. Maddocks waits. Last glances yet again at the clock.

LAST: All right, Cedric. I'll tell you how I see things and then I'll leave you, if you wish ... All right?

MADDOCKS: *(charming)* By all means, David. Can I get you a drink?

LAST: Thank you, no.

MADDOCKS: *(registering Brand's headshake)* I'll have a small gin, Jeremy ... and a tonic water, I think. *(to Last)* Sure, David?

Last smiles his headshake, sits patiently as Maddocks lights a cigar. Sandiford crosses to the drinks cabinet. Brand watches him, over the next exchange, is reminded of himself two nights ago.

MADDOCKS: *(puffing away, smiling, benign)* Mmm. Tell me how you see things, David ... and I'll tell you whether to go away ... Thank you, Jeremy. Help yourself ...

He turns back to Last, whose poise is total. Brand shifts uneasily, clocks the clock on the wall, edging past twenty to.

LAST: *(studying Brand's slip of paper in his fingers)* I take ... about thirty of Jim Wilks's votes to be personal to Jim. The rest come in a ratio of roughly three to two from Kearsley and Venables. Now, if we concentrate on those ... thirty, say, for the moment ... what are their options? They could vote for Venables, but that's not likely, he's too far to the right, with a view of the Labour Party very alien to their own. Or they could vote for Kearsley, who has just insulted and humiliated their candidate in public and would make the sacking of Jim Wilks possibly his first act in office. *(pause)* Or ...

Long pause. Maddocks begins to tap his deaf-aid, in the silence. The clock ticks. Brand's face is clenched. Sandiford is draped against a windowsill, looking at Maddocks.

LAST: ... they vote for me.

MADDOCKS: *(smiling, gnomish)* That's novel.

LAST: Perhaps. But not without a certain ... elegance? Especially since I offered to withdraw in their candidate's favour ...

MADDOCKS: ... But didn't.

LAST: *(gentle correction)* ... Wasn't allowed to.

MADDOCKS: *(eventually)* Is that all? The only reason?

LAST: *(unhurried)* No. *(pause)* They could also rest assured that if I were returned to power, Jim Wilks would still continue to make a contribution in ... high office.

MADDOCKS: How high?

LAST: I'm not sure I can answer that. You can hardly expect me ...

MADDOCKS: *(charming)* I expect nothing, David.

LAST: *(eventually, resisting the clock)* Shall we say Deputy Prime Minister?

MADDOCKS: And Leader of the House?

Big Ben chimes the three quarters. Last nods.

MADDOCKS: *(relentless)* Can rest assured, you say. You mean: they'd have your word.

LAST: They'd have my word.

He looks once at Brand, who sits flintily by, watching the two with potentially discomfiting concentration. Maddocks follows Last's look, smiles amiably at Brand.

MADDOCKS: How are you, young man? Feel like a bit of sprinting?

BRAND: I'm fine. I'm fine.

MADDOCKS: Good. Good. *(he's searching a drawer for some typewritten sheets; brings them out onto the desk)* It's ... twenty eight, actually. *(he pushes a sheet to Brand, one to Sandiford. Each studies the list of names)* I take it ... I'll be remembered in dispatches too, David ...?

LAST: Of course.

MADDOCKS: *(almost believably)* Not that it matters much any more. I begin to weary ... *(to Brand)* You take the top half ... *(to Sandiford)* ... you take the bottom. Meeting in Room 8 erm ... 1.15. Prompt. All of them. Tick tick gentlemen. *(he shows them his watch. Sandiford and Brand confer about who'll take what. Last stands)* Won't you have a drink now?

LAST: No thanks, Cedric. I've one or two people to see ...

MADDOCKS: *(hand out across the desk)* Good luck. Comrade. *(the smile hits Last like a hot poultice. He takes the hand. Smiles back)*

LAST: Thank you.

Last and Brand leave together.

MADDOCKS: Tick tick Jeremy.

Sandiford leaves smilingly. Maddocks sits. Clicks out a number on the phone. Waits.

MADDOCKS: Cedric. Just left ... *Buy* it? He came to *sell* it.

Maddocks laughs; one dry exultant bark.

Grand committee room. *Close shot of Last.*

BULLOCK: *(over)* Kearsley, Maurice. 99. *(close shot of Venables)* Last, David Russell. 106. *(close shot of Kearsley)* Venables, John Winston. 104.

The rest of Bullock's speech is drowned in the confused uproar. We stay on Kearsley's marooned face.

Last's office. *Kearsley and Last sit opposite each other in matching leather armchairs. The wall clock says 2.45. They've talked for some time. Kearsley lifts his scotch to his lips, pulls fairly heavily on it. Brand and Kearsley's PPS sit at a table on the other side of the room, just within earshot but detached. Brand makes calculations on a piece of paper, his attention largely on the two ministers. Kearsley's man consults a train timetable.*

KEARSLEY: There's no way, David. No bloody way. You're too clever by half. Should've been in the city, you'd've cleaned up.

LAST: *(decisive)* Maurice, for God's sake let's talk *politics.* You can't really mean you want to see the far right get its hands on the party ...

KEARSLEY: *(leaden irony)* No, I don't. That's one of the reasons I stood. The other was the possibility that it might fall into the hands of the far left. *(pause)* Of the two, since you press me, I think I have a marginal preference for Venables ...

LAST: *(tough)* ... Who will destroy this party. Your party. Mine. And split the movement. From which we both came.

KEARSLEY: *(dismissive)* No no ...

LAST: *(still tough)* Oh yes. You've heard him, you've read him, you know him. He wants to separate this party from its trade union base and launch it on a sea of floating voting consumers ...

KEARSLEY: Rhetoric, David. Two weeks as Leader – *dealing* with the unions – and all that ... verbiage ... won't be worth the air it came on. He'll bend to reality like everyone else. Like you even, eh?

LAST: *(eventually, face icing; a statement)* You don't believe that, do you.

KEARSLEY: Of course I believe it. What do you mean?

LAST: *(spilling a little)* Shit, Maurice. You wrote an article only last month in Labour Review attacking Venables' views on reorganising the movement and the party ... What're you talking about, he'll bend to reality? He wouldn't recognise our versions of reality if we hit him in the face with them ...

KEARSLEY: *(slight bluster)* Venables can be handled. I happen to know it.

LAST: He's offered already, you mean ...

KEARSLEY: Look, just leave it, David ...

LAST: You mean, you're preparing to sell the party down the river for the sake of your own career ...

KEARSLEY: *(standing abruptly)* No I'm not and I'd like you to retract ...

LAST: *(standing with him)* All right, how would you put it then ...?

KEARSLEY: I asked for an apology.

LAST: *(fast)* All right, I apologise, all right, let's hear it, come on, Maurice, let's hear it ...

KEARSLEY: I'll tell you this, Last. And then I'll go. The reasons – none of them shameful – I will give my supporters for not voting for you are as follows: one, a government led by you would invoke economic chaos, social disorder, political massacre and electoral suicide. Two, Venables has electoral charisma capable of defeating the Tories at the next election. Three, in any government formed by Venables, the interests of my section of the PLP would be fully represented in terms of office, with myself as Foreign Secretary and Deputy Prime Minister ... which is why I am able to reject your ... alarmist view that he seeks a policy of all-out confrontation with the unions ... *(pause)* And ... in the absence of any at least commensurate offer from you ... I believe they are reasons decisive enough to sway my supporters in the direction best suited to serve the needs of government, country and party. *(he waits for Last to answer. Nothing. No offer. Kearsley nods)* And in the unlikely event of those reasons proving insufficient, I would be forced to add a fourth – potentially the most decisive. *(pause)* If you were returned as leader of a party with no overall majority in the House, I don't believe for one moment that the Queen would send for you. *(pause)* John Venables is now our only chance of continuing in power at all. *(he nods to his PPS, who fastens his briefcase and makes for the door)* And now I'll go. *(he heads for the door)*

LAST: I hope, when this is written up in the histories, you get the attention you deserve, comrade.

KEARSLEY: *(over shoulder)* You too – comrade.

He goes. Brand stands, scans Last's face for the precise feeling. Last looks at the clock, turning his back on Brand. Big Ben strikes three. Brand sweeps his papers into his bag, still watching Last's back. Last glances up at Bevan's portrait. Crosses to the drinks cabinet. Pours himself a heavy scotch. Sips some, sips some more, his back still to Brand.

BRAND: We've lost then.

Last turns round fast, eyes ferocious, frightening.

Ministerial car, *parked up beyond No 10 and towards the neck of the cul-de-sac of Downing Street. Night. Sounds of people chattering and cheering desultorily. Outside the car window, Brand sees a News At Ten reporter doing a live piece on the situation. Lights, cameras, police, people.*

At a signal from down the street, the driver moves slowly forward. Brand sees Last emerge, disappear into a moil of reporters etc, reappear briskly, shaking his head, on his way to the car.

Brand holds the door open for him; they're away quickly, the fruits of the driver's long experience of such getaways.

Last leans back in the car, eyes closed for a moment. Sits up eventually. Picks up speaking tube.

LAST: To the House, Peter. *(the driver nods)* Thanks. *(to Brand)* I've got to see Starr and one or two others. Peter can take you home or wherever ...

BRAND: I'll come.

LAST: Fine. *(long pause)* He's asking us all to stay on. Partly because of the financial crisis, partly to 'unite the party'.

BRAND: Will you?

LAST: Yes.

BRAND: Why?

LAST: Because that's where the fighting's going to be. *(he looks at his watch)* I must ring home.

BRAND: I rang.

LAST: Thanks.

Silence. Last looks out of the window, bleak suddenly, very tired.

BRAND: Did you consider ... topping Venables' offer to Kearsley?

LAST: Yes.

BRAND: Why didn't you?

LAST: *(a blank list)* One: as Chancellor or Foreign Secretary – the only posts he'd've been prepared to accept – he'd've been in a position to sabotage any socialist programme we tried to introduce. Two: I'd already promised them to Trevor Brent and Edna Copple, as quid pro quos. Take your pick. I don't believe the offer on its own was it.

BRAND: What then?

LAST: He truly believed I wouldn't be sent for ... so my offer couldn't be made good. *(pause)* He really believed she had the power. Believed it.

BRAND: *(working it out)* And yet, objectively ... she sat there and never moved a finger.

LAST: *(looking at him, smiling bleakly)* Power indeed, eh?

He looks away, past his reflection, to the dank pavements. Brand watches him.

The car turns into St Stephen's Yard. A policeman salutes.

- *end* -

Episode 10

Revisions

was broadcast on Monday 9th August 1976

The cast was as follows:

Bill Brand   Jack Shepherd

Winnie Scoular   Rosemary Martin

Reg Starr   Douglas Campbell

McNab   James Giles

Renshaw   Peter Davidson

David Last   Alan Badel

Brent   John Woodnutt

Venables   Peter Howell

Albert Stead   John Barrett

Young Socialist   Ian Liston

Police Inspector   Lindsay Campbell

Walter Marland   Bernard Gallagher

Gus Lynch   Phil McCall

Moores   Ray Smith

Kearsley   Godfrey Quigley

Frear   Geoffrey Palmer

Edna Copple   Jean Boht

Wilks   John McKelvey

Maddocks   Peter Copley

Alf Jowett   Allan Surtees

Miriam Brand   Lynn Farleigh

Eddie Brand   Dave Hill

Mrs Brand   Anne Dyson

Stan   Bill Tasker

Designers: David Ferris, Harry Clark

Executive Producer: Stella Richman

Producer: Stuart Burge

Director: Stuart Burge

PART ONE

House of Commons. Small meeting room. Murk all but hides the river view from the window. Reg Starr stares out at it, deep inside himself. Behind him, a dozen or so Journal Group members prepare for the meeting. Winne Scoular hands round agendas; has a brief word with Renshaw (Under Secretary at the DHSS), who sits with Jim McNab and three others across the long polished table. A small group stand by the doorway.

Big Ben chimes mid-day.

SCOULAR: All right, Reg?

STARR: *(turning)* Mmm.

He resumes his seat at the top of the table. The standing members find their places.

STARR: OK, we'll make a start, comrades. Don't be depressed by the numbers – most of the Group won't be down until next Monday's Opening and the Queen's Speech. *(pause)* I cede the Chair then too; but I thought it important some of us at any rate should get together to discuss tactics for the new parliament – and the new government …

Brand and one or two others arrive.

STARR: Come in, comrades. Glad you could make it.

Brand sits at the opposite end of the table. Nods at Winnie, McNab. Begins removing file from his briefcase. He wears a Fight for Work Campaign badge in his lapel.

STARR: Winnie?

SCOULAR: *(grave, dry, some unresolved anger underneath)* It's hard to know where to begin, Reg. Last week we lost a decisive battle some of us didn't believe we should be fighting in the first place, but that was last week. If we have an initiative in the next battle, I'm damned if I can see it. Venables will do and we will react. Isn't that the way it is?

MCNAB: The question is: what's Venables likely to do? We may have made him leader but we didn't make him God. The whole of the movement – party, unions, constituencies – are to his left. He'll see that; or we'll make him see it. Whatever else he is, he's not stupid … A stupid man would've started by reconstituting the Cabinet, eh? I'm far from gloomy. We've got good cards …

SCOULAR: It's pretty obvious why he's kept the Cabinet intact, isn't it? New leader, need for unity. When he's stronger, he'll pick them off one by one. *(pause)* I don't think Trevor Brent's under any illusions. I was talking to Wally Armfield, his PPS, this morning.

RENSHAW: I think we need a statement getting out, don't we, Reg? Venables is bad news, however he plays it …

STARR: I'm not so sure, Charlie. About the statement, I mean. The party in the country's not going to thank us for rushing in with teeth bared, especially when he's not yet even opened his mouth.

MCNAB: I'm with Reg on that. I think we should ... dig in and see what his plans are ... No point wasting ammo on mere shadows ...

BRAND: Could I say something?

STARR: Surely.

BRAND: *(carefully)* I don't mean to be over-critical, but I can't help feeling this discussion has already become just a bit ... narrow in its perspective, that's to say, I've a feeling it's not what's going to happen here, but what's going to happen – or we can help make happen *out there (finger to window)* that's going to make the difference, as far as our new leader's concerned. *(pause)* Of course he'll ease himself into the job, of course he'll bow to pressures and the like, they all do, that's what it's about, 'leading'. But not *only* what it's about. Venables had committed himself – over three decades – to the 'modernisation' of this party, ie to the creation of a radical party of the *centre*, whose natural allies in the House will be the Liberals and the left of the Tory party, and in the country all those sane and reasonable voters who believe in moderation in all things but especially politics. *(pause)* When he'll start is speculative, I agree – in my view, sooner rather than later; *that* he'll start can't be in doubt. And I don't think we can stop him from here ...

He looks around him, catches Winnie's gaze.

SCOULAR: Go on.

BRAND: I believe we've got to bring pressure from outside on every Labour MP in the House to stand by the 1974 Manifesto. In the ward and constituency parties, in the unions and trades councils, in the National Executive Committee, in the TUC, in the grassroots movements and campaigns ... and I believe we must start now. If I were editing next Friday's Journal, I'd fill every page with the message: Hands off the Party, it doesn't belong to you ,,,

STARR: *(sceptical)* You think that's the mood of the movement, do you?

BRAND: Not yet. The movement's demoralised, doesn't know where the hell it is. We could help it find out; must.

SCOULAR: *(barbed)* What's David Last think about it?

BRAND: *(levelly)* I don't know. Why don't you ask him.

MCNAB: You say Venables'll move sooner rather than later. What's that based on, Bill? Or is it just a hunch.

BRAND: Hunch mainly, Jim. *(opening file, removing newspaper cuttings and press releases)* But I find it pretty significant that no less than three of his entourage – two in the Cabinet – have already been shooting their mouths off over the weekend about how different things were going to be under the new leader. I don't imagine they said what they did without clearing it first. Do you?

He's passed the stuff around the table.

STARR: *(studying pic of Frear at public meeting)* Frear. Aye, I read this.

Some mumbles around the table. Brand watches them.

BRAND: I think he'll go for the Queen's Speech.

Eyes switch sharply along the table.

STARR: What?

BRAND: Why not? He's got four days. Who's going to stop him?

STARR: *(face furrowed)* No no, Bill. He wouldn't dare.

Cabinet room. *Last studies a Cabinet agenda on the leather blotter before him. Around him, sounds of the Cabinet convening. Last's pen draws a circle round an item. His hand opens a file: Frear's face stares out from a cutting.*

Two secretaries enter, one with a pile of pamphlets, which she places on a desk behind and to the right of the PM's seat in the centre of the long table; the other carries typewritten messages, which she begins to hand out to some of the already seated members of the Cabinet.

Last looks round the table, past Frear, Kearsley and two others, to where Copple and Brent sit talking in whispers. Brent catches his eye, rises, comes over.

BRENT: *(quiet, casual; pointing to the agenda)* This it?

Last sniffs, says nothing.

Venables in, flanked by the Cabinet Secretary and other officials; greets the room with zest, cordiality, briskness and great charm. Brent returns to his seat.

VENABLES: Morning, David.

LAST: Morning, Prime Minister.

Victoria Bus Station. *The North-West contingent of the Fight for Work Campaign – hundreds of them – debouch. Brand waits by a barrier, watching them, exchanging the odd pleasantry with passing groups who possibly recognise him, or simply notice the Campaign badge in his lapel.*

Albert Stead, a battered suitcase in his hand, approaches, waving goodbye to a gang of comrades. He wears the badge, and another signifying Organiser.

STEAD: *(calling)* ... Midday sharp, Frederick. I'm counting on you ... Hello, Bill. Good to see you.

BRAND: And you, Albert. Give us your case ...

STEAD: *(grinning)* Get off with you. Cheeky sod. Have I got a bed or what?

BRAND: You've got a bed. Come on.

They walk off towards the stairs to the tube. Brand tries to take his case, Stead prevents him.

Clapham flat. *Brand's living room. Stead and Brand sit in armchairs opposite each other. Stead has a can of ale and a glass.*

STEAD: What'll we do for food? Will we go out?

BRAND: There's a Chinese on the corner. That OK?

STEAD: Yeah, that's fine. I could fancy a nice hot 73 ... *(holding can up)* Aren't you having one?

BRAND: *(shaking head)* Uhunh.

Stead drinks. Brand watches him, admiring the man. The mood steadies into seriousness.

STEAD: Well. This is a bugger, isn't it?

BRAND: Ahunh.

STEAD: So. What's happening this end?

BRAND: There's only a handful of us down. The mood on the left seems to be wait and see. Then, presumably, study it in action-replay, to see if you actually did see what you waited to see. And then wait to see if anybody else saw it ... and so on. It might lack a little, what shall we say, pace, but by Christ is it *inexorable* ... What I mean is: the Journal Group met this morning.

STEAD: What about the NEC?

BRAND: They meet Thursday. Winnie Scoular's asking for an Emergency Conference.

STEAD: Will she get it through?

BRAND: Not sure. Could. But doubtful. They'll want to wait and see too.

STEAD: What's happening with the Cabinet?

BRAND: God knows. I've spoken to David Last. There's a fight on, it seems. Over what, precisely ... *(he leaves it, expressively)* What's your reading, Albert?

STEAD: Tell you the truth, I've been so busy with the Campaign and this demonstration, I've barely had a chance to think it through. *(pause)* I thought a bit on t'bus though, coming down. Been through worse scrapes. Not many though ... And I'm not saying that this time we couldn't really fall apart ...

BRAND: Maybe that's what we should aim for.

STEAD: *(brow furling)* How do you make that out, lad?

BRAND: I don't know if I can explain exactly. *(sorting it out)* Listen, I met Venables at Ruskin during the summer. Spent a day with him. Saw him close up. As a stranger, for the first time, very detached. There was something in him

I admired. A very … proper adversary. In Watson it was something else you admired: the sly energy, the style, the passionate commitment to riding the swell, a cork among stones; the central, dazzling absence of belief. With Venables, the first thing that hits you is belief. In many ways he's a very literal man. And when he says nationalisation is a socialist fetish, he really means it. When he says the principal task of social democracy is to curb the power of the unions, he means that too. *(thinking)* Now, all the argument I've heard from the left seems to base itself on the apparently unchallengeable fact that Venables will at once find himself contained within the great web of governmental, party and trade union influence. That's to say, Venables will bend, like anyone else, to reality. That what the left will have to contend with is an emphasis here, a coloration there; at least until the next election. Also, the left argues that to carry the party in the House, he'll be forced to give ground all the way along the line. And if he wants industrial recovery – as he must – he's going to have to live with the unions, warts and all.

STEAD: So? *(pause)* You disagree?

BRAND: Supposing there's another way.

STEAD: What?

BRAND: What if he shows his colours right away and *defies* the party to refuse to back him.

STEAD: Then he's a madman. Christ, he was alive in 1931 …

BRAND: True. But so were many of the Parliamentary Labour Party. They won't be in any hurry to split from the leadership … *(Stead makes to interrupt; Brand anticipates)* … even if they are instructed by the constituencies to do otherwise.

STEAD: *(quite grave)* What are you saying, Bill?

BRAND: I'm saying – and I could be wrong – I'm saying … I think this is the crunch, Albert. Here. Now. I'm saying he's not there because he wants office, he's there because he wants power. And because, like the rest of us, he has no interest in a draw.

STEAD: I'll have to think about that one.

He belches suddenly, rubs his stomach.

BRAND: Fancy some food, then?

STEAD: *(dry)* Not particularly. Not after that little lot. I suppose I'd better, though. *(he gets up, frowning)* What's his first move, then, in this … scenario of yours?

BRAND: *(carefully)* If he *is* going to begin as he means to go on … I can't see him not wanting to rewrite the Queen's Speech. Can you?

STEAD: *(long pause)* Too many ifs, Bill. He's not a fool, whatever else he is …

BRAND: No.

STEAD: I'll go and get me coat.

He leaves, shaking his head. Brand crosses to the phone, dials. He picks up a wedding invitation from the dresser, studies the tawdry design on the front, looks inside.

BRAND: *(phone)* Hi, it's dad. Hang on, look, never mind the cartoons, is Mummy there? What? Where? Ahunh. Who's looking after you? Ahunh. No, no message. *Wait* a minute, is Jane there ... ? All right ... *Mike* ...

The phone has been hung up. Brand replaces his receiver, smiling wryly. The smile fades.

Morning. House of Commons tea room. *Fairly full. Brand and Last sit at a table in the window with coffee and croissant. They talk: low, intense, urgent exchanges, constrained by the place. The camera tracks in towards them.*

BRAND: ... It's bloody ridiculous to say wait and see. You *know*, for Christ's sake! What're you talking about?

LAST: *(patiently)* I'm talking about the importance of not being seen to be the one who aims the first blow.

BRAND: Is it aiming the first blow to pan somebody who's threatening to choke you to death?

LAST: Yes. If he can claim he was only trying to shake your hand.

BRAND: So. You think you can beat him from inside.

LAST: I can try. It's why I'm there. *(he looks at his wrist watch)*

BRAND: *(terse)* And you'll resign when?

LAST: *(tersish)* When it's necessary.

BRAND: Fine. I might pip you to it.

LAST: That's your privilege.

Last stands, fishes some money from his pocket, places it on the table with the bill.

LAST: I hope the march goes well.*(he ponders the next sentence rather carefully)* If you bump into Willie Moores at the TUC, ask him, in a quiet moment, how their talks with Venables went over the weekend ... particularly on our long-standing commitment to public ownership of the docks. I'd be very interested to hear his reply. *(he turns away, turns back)* Oh. Trevor Brent may resign today. That's wholly confidential, of course.

He leaves. Brand stares after him, rather angry.

PART TWO

The large Fight for Work march threads its way past the British Museum, heading for TUC headquarters. Banners proclaim local trades union sections, local parties, trades councils etc. The mood is sombre, angry; chants start up and pound the passing traffic: Thousands Out, Join the March, Fight for Work, No to Unemployment etc. March marshalls, armbanded, work at order unobtrusively, mingling with the police.

Brand carries one pole of the Leighley Trades Council banner, a woman the other. Their contingent, twelve strong, fans out behind them. A Young Socialist joins Brand.

YOUNG SOCIALIST: *(showing him the early edition Evening Standard headline)* What about it then, Bill?

Brand reads the headline: CABINET CRISIS: RESIGNATION RUMOURS.

BRAND: One thing at a time eh, comrade? *(he stares ahead)* Jesus, we're there. Here, cop hold of this, Peter …

Brand hands him the banner, starts legging along the pavement.

TUC headquarters. Chanting now very potent in the packed narrow street. Police cordon the entrance. Albert Stead talks to a police inspector, shows him his list. The inspector nods, checking against his own. Stead waves a man up the steps to join them. Finally, Brand appears, slightly out of breath.

STEAD: Thought we'd lost you.

BRAND: I was half a mile back. What's the hold-up?

INSPECTOR: *(pleasant)* Just checking credentials, sir. *(looking at list)* W. Brand, is it?

BRAND: That's right.

INSPECTOR: If I could just see some means of identification, gentlemen …

Stead pulls out his union card, passes through the police cordon to a huge cheer from the watching marchers. The second man (Lynch), a short, wiry Scot, National Organiser for the march, shows him his social security card. Another cheer. Brand shows his House of Commons pass. More cheering. The chants start up again.

INSPECTOR: Straight through, sir.

We close on the re-formed police cordon and the chanting, as the glass doors glint to after Brand. We watch them, through the glass, re-group, shake hands with an official, walk off up a corridor.

Office. Not sumptuous. The three sit in silence, on the interviewee's side of the desk. Two chairs have been set out on the other side. The room is at the back of the building, but the chants of the march can still be heard. Gus Lynch taps a thickish envelope against his knee, in time with the chants. Phones ring in an adjacent office.

STEAD: Hope to God it doesn't snow. *(silence)* Do you think it will?

BRAND: *(crossing to the window to look)* Could do anything.

The door opens sharply; Walter Marland in. He's General Secretary of the TUC; late 40s, slim, angular, dark, young-looking. He wears a serviceable grey suit over a pullover; carries a bunch of files in his hand.

MARLAND: *(Coventry voice, dragged towards received standard English)* Morning, brothers. Sorry to have kept you waiting about ... We've a Finance and General Purposes meeting on ... Walter Marland, General Secretary, TUC ...

LYNCH: Gus Lynch, National Organiser, Fight for Work Campaign ... *(they shake hands)* ... Brother Albert Stead ... Transport and Allied ... *(another handshake)*

MARLAND: *(hand out)* Bill Brand, yes?

BRAND: *(levelly, taking the hand)* That's right. How do you do.

MARLAND: OK, let's get cracking, shall we. Willie Moores is –

Moores in, tough, burly.

MOORES: Present. Morning, brothers. Bill. *(warmer)* How are you, Albert? Good to see you again ... *(he looks at Lynch)*

MARLAND: Brother Lynch, National Organiser.

MOORES: How are you?

LYNCH: I'm fine.

They resume their seats; Moores on Marland's left.

MARLAND: We've twenty minutes. I wish it could be longer, but we've a big agenda to work through up there ... *(leaning back in chair, friendly but tough)* All yours.

The three men look at each other. Lynch nods.

LYNCH: First off, I'll give you this then. *(he hands the envelope to Marland, who begins opening it)* That's a list of demands drawn up by our National Council on behalf of the Fight for Work Campaign membership. That's 37,000 men and women ... one in forty of those unemployed at the minute.

Marland studies the list of demands, hands the second copy of it to Moores.

MARLAND: All right. I'll see to it it's raised at the next Council meeting. *(makes a note in his diary)* Any comments, Willie?

MOORES: *(to group)* No. there's nothing here we haven't urged on government ourselves, I can assure you, in the Transport and Allied and at the TUC. Unfortunately the likes of us don't own the economy ... And there are undoubted problems ... World recession in trade, a sustained investment strike, loans with strings ... All that's not going to go away because we ask it to, is it?

The three remain silent, watch him carefully; their vigilance could well unnerve a smaller man. Moores merely pushes his lips out, concerned but firm.

MARLAND: For myself, I can't go beyond my General Council's statement of last month, copies of which ... *(hand in file)* ... I've brought down with me ...

He pushes one across the desk to each of the men.

MARLAND: You'll see there that we call unequivocally for further and decisive reflationary measures to be taken at the earliest possible moment ... so that new jobs can be created and this hideous rise in the unemployment graph can be reversed ...

Pause. The men study the statement coldly.

MARLAND: That's our position; and has been for well over a year.

Lynch places his paper on the desk, Stead his, Brand his.

LYNCH: *(a statement)* It's not good enough, is it.

MARLAND: Unemployment at 1.7 millions? Of course it isn't ...

LYNCH: *(deliberately)* I'm talking about your 'statement', brother.

MARLAND: *(cool, holding up Lynch's demands)* I think it covers the ground ...

LYNCH: Oh, it does that all right. But there's no point in covering the ground if you're not prepared to *occupy* it. You *talk* about the 'paramount need' to cut unemployment, but you don't actually *demand* it, do you ...

MARLAND: *(cool, patient)* Brother, we're not in a *position* to demand ...

LYNCH: Oh? And what about the employers, then? How come they *are*? You admit yourself they're forcing the government to keep unemployment high by refusing to invest. Why haven't the unions the right to make the hiring of their labour conditional upon unemployment being cut?

MARLAND: *(patient still)* Look, there's no point upping production unless we can sell the product. And we can't sell the product unless we get our prices right. Which means getting inflation *down*.

Lynch makes to reply, face wrinkling with distaste.

MARLAND: Look, I'm sorry to be so ... pedantic, but that's how it is in the real world, brother. And that's the basis of the compact between the trade union movement and the government. And if we do anything to undermine it, we'll have only ourselves to blame if the Labour government finds itself forced, however reluctantly, to use further unemployment as the sole remaining mechanism for controlling the new inflationary spiral that would ensue. *(pause)* Now I'm not asking for your pity, I'm asking for your intelligent understanding. And I'm saying: slogans are one thing, reality is another. *(deliberately)* We're doing what we can. *(he looks at his watch)* I must say, brothers, your own position is not without a certain, what shall we say, irony? I mean, one of your deputation is in fact the Parliamentary Private Secretary to the Minister for Employment ... I know Mr Brand is doing what he can too ... *(glancing at Lynch)* And who's to say whether it's 'good enough' or not ...?

Stead looks at Brand, who's studying the TUC statement.

BRAND: *(looking at Moores carefully, then Marland)* It's a somewhat ... inconclusive irony, I suspect. I've made it clear that my work in Parliament will in no way be inhibited by that connection. *(small pause)* I'm also on the point of resigning the post. Hoping, I suppose, that the Minister will move first and save me the trouble.

MOORES: *(brows alert)* Resign, you mean?

BRAND: Ahunh.

MOORES: That'd be bloody stupid, man. He's got to stay in there fighting as long as he can ...

MARLAND: *(smoothly)* I'm sorry, I seem to have got us off onto a tangent ... *(clearing his files)* Look, I'm going to have to get back up there ...

LYNCH: What do you suggest we tell the march then?

MARLAND: *(carefully)* Tell them: we sympathise; we're doing everything we can. Because that's the truth.

LYNCH: *(standing)* Well, my translation of that'll read someat like this: the TUC will continue to turn a blind eye to the unemployment situation for as long as this reactionary Labour Government tells it to. *(on the move, to Brand and Hilton)* I'll see yez outside ...

MARLAND: *(standing slowly)* Well, brothers, if I were you I'd get myself a new translator ...

He looks at Moores enquiringly.

MOORES: I'll follow you up, Walter. Five minutes.

MARLAND: Fine.

He shakes hands with Stead and Brand, wishes them good luck, the atmosphere now grave and unsmiling. Leaves.

MOORES: What time's the Albert Hall rally then, Albert?

STEAD: Eight.

MOORES: I'll see you mebbe.

Stead pauses a moment, looking at the window, though not for snow, then rises heavily, face distant.

STEAD: *(finally)* Aye. See you down there, Bill.

He leaves, buttoning his coat. Brand stays put, swivelled in his seat to watch Stead's departure. Moores locks his gaze onto an ornate paper-knife on the desk, picks it up eventually, toys with it. Brand watches him.

MOORES: Well then, boy, where do we go from here?

BRAND: *We* go to Downing Street. *(long pause)* I don't know where you go.

Long silence, broken by two deliberate sniffs from Moores.

MOORES: Anyone else from the House here with you?

BRAND: There'll be one or two for the Downing Street leg, I think.

MOORES: Ahunh.

BRAND: The gentleman's agreement? You do your bit in your sphere, we ours in ours.

MOORES: *(dry)* You can see their point, can't you.

BRAND: *(slow, distinct)* No. No I can't. Not any longer.

MOORES: Oh. I had you figured for bright, Bill. *(patient, searching)* Look, the unions are under attack from all sides. The mood's changing underneath us – my own Executive could fall to the Right at the next election, for Christ's sake. God knows, my members are suffering as much as anyone from unemployment … but you won't convince them the Tories'll be better, no way. The Tories'll cut public spending to the bone, impose an immediate wage standstill and start preparing a statutory incomes policy to back it up. *(pause)* I think we've got to give 'em another year, Bill. If things aren't better by next summer, we'll hit 'em. Hard. All of us. In the meantime, we stay out of it as much as possible. They know they're gonna have to deliver.

BRAND: *(quiet)* Does Venables know that?

MOORES: If he doesn't, he can't have been listening. We met him over the weekend at the NEDC. I think he knows it.

Brand gets up as though to go, then crosses to the window, stares out at the concrete car park. The chants are louder, more violent.

BRAND: There's five thousand out there, Willie. And there's millions behind them. And they're fed up with you and they're fed up with me. What do we do about that?

MOORES: *(quiet, unbending)* It'll pass. *(pause)* I'm not in this game for popularity.

BRAND: They think you've sold them out.

MOORES: *(very quiet)* Do they?

BRAND: *(turning, facing him)* They do.

Moores gets up slowly, walks towards the door, turns, hand on door-knob.

MOORES: That what you think?

Brand eyes him levelly; no answer.

MOORES: I'll tell you something, Bill. I've been a socialist since I was eleven. Where I come from, the Rhondda, they put it in the tea. When I was seventeen my dad and me packed a bag and took a train and a boat and a train again, three days it took, to Spain, see. Two years, fighting Franco's Fascists. Came back on my own. *(pause, carefully)* Now. I didn't fight and he didn't die – so that I could come back and betray my own class. OK?

They look at each other, deep, level. Moores turns again to leave.

BRAND: Willie. *(Moores turns)* A message from Last. He wants to know what happens if Venables drops the commitment to nationalising the docks.

For half a moment Moores' eyes crinkle, half disappear, something like venom washing what remains of them. When he nods, the face has resumed the enigmatic roundness of a man listening to news of distant counties on Lunchtime Scoreboard.

He leaves without answering. Brand studies the room. Notices a photograph on the wall. Studies it briefly. It's a picture of Lord Citrine, in robes. Bring up the chants of the march.

Close shot of Van Loo's portrait of Walpole *over the Adam fireplace in the Cabinet Room. The chants recede; bring up heated Cabinet exchange. Pull out to reveal table, full cabinet in attendance. Brent is arguing with Kearsley, with help from four or five others, of whom Frear is the most conspicuous. The tone is metallic, uncomradely, though familiarity and habitude restrain potential acidity. Venables watches, affable, relaxed, courteous. Last twiddles a pencil, looking at no one. Maddocks sits with Wilks; they mutter to each other at intervals.*

BRENT: ... I'm sorry, I will not accept that a British government is empowered to take instruction on how it will run its affairs from a German bank, Chancellor ...

KEARSLEY: That isn't what's being said, Trevor, and you know it.

BRENT: ... Well that's what I'm hearing and I think we should have none of it ...

FREAR: What, even if we need the money, as indeed we do, and desperately?

BRENT: *(tight; disliking Frear a lot)* Not at that price, no.

KEARSLEY: Trevor, you're like the Irishman asked how to get to Dublin says 'I wouldn't start from here'. We *have* to start from here. It's where we are ...

BRENT: *(tough)* ... No. It's where you are, Maurice ...

FREAR: If the Chancellor *shows* we need another £400 million bridging loan to see us through to the spring, that's good enough for me and I suspect for many others. And if he tells us our credit's good with next to nobody outside of the Reichsbundbank, I buy that too. And if the loan's conditional on certain ... guarantees of how the money's to be used, it's regrettable but there you are. Beggars never could be choosers ...

COPPLE: Brilliant. Did you think that up yourself, Malcolm?

Several people laugh at her end of the table. Frear makes to reply, catches Venables' eye, which minimally cautions against.

COPPLE: I think Maurice should go back to Bonn or wherever it is and start again. We're a sovereign state, for God's sake.

KEARSLEY: *(ill-tempered)* We're an *impoverished* sovereign state, Edna. We have a currency that melts in the hand. We have one of the lowest industrial outputs in Europe. We have a mountainous deficit on our balance of trade. We have an inflation rate – still – of 15 per cent, mm? Face a few facts for a change.

WILKS: *(formal)* I'm not sure this is getting us anywhere very fast, Prime Minister.

COPPLE: What, you mean we can't go on meeting like this, Jim?

Some general laughter, in which Venables chooses to join.

WILKS: *(smiling, awkward)* I merely point out, my dear Edna, that this is our second day in Cabinet. If it goes on much longer I'll begin *believing* the press talk about a Cabinet crisis …

VENABLES: *(easily)* All right. *(pause, as he waits for quiet, eyes poised over agenda)* Now. When I called this meeting, I knew we'd have much difficulty in reaching agreement on the way ahead. Which is why, when the BBC rang yesterday and asked me to be interviewed on their Panorama programme, I said no at once. *(pause)* I did, however, indicate that I could well be available for interview some time this evening. I think you'll all agree that with only two days remaining before the opening of the new parliament, and with a new leader, the country is entitled to a statement of intent.

Considerable agreement from Cabinet, though six or seven – including Last, Brent and Copple – remain silent.

VENABLES: The Deputy Prime Minister may dub me an incurable optimist, but I think we can achieve that agreement before we break. Because where there's talk, Jim, there's hope.

Some smiles from those on whom he smiles.

VENABLES: Of course, it helps if we all talk the same language.

More smiles. Frear looks mockingly up the table, vindicated, in the direction of Copple.

LAST: *(mild, unexpected)* Which language is that then, Prime Minister?

VENABLES: *(just managing to adjust)* The language of priorities, David. The language we were reared in.

LAST: *(as mild)* I thought our language was socialism.

VENABLES: *(no fuss)* I thought that's what I said. Isn't the language of socialism the language of priorities?

LAST: That's pidgin-socialism. A primitive trading patter developed in the twenties and polished in the fifties.

The room is very still now, hair invisibly standing as the smell of confrontation starts its slow spread.

VENABLES: *(at last)* Any … other comments, David?

LAST: *(very cool, quite still, contained, measuring his energy)* One or two. *(pause)* You say you look for agreement by this evening. That's to say, you want Cabinet approval of the German loan with strings, and of these extensive … modifications to our programme for the next session – further and immediate cuts in public spending, ie the social services, the 'temporary' reversal of the extremely modest reflationary measures we took last summer, the open acceptance of the present unemployment rate of 7% as 'realistic', the placing before parliament of a bill that will seek to fund political parties via the state, and thereby sever the historic link between the industrial and the political wings of our own movement, the dropping of our manifesto commitment to take the docks into public ownership, the further emasculation of the National Enterprise Board and the rechannelling of much of its funding into private industry.

He ticks them off, one by one, on the pad before him. Looks up at Venables, who remains impassive.

FREAR: What about strengthening the Race Relations Act? Prison Reform? The Theatre Levy? You make no mention of those …

LAST: *(deliberately)* I make no mention of them because in the main they're not contentious, Malcolm.

FREAR: But *there*, David. They're *there*, that's what I'm saying, part of the package!

Last stares at him, letting the word and its meanings sink in. Some sniffs around the room, a cough or two, discreet, timed.

VENABLES: *(ice beneath ease)* Let David finish if you would, Malcolm.

Frear sits back in his chair, defiant, unrepentant.

LAST: *(not waiting for Venables' permitting nod)* You say you want agreement on all this lot by five o'clock or so. Let me put a couple of hypothetical questions. Suppose you 'collect voices', but there are still people here who can't stomach it. What then?

VENABLES: I imagine such people would have to decide whether they could continue to serve.

LAST: Even though their … resignations would undoubtedly damage party unity and party morale.

VENABLES: *(carefully)* We must all do what we think right. The party is for the individual, not the other way round. Clearly the principle of collective cabinet responsibility will not be waived, in these or any circumstances. Naturally, I do not relish even the hypothetical prospect of resignations at this early juncture – we are the Cabinet we were, as Arthur Watson left us, more or less – and I must warn those who might be 'hypothetically' considering leaving us, that the responsibility for the effects upon party unity and morale will rest and will be seen to rest with *them* and not with those who remain.

LAST: I thank you for your candour, Prime Minister. I have one question more.

MADDOCKS: *(unexpectedly, out of a huddle with Wilks)* Might I say a word, Prime Minister?

VENABLES: I'd sooner David finished, if that's all right, Chief Whip.

MADDOCKS: It *is* germane, I think ...

VENABLES: *(pleasant)* I'm sure the Secretary of State for Employment will bear that in mind.

He nods at Last, the charming smile back on his lips.

LAST: *(deadly)* What happens if the Cabinet back the programme and the Parliamentary Party shoots it down? *(pause)* Hypothetically.

VENABLES: *(lightly)* I think we'd cross that hurdle when we came to it, David. Though I must say there are certain hypotheses so ... insecurely based as to border on the untenable.

MADDOCKS: *(insistence within the restraint)* Prime Minister ...

Venables continues to look at Last, who returns the look, level, composed. Finally turns up the table, to Maddocks.

VENABLES: Chief Whip. If it's your resignation, it's customary to put it in writing ...

The joke misfires, rather extraordinarily. Nerves stretch a little; spectres walk carefully behind the rows of eyes: bloody battles, factions, splits, electoral disasters, viral crisis. Venables hears its flat smack on the floor.

VENABLES: What was it, Cedric?

MADDOCKS: I've listened, I hope loyally, for the best part of two days to this debate. I have not spoken because, quite properly, I have neither vote nor voice in these counsels, save when a question is addressed to me. If I speak now, unbidden, I speak as your Chief Whip, Prime Minister, mindful of his responsibilities, and I speak in answer to a question not yet asked and only just now broached at all in these discussions. *(pause)* Prime Minister, I have studied and thought about these proposals, this programme, very carefully. It is my responsibility – no, it is my duty – to advise you that, should you proceed to the House with them, I can offer no guarantee that enough members of the party will support you to ensure a majority for them in division.

Long pause. Venables stares at him, frowning slightly, as though dazed. Chanting of marchers suddenly heard at the bottom of Downing Street, holding the floor for several moments.

MADDOCKS: I make no personal judgement on this proposed programme, you understand. I merely state what I feel to be the case with regard to its prospects of winning the approval of our supporters in the House.

Chanting again. Venables' head turns in its direction for a moment.

Several firecrackers go off, in dark sputters, down the street.

VENABLES: *(to young man near door)* See what that's about will you, Robin.

The young man leaves quietly.

VENABLES: Thank you, Cedric. I'm grateful to you for that. Can I be clear on one point? Is it your view that a sizeable number of Labour members will try to bring a Labour government down by voting against its agreed programme in the division lobby?

MADDOCKS: *(carefully)* Not quite, Prime Minister. It *is* my view that a substantial number of Labour members would vote *against* these measures and that the government may fall as a result.

VENABLES: It would, in fact, depend, would it not, on what countervailing support we could attract from other parts of the House. *(pause)* You agree?

MADDOCKS: Numerically, yes. *(dry)* My duties have not hitherto extended to the mustering of votes from other parties.

Silence. Venables scans the table carefully. His supporters frown. The centre looks glum, confused. Last sits tight, saying nothing, very alive. Brent has pushed back from the table, face hard and dangerous.

VENABLES: *(quiet, deliberate)* Colleagues, I hope in my desire to run this gathering as chairman and animateur rather than as leader and gauleiter I haven't misled you as to the nature and extent of my belief in this programme.

Chanting still, another short volley of firecrackers, more chanting. Robin re-enters, waits for a chance to speak with the Prime Minister.

VENABLES: These are grave, serious, dangerous times. It is not only the party, it is the country and social democracy itself that stand threatened. And the crisis – economic, political, social – will deepen unless we tackle it *now* and head-on. Every single one of these proposals, every single element of this programme, is a part of that solution. It's a programme that has emerged from long hours of discussion, with Maurice there, with Malcolm, with Andrew, Reg, John ... None of them, I'm sure, see in it any 'unprincipled break from the past', as Trevor puts it, any more than I do, or any more than I suspect the party in the House will, when it's had the matter properly explained. Much of what Arthur drafted and we as a Cabinet agreed remains. The new elements all arise as a response to the problems that *now* confront us, a month and more *after* the original programme was drafted; and, in particular, as I've gone to great pains to explain, the new urgent borrowing requirement and the conditions attaching thereto. *(pause)* If there is one break with the past – and I hope it will become this government's hallmark – it is that we propose to govern openly and honestly; so that when we all of us *know* that unemployment – however cruel and ugly in its social effects and however damaging to us electorally – when we all of us *know* that unemployment is a weapon in the fight against inflation, we will openly and honestly *acknowledge* the fact, instead of pretending we can do nothing about it, that it's wholly someone else's fault. And I am confident that when the people see a government at last coming clean, they'll thank us for it, because we'll have done something long overdue in politics: we'll have told the truth.

More chanting, more firecrackers.

VENABLES: As to ... party support in the House, I have only this to say: the House will support this programme. Of that I am quite certain.

He stops, pale, again composed, same keen feeling on nostril rims. Robin approaches, mutters in his ear. He nods once, twice, smiles at Robin, who retreats.

VENABLES: It seems there's a demonstration. Perhaps we might take tea now ...

The room breaks suddenly. Last sits for a moment, then crosses to the window. Brent joins him. Last studies the garden.

Downing Street. Up it, flanked by police, walk Brand and Lynch. Lynch carries an envelope. They arrive at the door. The escorting police speak with the police guarding No.10. Cameras flash, whirr, as Brand knocks on the door. The door opens. The envelope is duly passed. Huge cheer from the marchers on Whitehall. Focus on Brand: he has a cut under his left eye.

Cabinet Room. Last looks over his shoulder at Brent. Distant sounds of chanting from Whitehall.

LAST: *(reflective)* What are we doing here?

PART THREE

Leighley. The living room of Brand's house. Comfortable, lively paintwork, old and new effects living in precarious harmony. The television is on, though we hear only its sound. Brand sits at the piano, quietly improvising a blues from fragments of the News At Ten. His upper cheek-bone is red and pale blue, the sac under the eye a shade darker.

NEWSREADER: *(sound only)* Adverse reaction to contents of the Queen's Speech have not been confined to parliamentary circles. Trade Union leaders have almost unanimously condemned it ...

BRAND: Trade Union leaders ... Called it a load of crap ...

NEWSREADER: ... While Walter Marland, General Secretary of the TUC, had this to say when he came into our First Report studio this lunchtime ...

BRAND: TUC went blindfold ... Straight into that trap ...

He gets up suddenly, clicks the set off, stares at a poster over the mantelpiece, for Feminist Press Publications, with a large picture of Alex and two other women.

He returns to the piano. Sits. Stares at the keys. Might play something very sad, sweet, at any moment. Pulls down the lid.

Knocking at door. He crosses to it, admits Jowett, spattered up the legs with mud.

BRAND: Hello, Alf.

JOWETT: Just looka that. Bleeding cars. Look at it.

BRAND: Let it dry. It'll brush off.

JOWETT: I'd brain the sod if I got me hands on him. I only walked from the van …

BRAND: Sit down. I'll make a pot …

JOWETT: No, I can't stop, I've got some collecting to do. I was passing, saw the light on. Wondered if you'd heard owt.

BRAND: No. Save what I hear on the news.

JOWETT: So. You're out of a job.

BRAND: Ahunh.

JOWETT: So what are Last and Brent up to, now they've gone?

BRAND: Last's in Wales. Resting at his country cottage. Brent's back in his constituency, reporting to his E.C.

JOWETT: *(pointing to face)* How'd you get that?

BRAND: On the march. The Fascists tried to get in among us round Trafalgar Square.

JOWETT: I've spoken to Albert. He never mentioned it.

BRAND: He was in the thick. He got a bloody clout too.

JOWETT: Looks as if he was clouting 'em with you. You wanna get someat on that.

The phone rings on top of the piano. Brand answers.

BRAND: Hello. *(waits for pips)* Hello, Bill Brand … Yeah, sure … No, that's fine. Right. *(puts phone down)* My wife.

JOWETT: I'll get off.

BRAND: Hang on, Alf. What's happening here. In the party, I mean.

JOWETT: Emergency E.C. tomorrow. I sent you a letter. GMC midweek some time, if we can get it together. We're waiting on an Emergency National Conference.

BRAND: What are the chances of that?

JOWETT: Better than you might think. Albert Stead says the Regions have been bombarded with demands for one. It'll have to be reckoned with.

BRAND: *(eventually)* What's your reading, Alf?

JOWETT: *(dry smile, very serious)* How long have you got? *(pause)* I think we're in the mire, Bill. *(The knocker goes)* Up to there. *(hand at neck)* I'll let her in. We'll talk tomorrow. *(he opens the front door)* Hello, Mrs Brand. Nice to see you.

He leaves. Miriam comes in, almost shyly, pale, composed, young looking, almost lively. Studies the room with shy flirts of the head, smiles slightly at Brand as their eyes meet.

BRAND: Hi. Come in, sit down.

MIRIAM: *(sitting by the fire)* I was doing a home visit in Foundry Street.

BRAND: *(pause)* Oh yes. How're the kids?

MIRIAM: Fine. Michael had another tooth filled. They're staying at my mother's tonight. *(pause)* How are you?

BRAND: *(sitting)* OK.

MIRIAM: Last resigned then.

BRAND: Ahunh.

MIRIAM: *(smiling)* Didn't last long, did you?

BRAND: Ten days that didn't shake the world.

She laughs a little, almost fondly.

MIRIAM: Oh, listen. Are you going tomorrow?

BRAND: Yeah. To the wedding, you mean?

MIRIAM: Because I've been invited too. *(pause)* I thought you should know.

BRAND: Thanks.

Small silence.

MIRIAM: What have you got upstairs?

BRAND: Couple of bedrooms. Lavatory's outside.

MIRIAM: You could manage the kids then. Staying the night, I mean.

BRAND: Yeah. *(pause)* No sweat.

MIRIAM: You could use the camp beds.

BRAND: Yeah. Sure.

Another silence.

BRAND: Want some tea?

MIRIAM: No thanks. *(pause)* I'm thinking of re-marrying.

BRAND: *(just finding breath control)* Oh.

MIRIAM: He'll be there tomorrow.

BRAND: What's his name.

MIRIAM: Foster. Edward. I met him at the hospital. He's a pathologist.

BRAND: *(remote)* Doctor Foster.

MIRIAM: Yes.

Pause. Miriam pale, Brand tense, threatened.

BRAND: *(remote still)* What does he think of the kids?

MIRIAM: He likes them. Very much. *(pause)* And he knows that you're their father and they're your children. OK?

Brand says nothing. Doesn't look at her.

BRAND: What do they think of him?

MIRIAM: They like him.

BRAND: *(eventually; taking her eyes at last; smiling faintly)* Good. Sounds a nice feller.

MIRIAM: *(standing)* I'll get off. I'll see you tomorrow.

She makes for the door, shy again.

BRAND: Mim.

She stops, turns, eyes barely meeting his.

BRAND: You stopped hating me.

MIRIAM: No. I never hated you. I stopped hating myself.

She leaves. He turns, catches his pale, bruised face in the mirror.

C of E parish church, Leighley. *Noon. A cold day. Several dozen friends litter the pathway from gate to entrance. Festooned cars line up in the street. A lone photographer waits on the gravel square in front of the doors. The families and guests emerge, in twos and threes, begin their chat as they await bride and groom. Eddie's wife chats with other family. Miriam and Edward stand a little apart, arm in arm, talking quietly. Brand stands with several old uncles and aunts, nodding and smiling.*

Eddie, best man, busies himself with photographer and drivers.

Music swells up from the church organ. Family and guests turn in towards the doorway. The white-surpliced vicar leads bride and groom out into the damp day.

Eddie steps forward.

EDDIE: Thought you'd slipped off through the vestibule. Let's be having these photos then, it's freezing out here …

MRS BRAND: We were signing the book. I signed on the wrong bloody page, didn't I? What a kerfuffle, I've never seen anything like it …

EDDIE: Stan you here, right, Bill, over here … come on Margaret, *Margaret!* Bloody hell, somebody tell her, will you … *(to photographer)* Won't be a minute, love … Alfred, Nancy, over here …

Eddie laboriously assembles the immediate kin for the picture. Mrs Brand's hat blows off, several people make to go for it. Eddie intervenes.

EDDIE: Don't move, don't move for God's sake, it'll take me half an hour to get you all assembled again. I'll get it …

People click and chatter in the draughty porch, as Eddie follows the hat across the graveyard. A dog dives for his flapping trouser-leg; he aims a distempered punt at it with his right foot, catches it expertly in the ribs.

MRS BRAND: *(calling)* Stop that, our Eddie! Poor little thing!

STAN: *(meekish)* It did go for him, Edith.

MRS BRAND: It was *playing.*

Later. Eddie closes the door on the last car of guests, waves it off. Brand watches him. Eddie turns, mops his brow.

EDDIE: You'd think she'd have more bloody sense, wouldn't you. I know I wouldn't do it again, if I had me chances over.

Brand grins fondly. Eddie holds his hair against the wind.

A car starts up down the road. Brand turns, watches its approach. Miriam drives, Edward sits beside her. Brand waves, they wave back. Eddie says nothing. Brand says nothing.

EDDIE: Are you going back to me ma's or what?

BRAND: No. I'll call in and see 'em later. I've a meeting at the Labour Club.

EDDIE: I'll give you a lift if you like.

Brand asks a question with his face.

EDDIE: I've got old Johnson's delivery van – I do a bit of work for him through t'week, he lends me the van at weekends.

BRAND: Right.

The 15 cwt Bedford threads its way through side streets. Brand's voice over: 'Here'll do. Don't go out of your way …' The van draws into the kerb.

Van interior.

EDDIE: Are you sure? It's no trouble.

BRAND: No, this'll do fine, Ed. Thanks.

EDDIE: Hey, how'd you get the eye?

BRAND: Fight for Work march. Spot of trouble. Our section of it got … attacked.

EDDIE: Oh aye. Not a bad march, were it.

BRAND: Pretty good. See it on telly, did you?

EDDIE: No. I were on it.

Brand blinks. Looks at him.

BRAND: Were you?

EDDIE: Aye.

BRAND: Hey, that's great.

EDDIE: I'm not as thick as I look.

BRAND: No, I mean it.

EDDIE: I listen even when I'm arguing. D'you know what I mean?

BRAND: Yeah.

EDDIE: Anyway. *(long pause)* I learnt a lot. Quite a lot.

BRAND: Me too.

EDDIE: I met this feller on t'bus coming back up. He's one of your lot. Albert something. Said he knew you …

BRAND: Albert Stead.

EDDIE: Stead, that's it. Knew it began with an S. He's a pretty interesting feller.

BRAND: Yeah, he's that.

EDDIE: He was in Spain, you know. Told us about it, what they were fighting for.

BRAND: *(stunned; he didn't know)* Spain? Albert? Was he?

EDDIE: Yeah. He told us all about it. Well, I mean he didn't boast or owt, I had to keep asking him like, what it was like and that. *(pause)* I'd never really understood it before. You know? He were a right young feller when he went. First International Brigade. From Manchester. He's still got two machine gun bullets floating around inside him somewhere, he says. He was all right. *(pause)* And he's still bloody fighting, inne.

BRAND: *(slowly)* Yeah. Still fighting. I'll see you.

He holds his hand out, a sudden, odd movement. Eddie shares the slight embarrassment, takes the hand shyly.

EDDIE: See you, our kid. Take care.

Brand gets out of the van. Eddie draws away. Brand walks off down the soot-dark street towards the Labour Club. Turns a corner. Reaches a building. Stares at it for a longish moment. Goes in.

- end -

Episode 11

It is the
people who create

was broadcast on Monday 16th August 1976

The cast was as follows:

Bill Brand   Jack Shepherd

Jane Brand   Karen Silver

Jamie Finn   Jonathan Pryce

Winnie Scoular   Rosemary Martin

Sandiford   William Hoyland

Reg Starr   Douglas Campbell

Priest   Alan Partington

Gollimore   Colin Douglas

Researcher   Avril Marsh

Mboya   Salami Coker

Enoma   Willie Payne

TV presenter   Angela Easterling

Maddocks   Peter Copley

Venables   Peter Howell

Sian   Sharon Duce

Aya   Adelaida Arias

Cleo   Miranda Bell

Dink   Susan Glanville

Alf Jowett   Allan Surtees

Mrs Wainwright   Constance Chapman

Designers: David Ferris, Harry Clark

Executive Producer: Stella Richman

Producer: Stuart Burge

Director: Roland Joffé

PART ONE

Leighley Football Club car park. Brand locks his car door. Jane waits for him, wrapped up against the cool day. He carries kit in a small canvas bag. Ahead of them, a coach has begun emptying. As they approach it, a man of Brand's age, or a little younger, detaches from a group and moves towards him. He carries football boots in his left hand.

MAN: Bill! Bill Brand ... Jesus. How are you?

BRAND: *(recognising him almost at once, but puzzled)* Jamie ... Jamie Finn. Good to see you ... What're you doing here?

FINN: *(pointing to poster in coach window)* All Stars, son ... Don't say you're ...

BRAND: *(laughing)* Right. *(taking outstretched hand)* Well ... how about that ...

FINN: *(smiling at Jane)* Hello.

JANE: *(shy)* Hello.

BRAND: My daughter Jane. This is an old friend of mine from University, Jamie Finn.

FINN: *(to Brand)* How are you, comrade?

BRAND: I'll tell you at half-time. Terrible, I suspect. What're you up to?

FINN: Acting, you know. Directing a bit. *(they begin walking towards the gates to the ground)* We've got up a sort of group, touring our own shows, out of the Fringe ...

BRAND: What, political?

FINN: *(grinning)* What do you think? Come and see us, we're up this way soon. Playing the Trades Clubs, stuff like that.

BRAND: Terrific. Like to.

FINN: We're rehearsing the Space next week. Drop in if you like. Hey. Good to see you ...

They walk on through the gates, taking gentle punches at each other's shoulder. Jane frowns at their childishness. Close in on a wall-poster announcing North West Labour Party XI v. All Stars XI. Proceeds to Fight for Work Campaign.

Brand's car draws up *outside Miriam's house, behind a parked Renault 16 TS.*

Interior, Brand's car.

JANE: *(factual)* That's Edward's.

BRAND: So ... I'll see you when you get back, OK?

JANE: OK.

BRAND: Be sure to pack some warm clothes, it'll be seventeen degrees below in Leningrad this time of year.

JANE: You sound just like Mummy.

BRAND: And give Mike a kiss. Tell him I'm sorry I missed him and I'll see him when you get back.

JANE: I don't even want to go. Silly old medical conference, eeyugh.

BRAND: Go on, you'll enjoy it. Kiss.

JANE: Nose.

They rub noses gently.

JANE: If you'd scored that penalty, you'd've won, wouldn't you.

BRAND: Go on, scram.

She laughs, leaves the car, leans back into it. Gently:

JANE: Take care.

He smiles. She goes. He watches.

Brand's Clapham flat. *Morning. Brand dials a number, a list of Journal Group members on the table by his right hand. A Guardian beside it carries the headline: Labour Left Shows Teeth over Queen's Speech etc.*

He waits for a reply, studying the sheet before him. Names are listed alphabetically down the left-hand side; two columns to the right – headed Amendment and Main Question – carry ticks, crosses and question marks. In the Amendment column, ticks outnumber crosses by four to one. In the Main Question column, question marks predominate. He picks up a pen; has clearly been working his way methodically down the list.

BRAND: *(eventually)* Wilf, Bill Brand, hi. Did you think any more about the amendment? Ahunh. Good. Well, listen, see if you can get it signed today, it's important. *(he ticks the amendment column, against the man's name)* What about opposing the main question, if the amendment dips? *(listens, face setting as the familiar response develops. His pen scores a question mark, in the second column)* Well, have you read Winnie Scoular's piece in this week's Journal? *(he fiddles for it beneath the Guardian, finds it. It's a front page article headed: Fight The Revisionists Now'. Wilf isn't interested)* Well look Wilf, read it at least. OK. Fine. Thanks. Bye.

He puts the phone down, already tracing up another number from the list.

Winnie knocks and enters.

SCOULAR: Hi, it's me.

BRAND: Hi, Winnie, come in.

He leaves the table as she crosses to an armchair and sits down. He's on his way to the kitchen.

SCOULAR: No thanks.

He stops, turns, smiles.

BRAND: Sometimes I think you're not English.

SCOULAR: *(dry)* I had breakfast on the train up. A whole pot of tea to myself. So how's it going? The Times said forty four.

BRAND: Fifty two. It'll be seventy by tomorrow.

SCOULAR: It'll need to be. If we don't show Venables now, we can pack our things and go home.

He sits on a small chair to face her.

BRAND: Liked your piece. In the Journal.

SCOULAR: Has Trevor Brent signed?

BRAND: Ahunh.

SCOULAR: Edna Copple?

BRAND: *(factual)* Not yet. There's a rumour she's considering a peerage.

Scoular makes a minimal gesture of distaste with her mouth.

SCOULAR: Last? *(Brand shakes his head slowly)* Christ.

BRAND: *(no particular malice; factual)* He's planning an all-out attack on the Queen's Speech in the Chamber. But he won't vote with the amendment. Not the time. If the party's to split, it must be Venables who's seen to split it, not the left. Etc. etc. *(she looks away towards the window, says nothing. Brand studies her a moment)* What about Friday, Win?

SCOULAR: *(returning slowly)* I don't know. My GMC meets Tuesday. My EC's recommending them to advise me to do nothing that might bring down the Labour Government. *(silence)* What about you?

He crosses to the table, brings back the list he's been working on.

BRAND: I'm working on it.

SCOULAR: How many have you got? Prepared to vote against the main question, I mean.

BRAND: Not enough. Six.

SCOULAR: One's enough, if the Opposition gets out its full vote.

BRAND: *(quiet)* If the Opposition votes *against*.

SCOULAR: *(thoughtful)* Mmm. *(rising)* Well, we'll have to see. Think hard, Bill. That's all I ask. *(crossing to the door)* I've got a cab for half past, do you want to share?

BRAND: No thanks, I'd better finish this.

SCOULAR: Right. *(at door)* Oh, Venables offered me Minister of State at the DHSS at the weekend.

BRAND: *(quietly)* Yes?

SCOULAR: *(smiling bleakly)* I don't think he'll offer again. See you there, comrade.

She closes the door after her. Brand studies the list in his hand. Pencils in a question mark by Scoular's name.

Chief Whip's office. *Tuesday morning. Sandiford leans back in the Chief Whip's chair, feet elegantly lodged on a drawer, studying a list of names. Knock at door. Brand enters as Sandiford makes to call come in.*

SANDIFORD: *(straightening up)* Come ... Ah. Come in. Have a chair.

Brand stands by the door.

BRAND: Cedric asked me to call.

SANDIFORD: Yes, he's asked me to look after it. He's meeting the Opposition whips just now.

Brand dwells a moment, then takes a chair facing the desk.

SANDIFORD: So. *(long pause)* You're staging a revolt. *(he indicates the list of names)*

BRAND: *(bleak smile)* I'm moving an amendment, Jeremy.

SANDIFORD: To your own government's programme for the year.

BRAND: That's right.

SANDIFORD: What does your constituency party think of that?

BRAND: Why don't you ask them?

SANDIFORD: I will. *(pause)* What are you after?

BRAND: Socialism. *(pause)* Heard of it?

Sandiford smiles, easy, relaxed, confident; lies back in his chair, hands clasping back of head.

SANDIFORD: *(very mild, ironic)* Are you sure you're in the right party?

BRAND: *(weighing it carefully)* Are you?

SANDIFORD: Oh yes. Without a doubt.

Phone rings. Sandiford answers without hurry.

SANDIFORD: Chief Whip's office. *(listens)* He's out just now, Deputy Chief Whip speaking, can I ... ? Oh, certainly, yes ... *(slight but perceptible shift in posture and tone, as he learns who's about to come on at the other end)* Good morning,

Prime Minister, can I be of help, Cedric's ... *(he's interrupted; listens intently)* Sixty two, this morning. *(pause)* I'm ... looking into it now ... could I call you back? Yes. Yes indeed. I saw the Speaker this morning. No, not decided, but any time now, I should think. May I call you back? *(looks at watch)* Ten minutes. *(listens a moment; smiles, as the PM congratulates him on his new post)* That's very kind of you, Prime Minister, thank you.

He replaces the phone. Brand has stood towards the end of the call: looks down at him from behind the chair.

BRAND: *(slowly)* Yes. I suppose you are.

He turns to leave.

SANDIFORD: *(quietly)* The question is: is there room for both of us?

Brand turns to look at him, eyes dark, gleaming.

BRAND: *(finally)* Is it *just* career?

Sandiford leans back in his chair, a hair-line smile cracking his lower face.

SANDIFORD: What a silly ... silly question. Have you learned nothing?

The eye contact holds, hardens.

BRAND: You said all you want to say?

SANDIFORD: Not quite. *(phone rings. He picks it up without delay)* Chief Whip's office, Deputy Chief Whip speaking. *(reaching for his order paper file, opening it, picking up pen)* Yes indeed, go ahead. *(he begins ticking, starring and crossing out, as the list develops. Looks at Brand once, amost pleasantly, though the eyes are remote)* Thank you very much. I'll see he sees it the moment he gets back.

Phone down. He studies the paper a moment.

SANDIFORD: That was the Speaker's office ringing through the amendments he's decided to call. *(deliberate pause)* Yours isn't among them. *(he smiles suddenly, into Brand's face)* I've won a fiver on that. I said an amendment to a government motion from the government benches wouldn't be taken ...

Long silence. Brand blinks once, unprepared perhaps for this defeat.

SANDIFORD: Thanks for coming. Let's have a drink some time.

BRAND: One question.

SANDIFORD: Go on.

BRAND: Who *wouldn't* you serve?

Sandiford picks up phone carefully, checking a number on his pad.

SANDIFORD: *(finally)* You.

He taps out the number, waits, ignoring Brand. We hear the door close.

Tea Room, House of Commons. *Evening. Brand sits alone by a window, looking out across the river. The evening is wet, misty, the light well gone. Reg Starr enters with two other MPs, stands talking with them for a moment, his eyes on Brand. The two move off eventually up the room. Starr lingers a moment, then crosses to Brand's table. Stands, looking down at Brand, who slowly becomes aware of his bulk, turns to look up at him but doesn't speak.*

STARR: Mind if I join you?

BRAND: No.

Starr eases himself into a chair, joins Brand's gaze onto the slim glints of light that are the river.

STARR: *(finally, tired)* You should have stayed this morning. It got better.

BRAND: I'd had enough.

STARR: Brent took him on finally. Found a lot of support from the centre.

BRAND: Ahunh.

STARR: Venables promised to rethink the Party Funding Bill.

BRAND: That all?

STARR: *(not critically)* It's something. *(pause)* Did you see this? *(he's taken out an Evening Standard, folded, pushes it across the table to Brand. Brand looks at it, uninterested. It's the results of a national opinion survey in which Venables easily tops the list as most popular politician in the country. Last and Brent foot it)* They've got their man at last, eh?

BRAND: *(suddenly)* How will you vote on Friday, Reg? On the Main Question?

STARR: *(thinking a long time)* I don't know. *(pause)* Journal Group meets Thursday.

BRAND: *(insistent, not harsh)* You, Reg?

STARR: I don't know.

BRAND: *(getting up)* That's just what he's counting on, comrade.

Brand walks off, gathering pace. Starr sits on, not watching. Glances finally at the river.

BBC Lime Grove studios. *Small, cramped hospitality room. Several assorted chairs, a small hospitality cupboard, a colour tv in the corner.*

Brand and two other MPs, Priest and Gallimore, sit side by side along one wall, making eye-contact all but impossible. When they speak at all, it's in low tones, with minimal head shifts in the direction of the recipient. Brand has the middle chair.

A female researcher pours their drinks, carries them over. She's about 30, burly, attractive, not married.

RESEARCHER: Mr Priest. Mr Brand. Mr Gallimore. Five minutes, OK?

PRIEST: *(about 40, very thin, buoyant; on the revisionist wing of the party)* Fine. We're quite happy.

The researcher collects a solitary Roman Catholic bishop from the bottom of the room, where he sits watching the end of a Play for Today, leaves with him for the studio. Two black African emigré revolutionary politicians sit opposite the MPs arguing about the Russian presence in Central Africa. The dialogue is deeply familiar. Stalin is a neck ahead only, Mao closing fast.

Gallimore swigs his gin at one go, watching Brand from the corner of his eye. He's large, thick-necked, big-handed, a trades union MP from the dead centre of the party: a Londoner.

GALLIMORE: You vote against, mate, you're in dead trouble. You bring this government down, you're finished in politics, I'm telling you.

Brand sips his light ale, sniffs, says nothing, eyes on the two blacks.

PRIEST: *(casual; bright, airy)* He won't, Frank, don't worry. He knows which side his bread's buttered on. *(pause)* Too much of a risk anyway.

Brand half looks at Priest, gives him attention.

BRAND: *(calm, cold)* How's that, Peter?

PRIEST: *(sotto still)* Come on Bill. You know as well as I do. All the signs are the Opposition will at the very least abstain. So where does that leave you and your handful of kamikaze comrades? With your heads on the PM's block, I should've thought. No?

Brand turns back to the blacks, who are laughing suddenly, poking each other in the chest and arm, suddenly released.

GALLIMORE: The sooner John Venables carries out his pledge to wind up these sectarian groupings, the better it'll be for the party. No good's ever come of them, as far as I can see.

PRIEST: Won't be long, Frank. Won't be long.

The researcher returns.

RESEARCHER: All right, gentlemen? We're ready for you now ... I'll take you through to the studio. Stay close, won't you, it's easy to lose your way in this place ...

She leads them out. The blacks start arguing again, quite fiercely.

Chief Whip's office. *Night. Sandiford watches television, crosses to switch on the VCR beneath it as the Tonight interviewer introduces the discussion between the three Labour MPs (right, centre, left) on how they intend to cast their votes on the Main Question of the Queen's Speech tomorrow.*

Sandiford sits back to watch. We follow the discussion on his tv.

INTERVIEWER: In the Queen's Speech last Friday, the government unfurled its programme for the coming year. Although we know there are deep divisions within the ranks of the Labour Party, it appears that the new proposals could cause further dissent. In the studio tonight we have three Labour MPs, Frank Gallimore, William Brand and Keith Priest.

PRIEST: *(on screen; confident, buoyant)* Look, the first thing we'd better clear up is this business of a 'deep division' within the party. You know, with respect, we've heard it all before. We were a deeply divided party under Atlee, and he ruled for six years and changed the map of this society. We were deeply divided under Gaitskell, we were deeply divided under Watson ... *(ironic)* Let me answer this way, we're as divided as we ever were ... and I have a fiver says this Government will continue until Spring 1979.

INTERVIEWER: Well, that's a breezy enough start. Now, Mr Brand, you took the uncompromising step of voting against your own government. Do you share your colleague's optimisim for the future

BRAND: Let me answer this way. I came into Parliament less than a year ago as a socialist member committed to moving this society in socialist directions. Then as now, I deemed myself bound to the electorate by our Manifesto, which said – amongst other things – and I quote: 'Socialism is about helping the poor and eliminating poverty. It is also about achieving massive and irreversible shifts in the distribution of wealth and income in favour of working people. *(he's quoting from a pamphlet which he has in his hand, but pretty well knows the passage by heart)* For socialists, the creation of wealth is seen above all else as a *social* process – one which involves the co-operation of countless individual men and women, and of the community as a whole. No one person – or indeed any family or group of shareholders – can be said to create wealth, great companies or great estates. It is the people who create: it is the fortunate few, blessed by the custom and law of the land, who are deemed to *own*. It is time, we believe, to change these customs and laws. We must begin to load the scales in favour of equality. And this can only mean radical *socialist* measures.' *(he closes the pamphlet)* Now. The Government's programme for the coming year, which is at present under debate in the House, is in my view a cynical and deliberate breach of that promise. I shall consequently vote against it, when the Main Question is put.

Close shot of Sandiford, watching carefully.

INTERVIEWER: Even if, given the present strength of the parties in the House, it actually brings about the fall of your own government?

BRAND: I don't think there's any danger of that. I mean, after all, I didn't write the Queen's Speech. John Venables did.

PART TWO

Chief Whip's office. Day. Towards noon. On the television, a playback of Brand's reading from the 1974 Manifesto. Maddocks gives it half his attention. The remainder goes fitfully into clearing the office of his personal effects. He takes down the picture of the sheep, places it in an open cardboard box filled with other pics.

Knock on door, as Brand reaches 'I shall consequently vote against it ...'. He clicks the machine off, then the tv, and opens the door.

MADDOCKS: Come in, come in. *(Brand enters, pale, composed)* Move those boxes and sit down. *(he points to a chair. Brand shifts them, sits. Maddocks checks his watch by Big Ben – one o'clock; a reflex. Sits behind his desk)* Have a drink?

BRAND: No thanks.

Maddocks crosses to the cabinet, pours himself a large gin, splashes it with tonic.

MADDOCKS: Well, I'll have one. I fancy I'll have need of it.

BRAND: *(suddenly)* Do you have a beer?

MADDOCKS: Surely.

He hands him a can of Worthington 'E' and a glass. Brand strips the foil, pours. Maddocks resumes his seat, waiting. Raises his glass.

MADDOCKS: What shall it be? *(pause)* How about 'The Party'?

BRAND: *(unlaughing, slow)* How about ... 'The end of ... something'.

MADDOCKS: Why not? It's my last day. We'll drink to me.

Brand smiles.

BRAND: To you.

They drink. Maddocks goes deep, Brand sips.

BRAND: How do you feel about it? Going to the other place?

MADDOCKS: Not good. Not good. It's ... not what I wanted. But then, very little ever is ... in politics. Give and take. Here and there. Come and go.

Long silence. Rather sad. Brand watches Maddocks watch the rim of his glass.

MADDOCKS: I've had a good run. All in all. *(pausing)* I was a docker, you know, a tally clerk. Royal Albert. My father before me. He helped organise the big one – that's what they called it – 1889. Ben Tillett, Tom Mann, John Burns ... Mmm. *(pause)* A long time ago. A long way away.

Silence again. Brand places his glass carefully on the table. Maddocks looks at him suddenly, an anger welling momentarily, subsiding as quickly, unexplained.

MADDOCKS: You won't see it, Bill ... but we've changed this country. *We* have changed it. *(pause)* In 1931 *(he stops: hates the date, desperately)* ... In that year we could've just ... phtt ... finished, gone under. But we didn't. We got our heads down. And we stuck. And we were ready ... in '45 ... and we changed this country ... coal, railways, road transport, electricity, gas, steel, national health service, education, social welfare ... *(long pause)* But we could've gone under. Not stuck. *(long pause)* You're a good member, Bill. I've come to ... admire you quite a lot ... but there's something missing, something ... *(he teases it out from the webs of his mind)* You've got to love this party. You're in it, of it, but you don't ... love it. Not family. *(long pause)* Know what I mean?

Sandiford in, on knock, from connecting room.

SANDIFORD: Sorry, Cedric, didn't realise you were about. Can we talk about this afternoon some time?

MADDOCKS: Give me a minute, will you, Jeremy.

SANDIFORD: *(withdrawing; his own man)* Sure.

BRAND: *(finally)* And him?

MADDOCKS: *(studying his watch)* He's ... getting on. There's that too. S'what makes us ... human. Which I fancy you suspect rather a lot. *(he closes his watch)* You'll vote against us this afternoon?

BRAND: Yes.

MADDOCKS: Might I ask how many others will do the same?

BRAND: Six. Maybe eight.

MADDOCKS: *(standing)* So be it. *(he holds his hand out. Brand stands and takes it)* Go well.

BRAND: And you.

He leaves. Maddocks stares at the cardboard boxes on the desk. Takes out a glass-framed picture: the sheep. Stares at it for a moment.

Sandiford in again. Maddocks returns picture to box.

SANDIFORD: *(checking Brand's gone)* Eight at the most, I make it.

MADDOCKS: *(sitting again)* Ahunh.

SANDIFORD: Did you tell him the Tories are abstaining?

MADDOCKS: No.

SANDIFORD: Good thing. Make him sweat a bit.

He leaves. Maddocks sniffs. Drains his glass. Sets it down.

Living room, Clapham flat. *Brand's ready for off, his bags packed. The tv is on, showing a prime ministerial broadcast by Venables.*

VENABLES: *(on screen)* ... This week, as I say, your government has presented to Parliament the most extensive programme of social legislation ever placed before the House, certainly since the last war. It has one object: to make this country once again a place of freedom and enterprise and justice. A place we're proud to bring our children up in. A place where honesty and plain dealing are no longer derided. A place where compassion is once again a byword of our national life. In America's darkest hour, in the mid-thirties, a new phrase sprang up as if from nowhere, to beckon the promise of the future: the phrase was ... New Deal. In years to come, I hope this moment will be seen as a similar turning point in our national destiny; will be seen ... and felt ... as the year of *our* New Deal. Goodnight. *(he fades slowly from the screen)*

BRAND: *(crossing to turn tv off; sniffs)* You too, sunshine.

He searches for his car keys, finds them on the table, pockets them. Is checking his diary for an address when Winnie Scoular enters, on the knock.

SCOULAR: Hear him?

BRAND: Ahunh.

SCOULAR: Reg rang a while back. Did he call you?

BRAND: No.

SCOULAR: Mmm. There's a rumour Venables is planning to make the next division in the Chamber a vote of confidence in the Government.

Brand absorbs it, moving towards the drinks.

BRAND: Drink?

SCOULAR: Small one.

She sits down, tired, grey, uncertain. Brand brings her the drink, sits opposite her.

BRAND: Cheers.

SCOULAR: Cheers.

They drink in silence for a moment.

SCOULAR: He's going to bring us to heel.

BRAND: *(quietly)* He's gonna try.

SCOULAR: *(deliberately)* Comrade, I don't know about you, but my CLP's already poised to pass a vote of censure on me for voting against this afternoon. One more and I'm finished.

Brand gets up, splashes more water into his whisky at the sink. Scoular watches him.

SCOULAR: What about you?

BRAND: *(returning)* I don't know. I'm asking them to back me. All the way.

He sits down again, brows furrowing, his hand teasing his hair.

BRAND: Any news from the NEC?

SCOULAR: No. Tom Wiltshire's seeing Venables early next week. *(pause)* There's a general feeling Venables will come to his senses, once the oxygen begins to thin a little ...

BRAND: Willie Moores?

SCOULAR: Worried about his own General Council elections. Fears a shift to the right. *(pause)* He's lying low. *(silence again)* Will you go all the way?

BRAND: *(finally)* I'm not sure. *(long pause; half abstracted)* I might just go.

SCOULAR: *(smiling bleakly)* That'll be the day. *(pause)* You couldn't just ... go ... if you had a rifle at your head. Not in you.

He looks at her blankly for a moment, half hearing someone else.

BRAND: No. Probably not.

She gets up, sets her glass down.

SCOULAR: I'd better get off and face the constituency. Are you going up?

BRAND: *(sitting on)* Yeah. I've got to see a show first – well, a rehearsal. Mate of mine's putting it on round the Trades Councils ... Don't fancy, do you?

SCOULAR: What's it about?

BRAND: No idea.

SCOULAR: No, I don't think so. I've had enough theatre for one week.

BRAND: Yeah. I know what you mean.

SCOULAR: Are you driving?

BRAND: Ahunh.

SCOULAR: Take care, won't you.

She crosses to the door, breaking a rather keen eye-contact. Brand sits on, his back to her now.

BRAND: Win.

She stops, half turns.

SCOULAR: *(finally)* Mmm?

BRAND: *(close to innocent)* Why did we never make it?

SCOULAR: *(slowly)* I don't know. *(pause)* Maybe you just like me too much.

He turns to face her over the back of the chair. Smiles, half boyish. She smiles back at him, half shy. They laugh gently.

SCOULAR: Cheers, comrade.

BRAND: Cheers.

Brand parks his car on the vacant lot by the theatre venue. Walks towards the tiny back door entrance. Passes wall, lamplit, flaked with graffiti. Enters the building, climbs the narrow stairs, peers into a tiny office, where Jamie Finn is on the phone. Jamie sees him, waves a hand, continues the phonecall.

FINN: ... No, but listen, comrade, where are we gonna kip, for Christ's sake? ... Well, think about it, it's important. And park benches are out, we want a roof. And preferably a blanket or two. OK. See you Sunday. Cheers.

He puts the phone down.

FINN: You made it, great. Just started. S'OK, you haven't missed anything. I'm not on for ages. So. You've had a busy week ...

Points to Evening News, headline up, on desk: 'Rebels Routed' etc.

BRAND: *(smiling)* So so.

FINN: You're doing all right.

FINN: Hey. How're you fixed for some beds next weekend?

BRAND: How's that?

FINN: We're playing Manchester Trades Council Club. The digs've fallen through.

BRAND: Yeah, sure. You can have the house. Sunday'll be a bit tricky, but I should be able to sort something out.

FINN: Great.

BRAND: Where do I go?

FINN: It's through there. Hang on, I'll take you.

He leads Brand off down the passage, talking as he goes.

FINN: *(ironic apologetic)* It's erm ... on the politics of sexuality. *(pause)* It's called 'Come'. *(turns, grins drily)*

BRAND: *(nodding, game, not exactly bubbling)* Fine.

FINN: Watch out for me, I'm brilliant. Here we go.

He pushes into the small theatre space, dark save for the playing area. Brand follows.

A woman (Sian), young playing old, sits propped on a stool, a long cigarette holder in her left hand, a long phallic mic in the other. Behind her, a stage-wide screen, coloured light damson.

SIAN: Listen, you can stick your grace and dignity up your smarting arse, dear. I don't start with anything as trivial as desires, what I *want*. I start with *need*; stark, unadmirable, the base. Women *need* men. The reasons may vary, the need doesn't. A man is a woman's identity. Without one, she is a nullity. I start with fundamentals. Let's sort the merchandise, shall we?

As she works her way down her speech, Finn leads Brand to where the other three women (Aya, Dink, Cleo) sit and makes whispered introductions. The girls greet him fairly perfunctorily, busy watching and making notes. The woman in the acting area rearranges her long soignée dress suggestively, props her knee à la Dietrich, preparing for her song. We see the rose suspender against her heavy thigh.

SIAN: That's better. *(piano starts up; Weilian: sprechstimme. She sings)*

> When I was born
> I disappointed
> I was a girl

> When I was one
> I had a brother
> And felt the difference
> When I was two and three and four and more

> I waited and waited
> For a willy to grow
> And waited

> At six my mother told me
> To stop looking
> And slapped the hand I looked with

> When I was seven
> I met God
> Another father

> He confirmed that I was nobody
> I thanked him
> He stilled my fingers

> When I was eight and nine and ten
> Though I left myself alone
> Two uncles and a cousin
> Found me irresistible

> At twelve
> I bathed every day
> To watch my boobies grow

> At thirteen
> I found blood between my legs
> I knew I had sinned

> Fourteen, fourteen
> Changed my panties twice a day
> Terrified by change

> When I was fifteen
> My father rubbed my nipples in the hall
> Fastening a button on my blouse

When I was sixteen
When I was sixteen
I saw ... Marlene
And I've been sixteen ever since.

A huge pic of Dietrich, in the woman's identical position, on the screen.

Brand stares intently from the shadows, with Finn and the other women.

Cut to

Dink and Cleo on stage, in very brief bridal gowns, holding a demure posy each. We see that their wrists are handcuffed. They do their pieces deadpan throughout.

DINK: It pays, of course ...

CLEO: To learn ...

BOTH: Your commandments.

DINK: One: thou shalt not be thyself.

CLEO: Two: thou shalt abhor and put out of sight that which men abhor to see.

DINK: Three: thou shalt abhor and expunge that which men abhor to smell.

CLEO: Four: thou shalt abhor and eliminate that which men abhor to taste.

DINK: Five: thou shalt take no pleasure.

CLEO: Six: thou shalt be an object of pleasure.

DINK: Seven: thou shalt always commit adultery, but only behind locked eyelids.

CLEO: Eight: thou shalt be girl, boy, daughter, mother, whore, virgin, slave, nun, arab girl, cabin boy, schoolmistress, lady magistrate, victorian maid, companion, secretary, trophy, skivvie, thing, hot, cool, fat, thin, wet, dry, all things, and all manner of things, to men.

DINK: Nine: covet thy neighbour's penis.

BOTH: Ten: keep your hand on your ha'penny, in remembrance of me.

Brand, absorbed, enjoying it. Sian sits by him, leans across, touches his arm.

SIAN: Hi. I'm Sian.

BRAND: Bill Brand. Hi.

Cut to stage. Sian, in tight-fitting US Colonel's tunic, sheer tights, thigh-length leather boots. Dink, Aya and Cleo sit on the floor in front of her.

SIAN: *(American)* At ease, at ease. Now hear this. The major problem confronting the modern sex warrior is finding the enemy. Well, I got news for you, sisters. The enemy is you. The enemy is your own goddam body, right? Against which, in order to survive, you will wage total and unceasing *war.* Now, first off, all emissions and leakages gotta be plugged, staunched at all costs, OK? You gotta hack those thickets. Search and destroy. Deodorants, defoliants.

Technology on our side. Second: all ground overrun must be immediately colonised, pacified, against further insurgency. Depilation will continue to be handled as a long-term problem of growth. And since the battle for the mind begins with the belly, attention will be paid to that area; the cockpit, as it were, of the whole theatre of operations.

Brand laughs out loud, catches Finn (next to him) grinning. Brand lights a cigar.

Cut to

Finn on stage, a spot picking him out as he threads his arms into a jacket. He wears white tie and tails, a silver top hat with the day's Financial Times Share Index on it. His face is artificially whitened. He's greeted by a fast orchestral version (taped) of 'Money Money Money'.

FINN: Good eving, labies and mentalmen, labies and mentalmen, good eving. Tis my groat and sterling area this eving to reproduce for your dereliction and eventual consumption the Grossmazing, the Infibulous, the Fetish and Carry On of all spectation, fresh from their most recent traumas in Hamburg and Batley, the one and lonely – if you've got a hole, we'll help you fill it, if you've got something to fill a hole with, we'll help you find a hole … Seriously, frowns, for what you are about to perceive, may the law make you truly thankful. I prefer, of course, to the sensordinary, the sensificent, the exsexual, the percentual, the hypnerotic, the financial – the show of shows, what we don't show isn't there – labies and mentalmen – if you have eurodollars, prepare to shed them now … Or as Paul Raymond put it in his salivated ear pistol to the merchant bankers: 'What does it profit a man if he inherit the whole world and have not profit. It will be as the sound of empty cash registers, more doleful to the ear than the wailing and gnashing of teeth that will undoubtedly accompany it'. Gold is Beauty, Beauty is Taste, Taste is Profit. Profits are honoured, for they make one grow where two grew before, but on a regular basis … and those of us privileged enough to be living on the very frontiers of human liberation – you and I, comrades – know two paramount truths: nothing in God's little acre ever came free; and the only sin is the failure to consume. Wasn't it the extinguished poet-laureate Ernest Auden, sunloving marxist and homoffectual, who said we must screw one another or we die, and he did both, the craggy man, he was wrong about the or. We dedicate this next piece – entitled Miss World History – to that remarkable artist and his unforgettable epitaph. To you, Ernest Auden, for your brave true words, for helping us to see that Art, Sex, Freedom, Profit, Pragmatism and Progress are indivisible, we dedicate the following moving tableau.

Lights up on stairway, on which three girls stand, as beauty queens, numbers on the left wrist. They're dressed in appropriate historical costume but heavily fetishised.

Brand, amused, now leaning back a little after the bombardment.

FINN: *(forward, in spot)*And now, we present the first contestant for the Miss World History Prize, the duskily desirable Goddess Shiva, Miss India!

*The first girl (Aya) jerks into action, approaches centre stage and the mic.,
accompanied by taped piano version of 'A pretty girl is like a melody' in crude
Indian style.*

FINN: Welcome, goddess. Now tell me, do you like money?

GODDESS: Yes, I like money very much.

FINN: That's nice. Isn't that nice, ladies and gentlemen? Wonderful. And now tell
me goddess, do you have a hobby?

GODDESS: Yes. I like counting money. Every spare minute I have, I empty my
purse out onto the table or wherever and count it into neat piles.

FINN: Very good. How interesting. Isn't that interesting ladies and gentlemen? And
now perhaps, would you care to say something to our audience here in
Euroland in your own language?

GODDESS: Kanjesu dasi karnesu mantri rupe ka laksmi Ksamaya dharitri snena Ka
mata sayanesu Vesya sadkarma ukta kila dharma patni.

She smiles, walks back to her place.

FINN: *(fishing card from clipboard)* And the translation of that reads as follows: 'If
a man has commerce with a woman, having first rubbed his member with dung
dropped by a valgulibird on the wing, she will never have to do it with another
man'. Isn't that sweet? Contestant number two is Antony's Eden herself,
Cleopatra – Miss Egypt.

She takes her walk, to the same tune in crude Nile style.

FINN: Welcome, your Majesty. Nice to have you along. Do you have a burning
ambition, something you'd like to do more than anything else?

CLEOPATRA: Yes, I'd like to meet the man of my dreams and marry him and raise a
family and be extremely rich.

FINN: Bliss, bliss. I love your smile. Do it again. A quick word in your own
language, if you would.

CLEOPATRA: Abdul Gamil Nasser.

She returns to the staircase.

FINN: Short and sweet. And Miss Egypt said: 'Better the bourgeois revolution you
know than the proletarian one you don't'. Isn't she a charming girl? Finally,
and number three on your programme, the last contestant, the reigning Miss
World History herself, the selfless Miss Florence Nightingale, Miss United
Kingdom!

*The girl begins her walk to military version of 'A Pretty Girl etc'. The others
follow her down, as she finishes her walk, and line up diagonally across the
acting area, Miss India at the rear.*

FINN: Miss United Kingdom will now lead the contestants in the second stage of the contest to find the most everything girl in the history of the world. This, may I remind you, is the stage where the little ladies slip out of something less comfortable and show you their exciting flesh and organs.

Strip music begins, lights dim generally, focusing more concretely on the three girls. Miss UK begins to remove her scant nurse's uniform; after a moment Miss Egypt follows suit; as Miss India advances, a low muttering, murmuring sound starts up, rising in pitch, volume and intensity as the strips continue. The sound resembles human voices, hundreds of thousands of them, pressing upwards against their oppression, outwards against their misery.

The girls register consternation, concern, anxiety. The strips tail off. They stand awkwardly, half-dressed. Begin to gather up their clothes a little foolishly. Finn signals frantically for them to continue to strip. The noise is now deafening. Close shot of Brand, tense, watchful. At the very tip of the crescendo, a single image floods the screen behind them, a million Indians filling Calcutta city centre.

The sound stops suddenly. The image persists. The girls leave. Finn stares at the image, which fades very slowly. He walks forward finally into his spotlight. Lifts mic as if to speak, still dazed. Doesn't. Lights out.

House lights at once. Laughter from behind stage, relief at having cracked the first half. Brand stares at the stage, cigar gone out but still held.

FINN: What do you think of it so far?

BRAND: Wow.

The girls sit or sprawl or perch, forming a loose habitual discussion group, including Brand.

SIAN: That piece of yours is still too long, Jamie.

FINN: *(jokey)* Oh yeah.

DINK: *(serious)* Oh yeah. You'll have 'em tying their shoelaces and picking up old beer mats.

FINN: We'll see, eh.

SIAN: I think the whole bloody thing's too sophisticated, as a matter of fact. I mean, Jesus, Ernest Auden, I mean what's that about for Christ's sake!

FINN: Don't be so bloody élitist. You think you're the only one who's read a book.

CLEO: Jamie, she's right. We're gonna talk to working class men and women about sexuality, we're gonna have to include them *in* it. Their experience, you know what I mean. There's a good chance they won't have a bloody clue what we're on about …

DINK: I'm not sure *I* have, half the time.

FINN: *(used to it)* Oh Christ, here we go again. *(standing, very deliberate)* Persons, we are trying to present an entertainment, to make people laugh, to make people think, about their lives, about sex, about men's roles and women's roles, about sexual stereotypes ... *(he stops the weary list)* Listen, you wrote this pigging thing, why the hell do *I* always get it in the neck ...

SIAN: *(smiling, rather fond)* Because our stuff's fine. It's yours that's the problem ...

FINN: Oh, I give up. *(mock desperate)* Bill, what do you think?

BRAND: *(slowly)* You're going to play this where?

FINN: Trades Coucils. A few working men's clubs.

Silence. Brand begins to chuckle. The women join in after a moment or so, Finn too after further moments. It moves into laughter, warm, growing, unhysterical.

BRAND: *(finally)* Oh boy.

FINN: Yeah.

More laughter.

PART THREE

Jowett's office. Saturday evening. Jowett sits at his desk, working on the promotion of a party dance and listening to the six o'clock news on the battered red transistor radio by his right hand.

NEWSREADER: ... Finally, reports are just reaching us of a wave of mass arrests in Chile, following yesterday's unconfirmed reports of a general strike in the capital, Santiago. According to government sources, the arrests are an attempt to pre-empt a possible coup and to preserve law and order against the forces of anarchy in the country generally. We'll have more on that in our ten o'clock bulletin. And now the day's headlines again. In a tough speech in Birmingham today, the new Prime Minister has announced his intention to see things through 'come what may'. In a veiled reference to opposition in his own ranks, Mr Venables has promised to seek a vote of confidence from the whole House early next week. In a speech in Bristol, the Liberal Leader, Mr Blake, has offered the new government full backing in what he calls 'their principled struggle to knock sense into the heads of the backwoodsmen of all parties'. *(Brand in, carrying a ledger)* In Belfast, two elderly women and a five year old child died when a bomb exploded ...

Jowett switches off, puts down his pen.

JOWETT: Did you read them?

BRAND: Ahunh.

He puts the ledger down on the table, label up. It reads, in Jowett's hand, 'Leighley CLP General Management Committee: Minutes'. Brand sits down to face Jowett.

JOWETT: We're with you, Bill. *(pause)* We just think you should lie low for a while.

BRAND: Yeah.

Jowett hands him a sheet of paper with several handwritten notes on it.

JOWETT: A few messages, calls, you know, press mainly. *(pause)* Oh, the BBC want to know if you'd do one of them 'Word in Edgeways' things.

Brand grins wryly. Jowett sniffs.

JOWETT: I said it was doubtful.

He half returns to his work. Brand looks around him at the piled office, the habitat.

JOWETT: *(working on)* I think you did the right thing, stopping away ... the GMC, you know. They're always more likely to back you if you don't complicate matters by being there ...

He grins owlishly. Brand smiles, admiring but unsentimental.

JOWETT: *(pointing to radio)* It says Venables is gonna bring you to heel with a vote of confidence.

BRAND: Yeah. It's on the cards.

Jowett crosses to the filing cabinet, checking a raffle-ticket printer's address.

JOWETT: What'll you do?

BRAND: I dunno. We'll have to see.

JOWETT: The Tories'll vote against this time. They'll have to. *(pause)* If he loses, it's an election. *(looks at Brand, returns to his seat)* Nobody's gonna like that, I can tell you. *(long pause. He drinks from a mug of cold tea on the desk, pulls a face at it)* You're going on with it though, are you ... *(it's barely a question, properly unpointed)*

Long silence.

BRAND: Yes, fight the front you're facing ... *(he says it as though quoting)*

JOWETT: *(hesitant, half-diffident, almost shy)* Ethel thought you might care to come round for a bite to eat some time.

Sounds of band setting up in the main hall.

BRAND: Yeah, I'd like that.

JOWETT: How's tomorrow?

BRAND: Fine.

JOWETT: Right, I'll tell her. *(pause)* Are you coming to the social?

BRAND: Yeah, for a couple of hours. I've got some people staying.

JOWETT: Good. I'll see you there then. *(stands, begins clearing away, tidying the desk area. Brand watches him)*

BRAND: Will you stick, Alf?

Jowett blinks, stopped a little by the question.

JOWETT: *(finally)* Oh aye.

BRAND: *(quiet)* Why?

JOWETT: *(slowly)* Cos it's what I do.

BRAND: That all?

JOWETT: *(sitting down again)* No. *(pause)* I tell you, I've had the best part of twenty years here, right? I've seen 'em come and I've seen 'em go. Listen, in the 50s you could go on the knocker and ask if they were voting for Gaitskell and they'd say 'No, we're all Labour here'. We've had these buggers leading us before and we'll have 'em again, they're like dry rot; you clear one area, they break out somewhere else. But they can't win, Bill. They can't *win*. Not because you'll stop them, or Last, or Brent or owt like that. They can't win because reality's not on their side. They think capitalism's like a ... like a coat of paint, like a veneer, and underneath is the structure. But capitalism *is* the structure. The reality. And it splits us up, sets us against each other and against ourselves, in classes, in thought, in life-styles, in aspirations and all the rest of it ... And it breeds resistance, in every worker who goes down the road, in every tenant evicted, in every man and woman denied the chance to be human ...

He stops, half embarrassed at the moral passion he's asserted.

JOWETT: Any road.

Brand stands, nods.

BRAND: I'll see you later on.

JOWETT: Right. *(Brand's on his way. Jowett picks up a letter)* Oh, by the way, there's a theatre group want to do a show here, Red Letters or someat, do you know owt about 'em?

BRAND: Yeah, I know 'em.

JOWETT: Any good?

BRAND: *(a beat only)* Yeah. They're terrific.

JOWETT: Right. I'll book 'em then. Any idea what sort of thing?

BRAND: Oh, a bit of everything really.

JOWETT: Oh aye.

Brand grins, leaves. Jowett pencils some dates in his desk year-planner.

Brand's house. *Night. Brand walks up the ginnel at the back of his house, clicks open the wooden gate, crosses the tiny flagged yard. Sounds of laughter, talk, easy, alive, as he approaches the house.*

He lets himself into the lit kitchen. Finn, Sian, Dink and Aya sit around the big wooden table eating cheese, bread, crude crudités, and drinking wine. He's greeted warmly.

FINN: Come in, come in. Take your coat off, make yourself at home. Have a drink. *(pouring glass of white)*

BRAND: Thanks.

DINK: *(Miss UK, about 24)* Have you eaten? There's plenty.

BRAND: *(sitting at top of table)* I'm fine, thanks.

SIAN: *(Marlene Dietrich, late 20s)* Did we have a *night*, comrade.

BRAND: Yeah? How did it go?

FINN: We lost. About thirteen – nil.

SIAN: They were terrific. They listened and watched and patted us on the head and told us to piss off and get some in.

BRAND: I know the feeling …

DINK: I don't know about you, I learned quite a lot.

BRAND: Like what?

DINK: Well, for a start, we've gotta start from somewhere else. If you're gonna make connections, raise consciousness, you've gotta start where people are actually *at*, not from some notional spot in the middle of your own middle-class, guilt-ridden hang-ups …

FINN: Well, that was a good show while it lasted …

SIAN: Shit, Jamie, you know what she means. God, look at his little ego twitching away there …

FINN: Ego! What ego? We spend six weeks lashing up a piece about women's role in society and it gets two performances …

DINK: I'm not saying we should *scrap* it, I'm saying we should change it. Jesus Christ …

Brand watches the third girl throughout this (Goddess Shiva), who listens silently to the arguments but says nothing. She's in her young 20s, dark, dark-skinned, big eyes, composed yet vulnerable. She takes his eyes twice, smiles on the first, darts down and away on the second. The exchange putters off into the wine. They begin giving each other jokey notes. Some laughter again.

BRAND: *(half rising)* I'll sort out the beds …

FINN: Have a *drink*, man. Then we'll have a sing-song. Do you still play that thing in there … ?

BRAND: Now and again. The neighbours aren't too keen.

FINN: Saturday night. Saturday night. You brought your guitar, Dink?

DINK: In the front room …

FINN: *(ironic)* Ah, isn't this good. On the road. In the company of friends. Lodged in a fine hostelry … this is a great place you got here, comrade …

SIAN: Yeah, it's amazing. I mean why?

BRAND: Why do you think?

DINK: *(innocent, open)* Where does your family live?

BRAND: Somewhere else.

Slight silence.

DINK: I think it's terrific.

Brand catches the dark girl's eye. She stares at him steadily. He looks away, drains his glass.

BRAND: No. It's not terrific. It's a miserable little hutch. And there are about ten million people still live in them. And living here is a good way of not forgetting it. What about a song then?

DINK: OK, comrade. You gonna play?

BRAND: Ahunh.

FINN: Where's the other bottle, Aya?

AYA: *(crossing to sink)* It's here. I bring it.

Finn, Dink and Sian move off into the next room.

BRAND: *(opening table drawer)* Here, let me open it.

AYA: *(stripping foil)* It's OK. It has a cap.

The guitar begins to play in the next room. Jamie Finn launches a frolicky Irish rebel tune, the others join in.

BRAND: Where are you from?

AYA: South America. Chile. After Allende.

He nods. A small silence.

BRAND: Will you go back?

AYA: Yes. *(pause)* When we have won.

Knock at back door. Aya carries the bottle through to the front room, her eyes demurely down. Brand moves to open the door. A woman, about 50, stands on the doorstep, in pinnie and slippers.

WOMAN: It's Mrs Wainwright, Mr Brand.

BRAND: Come in, come in Mrs Wainwright. Look, if it's about the din, I've got some friends staying with me …

MRS WAINWRIGHT: Nay, I'm not worried about the din, it's Saturday night … *(she's holding several large envelopes and a parcel)* I took these in for you, postman couldn't get them through the box …

BRAND: *(taking them)* That's very kind of you, thank you …

MRS WAINWRIGHT: *(looking at kitchen)* You've got it quite nice now, haven't you? *(Brand nods, a little embarrassed)* I can't say I ... really understand it, mind you. I'd move tomorrow if I could get somewhere ... *(smiling suddenly)* But I'm glad you did.

BRAND: Will you have a drink with us?

MRS WAINWRIGHT: I'll not, if you don't mind. I'm baking. *(she's at the door, hand on latch)* We watched you on the box, Thursday, was it? *(she winks, very serious)* Keep it up, won't you.

He nods, smiling shyly.

MRS WAINWRIGHT: Good night.

BRAND: Good night.

He grows aware again of the package in his hand. Frowns; perhaps remembering the turd. Stares at it. Opens it diffidently. A sheaf of letters spill out. A covering letter from Gus Lynch, on the Fight For Work Campaign letterhead, comes to hand. 'Dear Bill, thought you'd like to see these. We've been flooded with applications for membership. Keep at it, comrade.'

He begins scanning the letters. Is attracted suddenly by the sound of a single bright voice singing in the next room. Carries the letters through. Dink accompanies Aya, who is singing Victor Jara's 'Venceremos' in a clear, lovely voice.

> Desde el hondo crisol de la patria
> Se levanta el clamor popular
> Ya se anuncia la nueva alborada
> Todo Chile comienza a cantar.
>
> Recordando el soldado valiente
> Cuyo ejemplo lo hiciera inmortal
> Enfrentemos primero a la muerte
> Traicionar a la patria jamas
>
> Venceremos, venceremos,
> Mil cadenas habra que romper,
> Venceremos, venceremos,
> La miseria sabremos vencer. ......

Brand stands and watches from the doorway; half moved by, half critically separate from the experience.

THE END

"Politically searching, dramatically compelling and superbly entertaining, *These Are The Times* does more to retrieve one of England's most magnificent radicals than anything that has ever been done before." **Terry Eagleton**

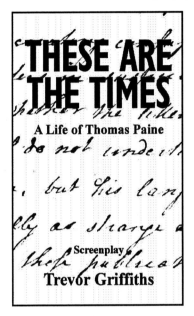

THESE ARE THE TIMES

A Life of Thomas Paine

Screenplay
Trevor Griffiths

"I am reading Griffiths with envy and admiration. *These Are The Times* reads like the greatest of novels and is the most thrilling read I've had in years. It is a gorgeous pageant of American idealism, of which we have been starved during the latter half of my lifetime." **Kurt Vonnegut**

These Are The Times
A Life of Thomas Paine
by Trevor Griffiths

ISBN: **0 85124 695 8** | Price: **£15.00**

Spokesman Books Russell House, Bulwell Lane, Nottingham, NG6 0BT, England.

www.spokesmanbooks.com

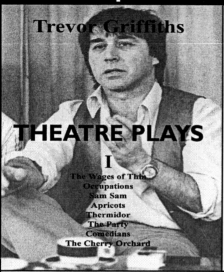
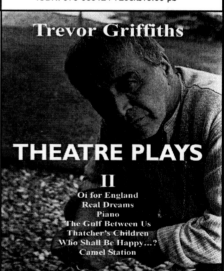